Re:Thinking Europe

I0129224

Re:Thinking Europe

Thoughts on Europe: Past, Present and Future

Edited by Mathieu Segers and Yoeri Albrecht

Routledge
Taylor & Francis Group
LONDON AND NEW YORK

First published in 2016 by Amsterdam University Press Ltd.

Published 2025 by Routledge
4 Park Square, Milton Park, Abingdon, Oxon OX14 4RN
605 Third Avenue, New York, NY 10158

Routledge is an imprint of the Taylor & Francis Group, an informa business

ISBN: 9789462983151 (pbk)
ISBN: 9781003702238 (ebk)
NUR 320 / 740

Cover photo: Jörg Brüggeman/OSTKREUZ

Cover design: Van Lennep, Amsterdam

Every effort has been made to obtain permission to use all copyrighted illustrations reproduced in this book. Nonetheless, whosoever believes to have rights to this material is advised to contact the publisher.

For Product Safety Concerns and Information please contact our EU representative: GPSR@taylorandfrancis.com
Taylor & Francis Verlag GmbH, Kaufingerstraße 24, 80331 München, Germany

Contents

Preface

Re-creating Europe

Yoeri Albrecht

On 1 January 2002, it seemed that the European project was complete. The euro had entered into circulation. The TV news showed the Minister of Finance withdrawing a few crisp new euro notes from a cash point, and that was that.

Few bothered to explain how and why there was a new currency. This was evidently unnecessary, because what Europe did, Europe did well; a superficial attitude on the part of the bureaucrats, politicians and intellectuals.

Around the turn of the century, though, the fact of Europe was still so self-evident that hardly anyone was talking about it. It was a background detail, part of the scenery. So self-evident and so out of sight that only specialists were truly interested in it.

But that time is certainly over. Europe has become controversial, and thus it is essential to talk and think about Europe once more. Countries, cultures, cities and political projects cannot advance unless the ideas that underlie them are developed, discussed, criticized, shared and supported.

Despite the urgent need, it has by no means become easier to talk about Europe. Much of the debate has degenerated into three topics that can be summarized as for or against migrants, for or against the euro and for or against centralized bureaucracy; but this is a dangerous oversimplification.

Europe is the continent that, like no other, has been able to translate the dreams and nightmares of humanity into reality.

Cities and landscapes, works of art, music and painting, the welfare state, the constitutional state and democracy: Europe has been able to polish each to perfection. But the downside of European history – genocide, war, exploitation and persecution – gives rise to constant tension when contemplating the present and the future. History offers many reasons to distrust Europeans at a fundamental level: ourselves, our motives and our political projects.

At the same time, our multi-coloured Europe has lived through a high summer of peace and prosperity for decades. Admittedly, there was a crisis in 2008, one that is still being felt. If we compare the standard of living among Europeans today with any other period in our thousands of years of history, though, we are enjoying an unprecedented degree of prosperity and freedom.

If we are dreaming, it is a sweet dream of prosperity and contentment. But is this the calm before the storm? Are we presently living through the last beautiful summer days, when the trees are laden with ripe fruit? And is the winter coming? Many think so.

For many decades, talking and thinking about Europe was put on hold, to a greater or lesser degree. There is an urgent need to catch up. It has been too long since the assumptions and ideals on which a united Europe was founded have been examined. That there was a need, after the great catastrophe of the world wars, for reconciliation and cooperation and to bury the savage, nationalistic aspect of the European soul is self-evident. But the fact that no new debate has been held on the utility of cooperation in Europe since the end of the Cold War in 1989 is perplexing. For too long in Europe, we have put all emphasis on, and all our hope in, the rationalist, bureaucratic approach.

In doing so, there has been a striking absence of artists, writers, and philosophers; in short, "public intellectuals".

After the abolition of the major, dangerous ideologies of the first half of the twentieth century, dreams and the imagination were largely left out of the equation. Back then, this was quite understandable, but now this situation is no longer tenable. We need to hold a far-reaching discussion about the added value that Europe brings for us, about the value of European culture, and about the way in which this culture can contribute to and form a foundation for peace, security and prosperity on our continent.

For it is also evident that there are dangerous depths. The pitch-black chapters of European history have taught us this all too clearly.

For centuries, European culture has steered a course between extremes of rationalism, expansionism and bureaucracy on the one hand, and romanticism, adventure and nationalism on the other. Somewhere between the Scylla and Charybdis of nationalism and internationalism, or romanticism and rationalism, there is a future for Europe; but then we have to be prepared to engage with the idea of Europe.

In this collection, a number of the most prominent European writers and thinkers of our time reflect on European culture. We have added a selection of speeches and essays, allowing the reader to trace the development of thinking about Europe from the post-war period to the present day.

The foundations of this book are formed by an essay by the liberal philosopher, Isaiah Berlin. In 1959, Berlin was already keenly aware of the problem of the two souls contained within the European body. As the child of Jewish refugees from the Baltic, he was deeply apprehensive of the centralizing, totalitarian side of the European utopia. Understandably, he was more drawn to liberalism and freedom. As a student in Oxford, however, I experienced first-hand in his tutorials on German Romanticism how important Berlin considered the national component of European culture to be.

For behind the rich diversity of European culture, behind the many differences and singularities, there lies a common characteristic. It is not in "for versus against", but in nuance, depth and many-layeredness that the power of European culture is to be found.

Introduction

Mathieu Segers

On 13 November 2015, a year of European recklessness was brought to a sombre conclusion by the terrorist attacks in Paris.
Shortly after the attacks, there was a run on Ernest Hemingway's *A moveable feast*; buying the book offered some consolation. In the book, the young Hemingway recounts his adventures among the American community in Paris in the 1920s. In those days, the *rive gauche* acted like a magnet for a select American elite.

After the shock of terror, the title and subject of Hemingway's book appealed to the imagination; that is to say, to those who were frequenting the outdoor cafes again while the pavements around Bataclan were still stained with blood. The short-lived popularity of *A moveable feast* is illustrative of today's mood of insecurity in Europe.

Europe was looking for support, for the umpteenth time. But in the context of the Parisian autumn of 2015, the title of Hemingway's book gave a false impression in this respect.

Hemingway and his friends saw Europe, traumatized in the wake of 1914-1918, as the *"banlieue* of Paris". *Their* Paris, to be precise, where like "iridescent flies" they were "caught in the black web of an ancient and amoral European culture", as Sinclair Lewis, one of Hemingway's fellow travellers, wrote; a world in which they could abandon themselves to the desire-driven charade, for an instant or for somewhat longer. This was something very different from American dreams; it was freedom.

But this is Europe in the eye of the beholder. Many ordinary Europeans are afraid of this Europe, where things are not as they seem; this cradle of the Enlightenment, where the basic condition is so often one of confusing surrealism, and a single question always gives rise to disquiet because it remains unanswered: what is Europe? After the fall of the Berlin Wall, Jacques

Derrida wrote in his essay, 'The Other Heading': "Old Europe seems to have exhausted all the possibilities of discourse and counter-discourse about its own identification." That is true.

And yet this soul-searching is the only certainty that Europe and Europeans have to hold on to. The pure clarity of "this strange white light, this far-away blue sky" on the other side of the Atlantic Ocean – as described so strikingly by Henry James in the nineteenth century, in his novella *The Europeans* – is a light that is not to be found above the Old Continent. Europe's light is a twilight; in Europe, Faust is never far away.

European brilliance stems from doubt, and from the hunger for knowledge and insight that accompanies it. From keeping on thinking and searching for roots. Continuing to create art, to write, to correspond, to speak and address, to teach and to research; it stems from culture and the art of politics. The day that Europe becomes lazy or complacent in such matters will be the day that catastrophe comes a step closer again.

This book is an exercise, in the Old European style, of doubting, thinking, re-reading and thinking again. It was precipitated by today's pressing situation. At its heart lies the unanswered question, "What is Europe?", and the accompanying search for an answer in our phase of "European unity and its vicissitudes", as Isaiah Berlin characterized Europe's history in his lecture to the Third Congress of the Fondation Européenne de la Culture in Vienna, on 21 November 1959.

That lecture by Berlin forms the starting point of this book. The thinkers, writers and scholars of today's Europe who collaborated on this book took Berlin's lecture as their inspiration when reflecting on the current situations in Europe and the role that culture plays within them.

Their contributions to this book have been illustrated with a selection of key texts, often half or entirely forgotten, from the incredible history of modern Europe, and from both sides of the integration divide. The selected texts also turn on the still-unanswered question. They have been included to enrich the search for Europe in this book and to put it in a historical context. In this introduction, we briefly introduce the key texts (the notes to the introduction contain a bibliography of the selected key texts that are available in English translation later in this book). At the same time, this serves as an introduction to the most important themes that are developed in the contemporary essays by the authors of this book.

*

Isaiah Berlin's lecture in Vienna in 1959 was one of the exceptional moments when Berlin ventured to tackle the problem of European unity. It was a problem that, for him, would always remain unsolvable – perhaps mainly, because Romanticism and the Enlightenment, each so embedded at the heart of European history and culture, proved irreconcilable in the absence of a stark choice for one or the other. That choice was precisely the one that Berlin did not wish to make. In his Vienna lecture, he avoided tackling this central matter directly.

Berlin did address a different issue more directly, however: that of Europe's constant vicissitudes. These formed the subject of his lecture. In a key passage, he explains their dynamic: "It is a truism that European history is a kind of dialectic between craving for public order and for individual liberty." The explanation with which Berlin accompanied this statement remains very topical today:

The quest for order is a kind of fear before the elements, an attempt to build walls and hedges against the chaos caused by absence of control, against the weakening of traditions, habits, rules of life, in an effort to preserve the banisters that human beings need to prevent them from toppling over into an abyss, to connect them with their past and point a path to the future. When institutions become too set and obstruct growth, order becomes oppression and worship of it self-stultifying; sooner or later it is broken through by an almost physiological desire to live, create, by the need for novelty and change.[1]

This dynamic of European vicissitudes forms the starting-point for this book. Its contemporary embedding is often just as Western as the transatlantic correspondence in Berlin's letters, such as that he maintained with the American diplomat George Kennan in the early 1950s. In this, the two discussed hope, sin and belief, against the oppressive spectacle of post-war Europe in the making.

1.   Letters

George Kennan was a prolific writer. This master-strategist of American government in the 1940s produced a vast quantity of memos, policy recommendations, memoirs and books. His feeling for the nuance of history was European, but his opinions were decidedly American – a compelling combination. His influence was often decisive and the fame of his Long Telegram of 1946 bordered on legend. Behind the superiority of his professional writings, however, lay Kennan the European; the breeding-ground for his doubt, his melancholy (that European disease[2]), and his romantic longing for the mystique of Scandinavia and the Baltic, his "mother-countries".

In order to keep these ghosts in check, Kennan wrote letters. Some were addressed to Isaiah Berlin, who, in addition to being a prominent Oxford don, had also been a refugee child from Riga.

Kennan and Berlin knew one other from the social circles of the American East Coast, and the English-American policy elite with which these were interwoven. In the final years of the war, Berlin had spent some time working for the British Foreign Office in New York and Washington. He had subsequently returned to the colleges and parks of academic life in Oxford. From this policy sideline, he grew to be the conscience of the West in the Cold War. It was also in this capacity that he became the recipient of Kennan's letters (which can be found in Berlin's published *Letters*).

In the spring of 1950, Kennan was unnerved by one of Berlin's publications. The American was affected by the fact that a recent *Foreign Affairs* article by Berlin ('Political Ideas in the Twentieth Century') implied, to his mind, that his friend was still dealing somewhat laconically with the phenomenon of totalitarianism. In the piece in question, Berlin had addressed communism at length. Kennan was disturbed by the fact that in doing so, Berlin had failed to explain that communism was an intolerable system, whereas such a thing could not be in doubt; for communism went counter to human nature.

In a letter to Berlin, Kennan explained himself in more detail. He argued that what the implementers of totalitarianism were doing was nothing less than committing "original sin". This represented precisely that which people should not do: taking advantage of human vulnerability to manipulation. Kennan explained his point further: in totalitarian regimes such as the Soviet Union, people acted as though problems would disappear without their being solved. This was trickery and deceit. In the end, it was simply "another form of taking human life arbitrarily and in cold blood, as a result of calculation", and there was no difference between this and Nazi practices.

According to Kennan, the success of a civilization depended "on the readiness to refrain from doing so: and on their sticking to the rational appeal which assumes that in the long run each man can be taught to rise above himself". He was prepared to concede that this was "perhaps the supreme make-believe", but ultimately, this did not trouble him. It was "the inexorable price of human progress" and *the* argument "for clinging to the belief that questions are important, are susceptible of solution by rational processes, and should be so approached and solved".

Kennan's written outburst formed an apt summary of the delusion of the age. It covered the whole programme of action for a new and improved post-war Western world: malleability, elevation and progress. And all without once mentioning the word "politics".

The intellectual historian Berlin was discomforted by his American friend's heartfelt cry. It would be almost a year before he could bring himself to communicate this to his friend, complete with long-winded and veiled argumentation.

According to Berlin, the world of "good cops and bad cops" described by Kennan was a simplistic denial of the tragedy of human nature and history. The European thus gave the pseudo-European a lesson on Europe: ambiguity and darkness belonged there; what is more, they swirled in the very essence of human affairs and the course of events. As far as Berlin was concerned, though, this lesson did not have to be understood *per se*; perhaps it would be better if it were not.

Nevertheless, in his reply, Berlin did his best to explain clearly where he stood. He agreed with Kennan that it was wrong to treat people, without their consent, as though one were "'moulding' them like pieces of clay". But, he continued:

> Our answer has to be that certainly all 'moulding' is evil, and that if human beings at birth had the power of choice and the means of understanding the world, it would be criminal; since they have not, we temporarily enslave them, for fear that, otherwise, they will suffer worse misfortunes from nature and from men, and this 'temporary enslavement' is a necessary evil until such time as they are able to choose for themselves – the 'enslavement' having its purpose not an inculcation of obedience but its contrary, the development of power of free judgement and choice; still evil it remains even if necessary.

According to Berlin, what Kennan had branded "Soviet evil" was ultimately "an extreme and distorted but only too typical form of some general attitude of mind from which our own countries are not exempt". And he warned: "we must avoid being inverted Marxists." In a subtle link to his substantive reply to Kennan, he moreover suggested that his friend was perhaps engaged in a battle above all with himself. After all, Kennan's letter had shown that his fiery plea for a "solution by rational processes" was built upon make-believe; pretence against one's better judgement. His American friend wanted to make an unconditional choice for rationality, to harness passion to do good. Such things did not convince Berlin.

2.   Desire

Few have described this transatlantic "clash of civilizations" more perceptively than Curzio Malaparte in his scandalous novel of 1949, *La Pelle*. As a liaison officer between the allied and Italian troops, the author sketched a disconcerting picture of the liberation of Italy in 1943. He described it as resulting in obscenity and bloodthirstiness; a macabre game between victors and vanquished, in which refugees, the starving, soldiers, traitors and merrymakers encountered one another in desire, disease and sin.

In *La Pelle*, Malaparte (a pseudonym for Kurt Erich Suckert, born in Prato) captures the essence of a Europe that will always elude non-Europeans; and Americans, above all.

And this is precisely why Malaparte loved Americans: "white or black, their souls are pure, much purer than ours. I like Americans ... because they believe that Christ is always on the side of those who are in the right; because they believe that it is a sin to be wrong." "In that terrible autumn of 1943", Malaparte was unable to do without them: "the pure and honest simplicity of their ideas and sentiments, and the genuineness of their behaviour, instilled in me the illusion that men hate evil, the hope that humanity would mend its ways." This represented the illusion and the hope that Europe was lacking. Europeans are different, and this is what makes them vulnerable.

Some pages later, Malaparte would complete the comparison when he wrote of *his* Americans: "They do not know, although they are in many respects the most Christian nation in the world, that without evil, there can be no Christ." Yet this also implies that contemporary Europe – like Malaparte in 1943 – can no longer do without America and American hope. That hope and that belief in goodness are addictive.

Europe has also become America, however much it might also not be America; it remains the American president who can speak most compellingly of European ideals.[3]

After the war, the small and troubled "West" of Europe became a bastion of solace and hope. An extremely shaky bastion, but a bastion all the same, complete with the pure division between an inner and outer world: we are one world, they another. It was a new, very real European surrealism. The British Embassy counsellor John Le Carré wrote of the *Small Town in Germany*, the heart of that now-vanished Western Europe: "In Bonn even the flies are official." In the present storm of European vicissitudes, that now-vanished region, in retrospect, is increasingly becoming a land of milk and honey; the memories of West Europeans remain vivid.

In 1983, Milan Kundera described the callous reality of Western Europe in his essay, 'The Tragedy of Central Europe'. Kundera began the piece by citing the battle cry of the director of the Hungarian Press Bureau in November 1956. The last telex that he sent ended with the sentence: "We are going to die for Hungary and Europe." The pan-European contact that this invoked proved to be a phantom. Shortly afterwards, the futility of his act of resistance was written in blood by the Red Army in the annals of European history.

But the hopeful mist of European solidarity continued to return at certain times. In the winter of 2014, the brave and the dead of Maidan saw the same fine spectre of European culture lingering above their square.

Reflecting on the telex of 1956, Kundera asked himself many years later: "When Solzhenitsyn denounces communist oppression, does he invoke Europe as a fundamental value worth dying for?" Kundera's answer was: "No". And he explained this further: "'To die for one's country and for Europe' – that is a phrase that could not be thought in Moscow or Leningrad; it is precisely the phrase that could be thought in Budapest or Warsaw", where "the word 'Europe' does represent a spiritual notion synonymous with the word 'West'"; their regions lie "culturally in the West", rooted in "Roman Christianity".[4]

When Joseph Roth, as a journalist travelling to Russia, arrived in the city of Lemberg in Western Ukraine (now Lviv) in November 1924, he observed a similar phenomenon. In his account of his travels (*Reisen in die Ukraine und nach Russland*), he wrote of this city: "Es ist die Stadt der verwischten Grenzen ... Hinter Lemberg beginnt Russland, eine andere Welt ... Zwischen Wien und Lemberg is heute noch, wie immer, der Radioaustausch der Kultur."

For decades, Eastern Europeans were not permitted to think, let alone to dream, of Europe; little else remained than "attempts to live within the truth", to use Václav Havel's striking phrase of 1978. When the "acceleration of history" in the autumn of 1989 made their forbidden dream come true from one day to the next, Eastern Europe became Europe again and Western Europe vanished, and a new dream glimmered: that of "European universalism projected into political reality", as described by Havel in 1994.[5]

We still do not know exactly what this meant. But Europe would notice that the Eastern European experience of tragedy is recent, and learn from it; although it would not be clear how.

3.   Make-Believe

Isaiah Berlin loathed the communist madness that plagued the regions of his youth. But it was also a stage where one could see how it worked, how the blueprints were implemented, and what became of them. In post-war Western Europe, the fatal threat of dogmatic make-believe lay dormant too; and wishful thinking about a European federation could prove a sophisticated disguise for this.

On the other side of the ocean, some had already realized this while the Second World War was still raging. On 1 May 1943, the Yale Institute of International Studies published a confidential report on post-war Europe. It concluded that there were good reasons for being very wary of a European federation. The most important of these was that Hitler had succeeded, in a certain sense, in bringing about European unity. The report described this as "the rape of Europe by Hitler", and argued that this showed that European unity was a bridge too far.

There was more, however; this experience of "rape" had created a deep longing in Europe to strengthen *national* aspirations and identity, rather than transcend them, particularly in the countries surrounding Germany. Moreover, it was realistic to assume that this fear of German leadership would continue to exist far into the future, and thus also the fear of a federation that could facilitate it. This fear would continue to colour European reality; something that proved to be true.

When, with the fall of the Berlin Wall, the bipolar freezing of international politics underwent an unstoppable thaw, there was little recourse to be found in international law. After all, the fact that no peace treaty had been signed "with and about" Germany after the Second World War formed the essence of the bipolar world. This began to shift on 9 November 1989.

In his time, Otto von Bismarck, the father of German unity in 1870, had already observed that self-control would be the great challenge for the Germans. The history of the first half of the twentieth century had subsequently shown this to be an impossible task.

Margaret Thatcher had her own reading of this history. During the earlier period of German unity, between 1870 and 1945, "Germany [had] veered unpredictably between aggression and self-doubt", she noted in her memoirs. Something like this was not without consequences. The European world wars had traumatized Germany's neighbours, but according to Thatcher, this was even truer of the Germans themselves. And that was the new German danger: the Germans were afraid of themselves. As a result, they had become gripped by the dangerous delusion that they would do well to voluntarily enclose themselves in a "federal Europe", which would in fact increase the German threat. For a federal Europe was the perfect driving wheel for the magnification of German power; it was a recipe for new German hegemony on the Continent.

Notwithstanding Thatcher's warnings, that was precisely the scenario she saw unfold ever more clearly from the autumn of 1989: a large and united Germany at the heart of a more deeply integrated Europe, as a guarantee of future security and stability after the Cold War. Europe's future was thus handed over to Brussels and Berlin: there is no tribe with greater make-believe ambitions than the Brussels technocrats and Europhiles; no people with more talent for going with this than the Germans.

In her notorious speech in Bruges in 1988, Thatcher had warned vociferously against a European "super-state", by drawing a parallel between the institutions of European integration and the Soviet Union.[6] No one had listened.

Other European leaders understood very well what Thatcher meant, but a sense of history and self-knowledge had taught most of them a different lesson.

The fall of the Wall was the plot-twist whereby a crushing Western victory in the Cold War could be achieved peacefully; an incredible turn, and one that a European could hardly oppose, certainly when the Americans were also backing it. For Europe, the Cold War thus ended with rapid German unification and a start on building the currency union; a gamble on the future that had to keep the past in check.

So the insight formulated by the authors of the Yale report was becoming reality: it was more and more difficult to conceive of genuine integration in Europe without German leadership.

The Yale analysis stemmed from 1943: the year in which Malaparte was shocked by the liberation of Italy, and in which he was torn by his desire for Atlantic leadership. This was the same deep desire that glowed in raped Europe. The sensation described by Malaparte was both liberating and terrible at the same time. There was a reason for this ambiguity: Malaparte sensed that the glowing desire represented an illusion.

This was something that became clear less than five years later. Europe was in the grip of the Cold War, and it was the United States that made the turn. In exchange for Marshall Aid, the American government now asked explicitly for European integration, even in the form of a federation. The Americans took a small step back from the European quagmire; also because the order that had been established at Yalta was adequate for this new phase in the "European civil war", as Norman Davies has described the period between 1914 and 1990.

The promise of an Atlantic world was transformed into a Western-European fairy tale, but one that continued to inspire dreams until far beyond the Berlin Wall and 9/11.[7]

4.   Occident

More economic cooperation within Europe was direly needed, in the American view. The liberalization of trade in Western Europe could boost production, growth and consumption, leading to the elimination of the pressing dollar deficit and an influx of American influence. What is more, this would offer greater capitalist unity against the communist danger and the threat from the Soviet Union. European integration thus became the overriding aim of Marshall Aid.

But this did not solve Europe's major problem: how to deal with Germany? During internal consultations in August 1947, the American francophile Charles Bohlen – one of Marshall's main advisors – formulated a new insight that would play a key role in Washington. He turned things around: the German problem was not an occupation issue that was limited to German territory; it was a European issue! The three Western occupation zones should be seen "not as part of Germany, but as part of Western Europe".

From the end of 1947, Washington embraced a new post-war mission: that of building Europe. How this was to be done was not so important, so long as it happened. Will Clayton, a driving force behind the Marshall Plan, had travelled in Western Europe for several days and had been shocked by the misery and poverty that he had found in Malaparte's Europe. Something had to be done. (Clayton's conclusion at the time was published in full in the *Political Science Quarterly* in 1963.)

It became an American priority to set up a West German state to facilitate Western Europe unity, and to prop up this state not only politically, but also mainly economically, so that it could form a long-term line of defence against the Soviet Union. The founding of the Federal Republic of Germany (FRG) would be essential for post-war Western European cooperation. It was the framework in which Bismarck's self-control could be exercised once more.

More than anything, this *Weststaatsgründung* of the FRG formed the foundations that underlay the process of European integration. The German Constitution literally states that it was founded "von dem Willen beseelt, als gleichberechtigtes Glied in einem vereinten Europa dem Frieden der Welt zu dienen". It is this sentence that enabled Chancellor Merkel to maintain that "Germany has always understood European unity as part of its reason of state", and to acknowledge that she does not wish to return "to that seemingly simple way of doing things" that characterizes the worlds beyond democracy. Her distinguished predecessor, Helmut Schmidt, also captured this in an influential crisis speech in December 2011: "Germany in and with and for Europe".[8]

One year after the founding of the FRG, European integration took off in unprecedented fashion. On 9 May 1950, the French Minister of Foreign Affairs, Robert Schuman, launched a revolutionary plan for the founding of a European Coal and Steel Community (ECSC). This plan had been secretly coordinated with the American Secretary of State, Dean Acheson, and prepared with Konrad Adenauer, the first West German Chancellor. On the day on which the French minister called for concrete steps "créent d'abord une solidarité de fait", the rest of the world was confronted with *la bombe Schuman*, as it was described by one Belgian daily, *La Relève*.

The plan for the ECSC was conceived and drafted by Jean Monnet. Monnet was no ordinary Frenchman. During the war he had worked for the British government and cooperated with American production planning. When he joined the leaders of the "Free French" in the course of the Second World War, he acted as a liaison for the American President Roosevelt, no less, from whom he directly received secret instructions.

Monnet's close ties with the Anglo-Saxon world sometimes caused frowns on the faces of his compatriots, including General de Gaulle, the leader of the "Free French". But when the same Charles de Gaulle became the first prime minister of post-war France, he gave Monnet the key role of leading the planners of the *Commissariat au plan,* which was tasked with restoring the material aspects of French grandeur. Monnet's network and modernism proved indispensable.

Monnet wanted more, however: "to change the existing order in Europe." He had already described how this should be done in a memo to himself in 1943.[9] He believed that it could be done by striving for Western-European integration, step by step; it could be achieved through economic cooperation in an increasing number of sectors. For this, it was essential for cooperation to be anchored in supranational institutions. This formed the core of Monnet's vision; this was the revolution. The ECSC had to be the first and crucial step on the way to supranational community.

Monnet believed that only in this way would Europe be able to wrest herself from her tragic history. The new supranational institutions that would be established were to be the bearers of this promise. They had to provide a place in which to build a collective memory of peaceful and profitable cooperation. This would form an antidote to fanatical nationalism, something that was written so overpoweringly into the fabric of the other institutions (the nation states), and which had become manifest in Europe, time and again, in an escalating spiral of mutual distrust, protectionism and cynical power politics.

During his speech to the European Parliament in January 1995, François Mitterrand echoed Monnet's analysis when he said: "le nationalisme c'est la guerre."[10] Monnet thought that supranational institutions could be used to influence the European *condition humaine*; and in post-war Western Europe, that idealism would also become realism.

5.   Therapy

When building his vision of Europe, Monnet drew inspiration from an idea expressed by the Swiss philosopher, Henri-Frédéric Amiel. It concerned an observation that Amiel had made in his *Journal Intime* on 4 October 1873:

> Each man begins the world afresh, and not one fault of the first man has been avoided by his remotest descendant. The collective experience accumulates, but individual experience dies with the individual, and the result is that institutions become wiser and knowledge as such increases; but the young man, although more cultivated, is just as presumptuous, and not less fallible to-day than he ever was. The whole is better, perhaps, but man is not positively better – he is only different ... A thousand things advance, nine hundred and ninety-eight fall back: this is progress. There is nothing in it to be proud of, but something, after all, to console one.

In the 1940s, time was becoming ripe for Monnet's concept of European integration. This became manifest in a pre-eminently modern phenomenon of that time: policy.

Policy was associated with rationalism and a problem-solving approach, with a progressive yet essentially apolitical demeanour. At the same time, its apolitical outlook was especially appealing and comforting, as the brute facts of recent history prescribed that politics should not be allowed to run wild again. New bureaucracy and state planning appeared capable of building a trustworthy fortress against the evils of polarization and fragmentation, thereby enabling societies to contain their feelings and sentiments by means of reason and moderate societal excitement, as described by the American historian Charles Maier in his 1987 book, *In Search of Stability*. The "policy approach" offered a form of purifying therapy, feverishly longed for after the incomprehensible horrors of war.

The essence of the resulting new grand design for the post-war capitalist order was twofold: planning and multilateralism. The primary and overarching goal was stability through control, at home and abroad. A relatively small but coherent group of transatlantic "policy therapists" guided the construction of post-war Western multilateralism, John Maynard Keynes being the most brilliant among them in the art of persuasion.

These men engaged in the core paradoxes of free-world capitalism, such as domestic versus international stability, market growth versus state control, and welfare and social cohesion versus competitiveness.

Their struggles with these paradoxes shaped the post-war West. The flagships of post-war Western multilateralism, such as Bretton Woods, General Agreement on Tariffs and Trade (GATT) and European integration, were all in essence concerted efforts of multilateral institution-building in order to reconcile resilient capitalism and democracy after the Great Depression and the Second World War. This quest for a historical compromise still remains very much at the core of the post-war Western world.

The "policy therapists" gained huge influence, as they were able to offer that which was being demanded: political modesty mixed with a convincing rationalism that was strongly driven by idealism; something new in which to believe. Be that as it may, many of their policies and fantastic societal plans could equally be described as plain escapism. Joseph Schumpeter, for one, did so; he hinted at a new fatal attraction. The overwhelming passion for a post-fascist utopia went hand-in-hand with an obsession with policy, the perfect seduction of make-believe. According to Schumpeter, this implied a blind "march into socialism", towards the end of freedom (as he argued in his infamous 1942-book *Capitalism, Socialism and Democracy*); yet it was revitalizing therapy all the same.

The "therapy" admittedly included "counter-planners", such as the German *Ordoliberals* who would become the inspiration of post-war Western Europe's *soziale Marktwirtschaft* (social market economy), that distant *finalité politique* that emerged in the slipstream of the Marshall Plan and the *Wirtschaftswunder* of their spokesman, the West German Finance Minister Ludwig Erhard. As the defenders of free enterprise anchored in framework treaties (guaranteeing respect for property and law, protecting free competition and honouring monetary prudence), the Ordoliberals were convinced that only a free market and a process of price correction through deflation could point the way to a new and stable (and more spontaneous) order.

This was exactly the opposite of the interventionist policies of planning, *dirigisme*, lending and price-fixing that were in vogue in Keynes' emerging wider Western world. According to the Ordoliberals, national governments, rather than international organizations, ought to be held responsible for setting the framework conditions for national order. International order then would emerge out of this subsidiarity as a "by-product", on the grounds that well-functioning nations would provide a beacon of light that other governments would follow through competitive emulation. In their view, not a European federation, but a competitive economy (such as the German one) would lead by example.

As the promises of an Atlantis grounded in solidarity faded, the Ordoliberal grip on Europe grew stronger. In many respects, Wolfgang Schäuble is the last *Ordoliberal*. His *kern-Europa* – rooted in his *Überlegungen zur europäischen Politik* of 1994 – forms the true, and very Western European, Ordoliberal legacy.

6. Consolation

Like Isaiah Berlin, Jean Monnet was sponsored by the Ford Foundation. In the mid-1950s, when Jean Monnet decided to leave the High Authority of the European Coal and Steel Community (the predecessor of today's European Commission, of which he was the first chair) in order to devote himself more specifically to promoting his European ideals, he was able to count on his American friends. They supported the founding of his Action Committee for the United States of Europe, a lobbying organization unlike any other, and one in which the Dutchman Max Kohnstamm played a key role.

Kohnstamm had been branded by the horrors of war, but not broken; for him, Europe provided a new sense of purpose. In the European integration project, he saw the power of the potential for harmony and the mutual strengthening of social order and individual liberty. This could be achieved through democracy and the constitutional state, as the American theologian Reinhold Niebuhr explained in *The Children of Light and the Children of Darkness* in 1944 – a lasting source of inspiration for Kohnstamm. Europe gave new meaning to his life.

This explained the panic that could seize Kohnstamm, when the integration process was in crisis; or when the banished memories of the nightmares of 1940-45 crept back into his thoughts, and Malaparte would oust Niebuhr, and European horror would replace transatlantic hope.

This happened too on a morning in April 1961, in an aeroplane above the Atlantic Ocean. Before his departure, when he had said goodbye to his teenage daughter in her bedroom, fear had gripped his heart. The book that he thought he had seen in her hands was *The 25th Hour* by the Romanian writer Constantin Virgil Gheorghiu. During the flight, he wrote about the incident in his diary: "I have no right to leave her alone with such things, but what is there to explain?"

During the early years of the Second World War, the theologian and philosopher Gheorghiu worked for the Romanian Minister of Foreign Affairs. When Soviet troops marched into Romania in 1944, he fled his native country. He was subsequently taken prisoner by the American army. During his imprisonment, he wrote the novel *Ora 25*, which was published in French in 1949.

The novel contained strong parallels with his own experiences in the blood-lands of Central Europe, that hell's gate of Europe's dismemberment. *The 25th Hour* is a lamentable tale of the hopeless wanderings of people in the sinister worlds beyond citizenship and the uncompromising ideals of social engineering.

It touches on the issue about which Isaiah Berlin tried to warn his friend George Kennan: if the chaotic mix of opinions and ideas that shapes Western civilization is watered down into something that has to be understood in an entirely rational way, appalling disasters will threaten.

The refugee and philosopher Berlin described the contradictions of the chaotic mix of Western civilization and culture as something tragic, but mainly as a thing of beauty that was still worth defending. The refugee and writer Gheorghiu was ordained as a priest in 1963, and he became the patriarch of the Romanian Orthodox Church in France in 1971. Both sought consolation in European culture and its institutions, as did Max Kohnstamm and Jean Monnet in their own ways. *Les hommes politiques* of early post-war Western Europe found inspiration in them.

7.   Reconciliation

The Catholics Konrad Adenauer and Robert Schuman spoke each other's language. Schuman spoke German well. He had been born in Luxemburg and had grown up in Lotharingen at a time when this *Reichsland* still belonged to the German Empire. He studied law in Bonn, and during the First World War he served in the German army. After the war, Elzas-Lotharingen became French and Schuman became a French citizen.

A born politician from the Rhineland, Konrad Adenauer had previously been the mayor of Cologne. After the Second World War, he had risen rapidly through the political ranks as the chair of the Christian Democratic Union (CDU) in the British occupation zone, to become, at the age of 73, the first Chancellor of the FRG in 1949.

Adenauer met a contemporary in Schuman, but also a kindred spirit in what he called the core principles of the "Abendländische Christentums": individual freedom, democracy and social cohesion – along with the seed-bed of the social market economy inherent to the Rhineland model, and so different from its Anglo-Saxon sibling.

Schuman and Adenauer were in complete agreement that the individual, the human being, must once more be at the heart of things. This would only be possible through democracy. And in order to achieve this in the long term, Christian values would be essential. Only in this way could the state and market be put at the service of the individual; and not vice versa, as had happened in the interwar period. A new Europe resting on Christian foundations would also be able to provide the essential stability for the West German future.

That West German future was primarily a regional future, and mainly Franco-German, in Adenauer's view. Shortly after the war, he tried to re-launch an old plan for French-Belgian-German federalization, a *Rhein-Ruhr-Staat*. It proved too early. At that time, the plan came over as an obscure form of Rhineland separatism. For the British occupation authorities, this proved reason to sack Adenauer as the mayor of Cologne. The British saw him as "dangerous" and a "born intriguer" (as revealed by Charles Williams in his biography of Adenauer).

Adenauer's vision remained unchanged, however, when a few years later, along with Schuman and Monnet, he began to build a form of European integration in which the British did not participate. For Adenauer, a step such as that of the ECSC represented the great hope for Germany *and* Europe; something that he had proclaimed back in the ruined auditorium of Cologne University in the bleak spring of 1946.[11] His hope became a reality in the years that followed, and was developed further in the institutions of Franco-German reconciliation that he managed to establish in the final days of his chancellorship, together with Charles de Gaulle and against the Americans. They would be cherished by all of his successors, to this very day.

But a major part of the European promise was not redeemed; something realized even by the very first Europeans, such as Monnet and Kohnstamm. Although Monnet had claimed in a speech in Washington in 1952, "We are not making alliances between states, we are uniting people", in the practice of European integration, little unification of people was to be found. And the longer this continued, the more difficult it would become. Something else did work, though: the socialization and lionizing of European policy elites. If one wanted to be cynical, this was not exactly difficult.

Nevertheless, there was also the singularly pleasing and increasingly sustainable outcome of all that wheeling and dealing: an integration process unequalled in history; a peace project that commanded increasing respect in the world and sent out messages of reconciliation. That Europe was something worth fighting for. But how long could this continue? How long could one keep appeasing the people in this fashion? (With the very best of intentions, of course.)

Even model Europeans didn't know the answers to these questions. Perhaps 'their' Europe would only be able to keep going so long as prosperity continued to grow – maybe it was already infected with a fatal dose of make-believe.

8.   Twilight

The philosopher Gabriel Marcel wrote an unsettling foreword to the French edition of *The 25ʰ Hour*. According to this ultra-existentialist, Gheorghiu's novel was "the literary expression" of where Europe was heading: "a world in which 'citizens' threaten to replace people." Marcel believed that this would end in a fight to the death between "real" and "paper people".

In France and Western Europe, the problem was particularly urgent. *Planisme* was spreading insidiously and assuming "more dangerous forms by the day". If there was one person in Marcel's time who personified this, it was his compatriot, the arch-planner Jean Monnet, the brain behind post-war European integration.

The French president De Gaulle shared Marcel's concerns, with a feeling for the European reality of surrealism. He saw Monnet as a straw man who had been created by the United States (there were enough indications of this); someone who had brought a reprehensible and hollow Americanization to Europe under the cloak of technocracy. Through the supranational institutions of the integration process, this had infected and weakened France and Western Europe.

The manner in which De Gaulle would lash out at the supranational institutions of European integration at press conferences now seems strikingly topical. He was concerned about a dangerous technocratic and democratic "chimère".[12] De Gaulle contrasted this with a Europe of states and referenda: more politics, more vagaries, more Europe.

De Gaulle called the Europe of the institutions "ce machin"; this "thing" that, it was said, would threaten European culture and civilization if it were allowed to have its way, and if the weakness were allowed spread. For then governance would increasingly be left to non-Europeans brimming with self-confidence. This doom-scenario of European weakness, caught in the faceless institutions of the constitutional state and democracy, is also topical. It forms a major theme in Michel Houllebecq's *Soumission*, in which the Saudis play the role of De Gaulle's Americans.

In order to keep these and other European weaknesses in check, in thought and deed, Europe cannot do without the self-awareness that comes with self-knowledge, with knowledge of the Europe of the past. That hidden Europe is still alive, but it is difficult to find and perhaps, as a result, all too often neglected and poorly understood.

The chaos and agitation of today's Europe reflect many things, but they certainly also reveal an anxious need for greater self-understanding. Our Europe sometimes shows parallels with the Europe of before the great wars; the Europe that Roger Martin du Gard, in the family epic *Les Thibaults*, compares with the over-strung French diplomat Rumelles, who literally "buckled under the confusing torrent of thoughts".

Under the pressure of circumstances, pretence is becoming a less and less viable alternative.

With this book, the authors and editors wish to focus on self-knowledge, driven by the assumption that for Europe, hope is to be found through the ambiguities of culture and history; "the

special quality of Europe is culture", to quote György Konrád.[13]
For Europe, grace comes through contact with the other side.

Notes

1. Isaiah Berlin, 'European Unity and its Vicissitudes', *The Crooked Timber of Humanity. Chapters in the History of Ideas* (Princeton, N.J.: Princeton University Press, [1959] 2013).
2. Tomasso Padoa-Schioppa, 'The Europe of Melancholy', *The Federalist* (2006).
3. Barack Obama, *President Obama's Remarks in Turkey*, 6 April 2009.
4. Milan Kundera, 'The Tragedy of Central Europe', *New York Review of Books* 31, 7 ([1983] 1984).
5. Václav Havel, *Speech to the European Parliament*, Strasbourg, 8 March 1994.
6. Margaret Thatcher, *The Bruges Speech*, 20 September 1988.
7. Édouard Balladur, 'Pour une Union Occidentale', *Revue internationale et stratégique* 4, 72 (2008).
8. Helmut Schmidt, 'Germany in and with and for Europe', *Speech in Berlin*, 4 December 2011.
9. Jean Monnet, *Note de réflexion*, Algiers, 5 August 1943.
10. François Mitterrand, *Speech to the European Parliament*, Strasbourg, 17 January 1995.
11. Konrad Adenauer, *Rede in der Aula der Universität zu Köln*, Cologne, 24 March 1946.
12. Charles de Gaulle, Conférence de presse, Paris, 5 September 1960.
13. György Konrád, 'The Special Quality of Europe is Culture', in: Wolfgang Beck, Laurent J.G. van der Maesen, Fleur Thomése, and Alan Walker (eds.), *Social Quality: A Vision for Europe* (The Hague, London, Boston: Kluwer Law International, 2001), pp. 369-374.

European Unity and its Vicissitudes[1]

Isaiah Berlin

Vienna, 21 November 1959

I

It is by now a melancholy commonplace that no century had seen so much remorseless and continued slaughter of human beings by one another as our own. Compared with it, even the wars of religion and the Napoleonic campaigns seem local and humane. I am not qualified to undertake a general examination of the causes of hatred and strife in our time. I should like to direct attention to only one aspect of this situation. We live in an age in which political ideas, conceived by fanatical thinkers, some of them very little regarded in their won day, have had a more violently revolutionary influence on the human lives than at any time since the seventeenth century. I should like to discuss one group of such ideas, by which our own lives have been profoundly affected both for good and evil.

Our ideas about the ends of life are, in one essential respect, unlike, and indeed opposed to, those of our forefathers, at least those prevalent before the second half of the eighteenth century. According to these the world was a single, intelligible whole. It consisted of certain stable ingredients, material and spiritual; if they were not stable they were not real. All men possessed certain unchanging characteristics in common, called human nature. And although there existed obvious differences between individuals, cultures, nations the similarities between them were more extensive and important. The most important common characteristic was considered to be the possession of the faculty called reason, which enabled its possessor to perceive the truth, both theoretical and practical. The truth, it was assumed, was equally visible to all rational minds everywhere. This common nature made it not only necessary, but also reasonable, for human beings to attempt to communicate with each other, and to try to persuade one another of the truth of what they believed in; and, in extreme cased, to inflict compulsion upon others, on the assumption (made, for example, by Sarastro in the great fable of the age of reason, Mozart's *Magic Flute*) that if men obeyed orders (or were, if all else failed, forced to obey) they would, as a result of this, perceive the validity of what their educators or legislators or masters themselves knew to be true; they would follow this, and be wise and good and happy. In the twentieth century this claim to universality, whether of reason or any other principle, is no longer taken for granted; what Walter Lippmann had called the public philosophy has ceased to be the automatic presupposition of politics or social life, and this has vastly transformed our lives.

This is most obvious in the case of Fascism. The Fascists and National Socialists did not expect inferior classes, or races, or individuals to understand or sympathise with their own goals; their inferiority was innate, ineradicable, since it was due to blood, or race, or some other irremovable characteristic; any attempt on the part of such creatures to pretend to equality with their masters, or even to comprehension of their ideals, was regarded as arrogant and presumptuous. Caliban was considered incapable of lifting his face to the sky and catching even a glimpse of, let alone sharing, the ideals of Prospero. The business of slaves id to obey; what gives their masters their right to trample on them is precisely the alleged fact – which Aristotle asserted – that some men are slaves by nature, and have not enough human quality to give order themselves, or understand why they are being forced to do what they do.

If Fascism is the extreme expression of this attitude, all nationalism is infected by it to some degree. Nationalism is not consciousness of the reality of national character, nor pride in it. it is a belief in the unique mission of a nation, as being intrinsically superior to the goals or attributes of whatever is outside it; so it hat if there is a conflict between my nation and other men, I am obliged to fight for my nation no matter at what cost to other men; and if the others resist, that is no more than one would expect from being brought up in a n inferior culture, educated by, or born of, inferior person, who cannot ex hypothesi understand the ideals that animate my nation and me. My gods are in conflict with those of others, my values with those of strangers, and there exists no higher authority – certainly no absolute and universal tribunal – by which the claims of these rival divinities can be adjudicated. That is why war, between nations or individuals, must be the only solution.

We think, for the most part, in words. But all words belong to specific languages, the products of specific cultures. As there is no universal human language, so there exists no universal human law or authority, else these laws, this authority, would be sovereign over the earth; but this, for nationalists, is nether possible nor desirable; a universal law is not true law: cosmopolitan culture is a sham and a delusion; international law is only called law by a precarious analogy – a hollow courtesy intended to conceal the violent break with the universalism of the past.

This assumption is less obvious in the case of Marxism, which in theory, at least, is internationalist. But Marxism is a nine-teenth-century ideology, and has not escaped the all-pervasive separatism of its time. Marxism is founded on reason; that is to say, it claims that its propositions are intelligible, and their truth can be "demonstrated" to any rational being in the possession of the relevant facts. It offers salvation to all men: anyone can, in principle, see the light, and denies it at his own peril.

In practice, however, this is not so. The theory of economic base and ideological superstructure on which Marxist sociology is founded teaches that the ideas in men's heads are conditioned by the position occupied by them, or by their economic class, in the productive system. This fact may be disguised from indi-vidual person by all kinds of self-delusions and rationalisations, but "scientific" analysis will always reveal that the vast majority of any given class believe only that which favours the interests of that class – interests which the social scientists can determine by objective historical analysis – whatever reason they may choose, however sincerely, to give for their beliefs; and conversely they disbelieve, reject, misunderstand, distort, try and escape from, ideas belief in which would weaken the position of their class.

All men are to be found, as it were, on one of two moving stairs; I belong to a class which, owing to its relationship to the forces of production, is either moving upwards towards triumph, or downwards towards ruin. In either case my beliefs and outlook – the legal, moral, social, intellectual, religious, aesthetic ideas – in which I feel at home, will reflect the interests of the class to which I belong. If I belong to a class moving towards victory, I shall hold a realistic set of beliefs, for I am not afraid of what I see; I am moving with the tide, knowledge of the truth can only give me confidence; if I belong to a doomed class, my inability to gaze upon the fatal facts – for few men are able to recognise that they are destined to perish – will falsify my calculations, and render me deaf and blind to truths too painful for me to face. It follows that it must be useless for members of the rising class to try to convince members of the falling order that the only way in which they can save themselves Is by understanding the necessities of history and therefore transferring themselves, if they can, to the steep stair that is moving upwards, from that which runs so easily to destruction. It is useless, because ex hypothesi members of a doomed class are conditioned to see everything through a falsifying lens: the plainest symptoms of approaching death will seem to them evidence of health an progress; they suffer from optimistic hallucinations, and must systematically misunderstand the warnings that persons who belong to a different economic class, in their charity, may try to give them; such delusions are themselves the inevitable by-product of clinging to an order which history has condemned. It is idle for the progressives to try to save their reactionary brothers from defeat: the doomed men cannot hear them, and their destruction is certain. All men will not be saved: the proletariat, justly intent upon its own salvation, had best ignore the fat of their oppressors: even if they wish to return good for evil, they cannot save their enemies from "liquidation". They are "expendable" – their destruction can be neither averted nor regretted by a rational being, for it is the price that mankind must pay for the progress of reason itself: the road to the gates of Paradise is necessarily strewn with corpses.

Although it has been reached by a different road, this conclusion is curiously similar to the nationalist or Fascist point of view, and different from the outlook of previous ages. However bitter the hatreds between Christians, Jews and Muslims, or between different sects within these faiths, the argument for the extermination of heretics always rested on the belief that it was in principle possible to convert men to the truth, which was none and universal, that is, visible to all; that only a few individuals were lost beyond redemption, being too blinded and perverted to be saved by anything but the sufferings of death. This rests on the assumption that men, as such, have a common nature, which makes communication in principle always possible and therefore always morally obligatory. It is this assumption that was at first questioned, and the altogether collapsed. The sheep must not try to save the goats – that is irrational and unrealisable.

The division of mankind into two groups – men proper, and some other, lower, order of beings, inferior races, inferior cultures, subhuman creatures, nations or classes condemned by history[2] – is something new in human history. It is a denial of common humanity – a premise upon which all previous humanism, religious and secular, had stood. This new attitude permits men to look on many millions of their fellow men as not quite human, to slaughter them without a qualm of conscience, without the need to try to save them or warn them. Such conduct is usually ascribed to barbarians or savages – men in a pre-rational frame of mind, characteristic of peoples in the infancy of civilisation. This explanation will no longer do. It is evidently possible to attain to a high degree of scientific knowledge and skill, an indeed, of general culture, and yet destroy others without pity, in the name of a nation, a class, or history itself. If this is childhood, it is the dotage of second childhood in its most repulsive form. How have men reached such a pass?

V

It is a truism that European history is a kind of dialectic between craving for public order and for individual liberty. The quest for order is a kind of fear before the elements, an attempt to build walls and hedges against the chaos caused by absence of control, against the weakening of traditions, habits, rules of life, in an effort to preserve the banisters that human beings need to prevent them from toppling over into an abyss, to connect them with their past and point a path to the future. When institutions become too set and obstruct growth, order becomes oppression and worship of it self-stultifying; sooner or later it is broken through by the almost physiological desire to live, move, create, by the need for novelty and change. Romanticism was just such an outbreak against a moral and political structure that had become a suffocating straitjacket: in due course this became decayed, and one fine day burst asunder in country after country. Like all revolutions, romanticism revealed new truths, endowed men with insights which they were never wholly to lose again, renovated the ancient establishment, and went too far and led to distortions and excesses, its own tyranny and its own victims. The distortions are all too familiar: our generation has paid for them more heavily, perhaps, than any other human society has ever paid for an aberration of the spirit.

The origins of this revolt are well known. The armies of Richelieu and of Louis XIV had crushed and humiliated a large part of the German population, and stifled the natural development of the new culture of the Protestant renaissance in the north. The Germans, a century later, rebelled against the dead hand of France in the realms of culture, art and philosophy, and avenged themselves by launching the great counter-attack against the Enlightenment. It took the form of glorification of the individual, the national and the historical, against the universal and the timeless; of the exaltation of genius, of the unaccountable, of the leap of the spirit that defies all rules and conventions, of the worship of the individual hero, the giant above and beyond the law, and an assault upon the great impersonal order with its unbreakable laws, and its clear assignment of its own place to every human function and group and class and purpose, which had been characteristic of the classical tradition, and had entered deeply into the texture of the western world, both ecclesiastical and secular. Variety in the place of uniformity; inspiration in the place of tried and tested rules or traditions; the inexhaustible and the unbounded in the place of measure, clarity, logical structure; the inner life and its expression in music; worship of the night and the irrational: that was the contribution of the wild German spirit, which broke like a fresh wind into the airless prison of the French Establishment. This great revolt of the humiliated Germans against the dead and levelling rationalist pedantry of French thought and taste in the mid-eighteenth century had, in its beginnings, a life-giving effect upon art and ideas about art, upon religion, upon personal relationships between human beings, upon individual morality. Then the tidal wave of feeling rose above its banks, and overflowed into the neighbouring provinces of politics and social life with literally devastating results. All forms of going to the bitter end were thought more worthy of man than peaceful negotiation, stopping half-way; extremism, conflict, war were glorified as such.

Few things have played a more fatal part in the history of human thought and action than great imaginative analogies from one sphere, in which a particular principle is applicable and valid, to other provinces, where its effect may be exciting and transforming, but where its consequences may be fallacious in theory and ruinous in practice. It was so with the romantic move-ment and its nationalist implications. The heroic individual, the free creator, became identified not with the unpolitical artist, but with leaders of men bending others to their indomitable will, or with classes, or races, or movements, or nations that asserted themselves against others, and identified their own liberty with the destruction of all that opposed them. The notion that liberty and power are identical, that to be free is to make free with whatever stands in your path, is an ancient idea which the romantics seized on and wildly exaggerated. Even more typical of romanticism is the insane, egomaniacal self-prostration before one's own true inner essence, one's of one's own skull, the place of one's birth, as against that which one shares with other people – reason, universal values, a sense of the community of mankind.

The neo-rationalism of Hegel and of Marx, in a sense, tried to oppose the unbridled subjectivism of the romantics, and their self-worship, by an effort to discover objective standards in the inexorable forces of history, or the laws of the evolution of the human spirit or the growth of productive forces and relations. But they were themselves sufficiently infected by romanticism to make progress consist in the defeat and absorption of the rest of society by one victorious section of it. For Hegel, progress and the liberation of the human spirit consist in the triumph of reason as embodied in the state over other forms of human organisation, the victory of the historic nations over the unhistoric, of "Germanic" culture over the rest, and of Europe over other "discarded" human cultures, the "dead" civilisation of China, for example, or the barbarous Slav nations. Without conflict, struggle, strife (so Hegel tells us) progress ceases, stagnation sets in. Similarly for Karl Marx, the proletarians can only become free by suppressing their adversaries with whom they, ex hypothesi, can have nothing in common. Progress is self-assertion, the conquest of an area in which the agent can freely develop and create by eliminating (or absorbing) whatever obstructs it, both animate and inanimate. In Hegel it is the nation organised as a state. In Marx it is the class organised as a revolutionary force. In both cases a large number of human beings must be sacrificed and annihilated if the ideal is to triumph. Unity may be the ultimate goal of humanity, but its method of attaining it is war and disintegration. The path may lead to a terrestrial paradise, but it is strewn with the corpses of the enemy, for whom no tear must be shed, since right and wrong, good and bad, success and failure, wisdom and folly, are all in the end determined by the objective ends of history, which has "condemned" half mankind – unhistoric nations, members of obsolete classes, inferior races – to what Proudhon called "liquidation", and Trotsky, in an equally picturesque phrase, described as the rubbish heap of history.

Yet there is a central insight given us by romantic humanism – this same untamed German spirit – which we shall not easily forget. Firstly that the maker of values is man himself, and may therefore not be slaughtered in the name of anything higher than himself, for there is nothing higher; this is what Kant meant when he spoke of man as an end in himself, and not a means to an end. Secondly, that institutions are made not only by, but also for, men, and when they no longer serve him they must go. Thirdly that men may not be slaughtered, either in the name of abstract ideas, however lofty, such as progress or freedom or humanity, or of institutions, for none of these have any absolute value in themselves, inasmuch as all that they have has been conferred upon them by men, who alone can make things valuable or sacred; hence attempts to resist or change them are never a rebellion against divine commands to be punished by destruction. Fourthly – and this follows from the rest – that the worst of all sins is to degrade or humiliate human beings for the sake of some Procrustean pattern into which they are to be forced against their wills, a pattern that has some objective authority irrespective of human aspirations.

This conception of man, inherited from the romantic movement, remains in us to this day: it is something which, despite all that mankind has lived through, we in Europe have not abandoned. For this reason, when Hegel and Marx prophesied inevitable doom for all those who defied the march of history, their threats came too late. Hegel and Marx, each in his fashion, tried to tell human beings that only one path to liberty and salvation lay before them – that which was offered them by history, which embodied cosmic reason; that those who failed to adapt themselves, or to realise that rationality, interest, duty, power, success were, in the long run, identical with one another and with morality and wisdom, would be destroyed by "the forces of history", to defy which was suicidal folly. But this line of metaphysical intimidation proved on the whole ineffective. Too many men were prepared to defend their principles even against the irresistible power with which Marx threatened to annihilate them. The ideals of individual human beings commanded respect and even reverence, even if no guarantees of objective validity could be provided. Fidelity to an ideal, indestructible regard for what a man himself, whatever his reasons, believed to be true, or right, became something in the name of which men were prepared to defy the big battalions, even if these were identified with the mysterious power of history or reality itself. It was no longer possible to persuade men that Don Quixote was not merely foolish and unpractical and obsolete (which no one had denied), but that because he had ignored the historic position of his nation, or race, or class he was defying the forces of progress and was therefore vicious and wicked too. Men stood up, as they had always done, and became martyrs for their beliefs, and were admired for it, at times even by those who destroyed them. They were tortured and died for principles which, so at any rate they believed, were universal and binding on all men, part of the human essence in virtue of which men were rightly called men. They could not break these principles, without feeling that they had forfeited all right to human respect. They could not betray them and face themselves or others. For this reason the appeals to realism made to defeated countries in 1940 by victorious German leaders, who said, reasonably enough, that resistance was useless, that the new order was coming, that this new order would transform the values of all the world, that to resist was not only to be crushed, but to be written off as fools or enemies of the light by later generations, inevitably conditioned by the morality of the victors – this type of argument failed to break the spirit of those who truly believed in universal human values. Some resisted in the name of universal ideals enshrined in churches, or national traditions, or objective knowledge of the truth, others stood up for goals which were none the less sacred because they were individual and private to their possessors.

This dedication to ideals, irrespective of their "source" – it is sometimes even denied that there is a source to seek – has an affinity with the modern existentialist position, which declares that the attempt to seek guarantees for moral beliefs in some vast, objective metaphysical order is no more than a pathetic attempt on the part of men to look for help outside themselves, to lean on something stronger than themselves, to derive rational justification for their acts by proving that they are ordained by some objective establishment; that they do this because they have not the courage to face the fact that there may exist no such establishment, that their values are what they are, and men commit themselves as they do, for no reason, or rather for the only reason that can, in principle, be given, namely that, being what they are, this particular end – whatever it may be – is what they have chosen, is their ultimate goal; that is what choice entails – and beyond it there is no other, and since a final goal justifies all else it cannot itself need justification. Such existentialists are legitimate descendants of that humanist romanticism which declares that man is independent and is free, that is to say, that the essence of man is not consciousness, nor the invention of tools, but the power of choice. Human history, as a famous Russian thinker once remarked, has no libretto: the actors must improvise their parts. Reality bursts through the patterns in which we try – in our effort to find assurance and comfort – to arrange it. The universe is not a jigsaw puzzle, of which we try to piece together the fragments, in the knowledge that one pattern exists, and one alone, in which they must all fit. We are faced with conflicting values; the dogma that they must somehow, somewhere be reconcilable is a mere pious hope; experience shows that it is false. We must choose, and in choosing one thing lose another, irretrievably perhaps. If we choose individual liberty, this may entail a sacrifice of some form of organization which might have led to greater efficiency. If we choose justice, we may be forced to sacrifice mercy. If we choose knowledge we may sacrifice innocence and happiness. If we choose democracy, we may sacrifice a strength that comes from militarisation or from obedient hierarchies. If we choose equality, we may sacrifice some degree of individual freedom. If we choose to fight for our lives, we may sacrifice many civilised values, much that we have laboured greatly to create. Nevertheless, the glory and dignity of man consist in the fact that it is he who chooses, and is not chosen for, that he can be his own master (even if at times this fills him with fear and a sense of solitude), that he is not compelled to purchase security and tranquillity at the price of letting himself be fitted into a neat pigeon-hole in a totalitarian structure which contrives to rob him of responsibility, freedom and respect both for himself and others, at one single stroke.

VI

The disintegrating influence of romanticism, both in the comparatively innocuous form of the chaotic rebellion of the free artist of the nineteenth century and in the sinister and destructive form of totalitarianism, seems, in western Europe at least, to have spent itself. The forces that make for stability and reason are beginning to reassert themselves. But nothing ever goes back completely to its starting-point; the progress of humanity appears to be not cyclical, but a painful spiral, and even nations learn from experience. What has emerged from the recent holocausts? Something approaching a new recognition in the west that there are certain universal values which can be called constitutive of human beings as such. Romanticism in its inflamed state – Fascist, National Socialist, and communist too – has produced a deep shock in Europe, less by its doctrines than by the actions of its followers – by trampling on certain values which, when they were brutally thrown aside, proved their vitality, and returned like war cripples to haunt the European conscience.

What are these values? What is their status, and why should we accept them? May it not be true, as some existentialist and nihilist extremists have maintained, that there are no human values, still less European values? Men simply commit themselves as they commit themselves, for no reason. I dedicate myself to being a poet, and you to being a hangman: this is my choice and that is yours, and there are no objective standards in terms of which these choices can be graded, whereby my morality is superior or inferior to yours. We choose as we choose, that is all that can be said; and if this leads to conflict and destruction, that is a fact about the world which must be accepted as gravitation is accepted, something which is inherent in the dissimilar natures of dissimilar men, or nations, or cultures, That this is not a valid diagnosis has been made clear if only by the great and widespread sense of horror which the excesses of totalitarianism have caused. For the fact of shock reveals that there does exist a scale of values by which – the majority of mankind – and in particular of western Europeans – in fact live, live not merely mechanically and out of habit, but as part of what in their moments of self-awareness constitutes for them the essential nature of man.

What is this nature? Physically it is not too difficult to say: we think that men must possess a certain physical, physiological, and nervous structure, certain organs, certain physical senses and psychological properties, capacities for thinking, willing, feeling, and that anyone who lacks too many of these properties should not properly be called a man, but an animal or an inanimate object. But there are also certain moral properties which enter equally deeply into what we conceive of as human nature. If we meet someone who merely disagrees with us about the ends of life, who prefers happiness to self-sacrifice, or knowledge to friendship, we accept them as fellow human beings, because their notion of what is an end, the arguments they bring to defend their ends, and their general behaviour, are within the limits of what we regard as being human. But if we meet someone who cannot see why (to take a famous example) he should not destroy the world in order to relieve a pain in his little finger, or someone who genuinely sees no harm in condemning innocent men, or betraying friends, or torturing children, then we find that we cannot argue with such people, not so much because we are horrified as because we think them in some way inhuman – we call them moral idiots. We sometimes confine them in lunatic asylums. They are as much outside the frontiers of humanity as creatures who lack some of the minimum physical characteristics that constitute human beings. We lean on the fact that the laws and principles to which we appeal, when we make moral and political decisions of a fundamental kind, have, unlike legal enactments, been accepted by the majority of men, during, at any rate, most of recorded history; we regard them as incapable of being abrogated; we know of no court, no authority, which could, by means of some recognised process, allow men to bear false witness, or torture freely, or slaughter fellow men for pleasure; we cannot conceive of getting these universal principles or rules repealed or altered; in other words, we treat them not as something that we, or our forefathers, freely chose to adopt, but rather as presuppositions of being human at all, of living in a common world with others, of recognising them, and being ourselves recognised, as persons. Because these rules were flouted, we have been forced to become conscious of them.

This is a kind of return to the ancient notion of natural law, bur, for some of us, in empiricist dress – no longer necessarily based on theological or metaphysical foundations. Hence to speak of our values as objective and universal is not to say that there exists some objective code, imposed upon us from without, unbreakable by us because not made by us; it is to say that we cannot help accepting these basic principles because we are human, as we cannot help (if we are normal) seeking warmth rather than cold, truth rather than falsehood, to be recognised by others for what we are rather than to be ignored or misunderstood. When these principles are basic, and have been long and widely recognised, we tend to think of them as universal ethical laws, and we assume that when human beings pretend that they do not recognise them, they must be lying or deceiving themselves, or else that they have in some way lost the power of moral discrimination, and are to that extent abnormal. When such canons seem less universal, less profound, less crucial, we call them, in descending order of importance, customs, conventions, manners, taste, etiquette, and concerning these we not only permit but actively expect wide differences. Indeed we do not look on variety as being itself disruptive of our basic unity; it is uniformity that we consider to be the product of a lack of imagination, or of philistinism, and in extreme cases a form of slavery.

The common moral – and therefore also political – foundations of our conduct, so far from being undermined by the wars and the degradation of human personality that we have witnessed in our time, have emerged as something more broadly and deeply laid than they seemed to be during the first forty years of this century. I say "our" conduct; I mean by this the habits and outlook of the western world. Asia and Africa are today boiling cauldrons of disruptive nationalism, as Germany and perhaps France still were after Britain and Holland and Scandinavia had attained relative equilibrium. Humanity does not seem to march with an even step, the crises of national development are not synchronised. Nevertheless, after the violent aberrations of the recent European experience, there are symptoms of recovery: of a return, that is to say, to normal health – the habits, traditions, above all the common notions of good and evil, which reunite us to our Greek and Hebrew and Christian and humanist past; transformed by the romantic revolt, but essentially in reaction against it. Our values today tend to be, increasingly, the old universal standards which distinguish civilised men, however dull, from barbarians, however gifted. When we resist aggression, or the destruction of liberty under despotic regimes, it is to these values that we appeal. And we appeal to them without the slightest doubt that those to whom we speak, no matter under what regime they live, do in fact understand our language; for it is clear, from all evidence, whether they pretend otherwise or not, that in fact they do so. The spokesmen of despotism may profess (it may be not always sincerely) that the brutalities and repression which they practise are designed to make these same values shine the more strongly in the new world which they are about to build. If this does not ring true, it is at any rate not cynicism but hypocrisy: an attempt to seem virtuous; a tribute to the restored prestige of humanism.

This was not so in the 20s and 30s of our century, when totalitarians of both the right and left affected to reject humanistic values as such – the good and the bad together – and did not say, as they now say more and more frequently, that they were serving them better than we. This seems to me genuine gain, genuine progress towards an international order, based on a recognition that we inhabit one common moral world. Upon this our hope must rest.

Notes

1.   Address at the third Congress of the Fondation Européenne de la Culture. In: Isaiah Berlin, *The Crooked Timber of Humanity. Chapters in the History of Ideas* (Princeton, N.J.: Princeton University Press, 2013). Parts of the original text have been omitted in this publication.

2.   Even if it is allowed that individuals can save themselves by a great leap on to the upward-moving stair – as, after all, Marx and Engels themselves and many another bourgeois revolutionary did – this is a step which can be taken only by individuals, but never by entire classes or even large parts of them.

Contemporary essays

Homogeinity and Diversity

Tom Holland

For many years, German leaders had been struggling to cope with an influx of peoples across their borders. While the crisis was one that had afflicted much of Europe, it was Germany that bore the brunt. Year after after year they had been coming, crossing from the steppes of the Carpathian Basin into Swabia and Bavaria, a relentless tide of migrants who, while they shared neither the religion nor the customs of the native Germans, were irresistibly drawn by perceptions of their wealth. Various policies had been attempted to stem the flow. Carrots, in the form of financial subsidies, and sticks, in the form of refurbished border controls, had both been judiciously applied. Nothing, though, seemed to work. Indeed, the determination of those beyond the limits of Germany to cross its frontiers appeared, if anything, to be stiffening. As a result, for the German authorities, the moment of truth was drawing near. The choice they faced was a stark one: either to secure a definitive solution to the crisis, or else to lose control of their borders altogether.

The storm finally broke in the summer of 955. "A multitude of Hungarians, such as no living person can remember having seen in any one region before, invaded the realm of the Bavarians which they devastated and occupied simultaneously from the Danube to the dark forest on the rim of the mountains."[1] It was not only the scale of the invasion force which filled the Germans with dread, though, but the evident scope of its preparations. Previously, when the Hungarians had come sweeping out of their steppe lands, they had done so exclusively on horseback, setting a premium on speed, the better to strip a landscape bare, and then to retreat back to the Danube before the more heavily armoured German cavalry could corner them. Plunder, not territorial acquisitions, had been their goal. Now, though, it seemed that they had a different strategy. Crossing into German territory, their horsemen rode at a measured pace. Alongside them marched huge columns of infantry. Siege engines creaked and rumbled in their train. This time, it seemed, the Hungarians had come to conquer.

Early in August, they arrived before the walls of Augsburg. The city, rich and strategically vital though it was, stood perilously exposed. Otto, the German king, had been campaigning far in the north, and no one knew when, if at all, he could be expected to come to its relief. Instead, in the hour of its darkest peril, it was Ulrich, the city's formidably learned bishop, who took command of its defence. While men laboured to shore up the walls, and women walked in procession, offering up fearful prayers, Ulrich toured the battlements, inspiring the garrison under his command to trust in Christ. Yet so overwhelming were the forces besieging the city, and so menacing their preparations, that it seemed to many that Augsburg was bound to fall. On 8 August, as siege engines crawled towards the fortifications, and infantry were driven forwards under the lash, a gateway above a river named the Lech was breached. Ulrich, "wearing only his vestments, protected by neither shield, nor chain mail, nor helmet,"[2] rode on his horse to block the Hungarians' path. Miraculously, despite the hissing of arrows all around him, and the thudding of stones, he succeeded in holding the attackers at bay. The open gate was secured. The Hungarians did not enter Augsburg.

And already, in their trail, relief for the imperilled city was on its way. Otto, informed of the Hungarian invasion of Bavaria, had ridden fast and furiously to confront it. With him he brought 3,000 heavily armoured cavalry and the single most potent treasure in his entire realm: the very spear which had pierced the side of Christ, and which, adorned as it was by the nails used in the Crucifixion, served to "join the realm of the mortal to that of heaven".[3] These advantages, in the terrible battle that followed, would prove sufficient to gain Otto a stunning victory against all the odds. A great surging cavalry charge crushed the Hungarians; the German horsemen, pursuing them across the floodplain of the Lech, then hacked and speared them down; of the mighty force that had laid siege to Augsburg almost nothing was left. Such was the glory of Otto's feat that his troops, standing on the battlefield amid the tangle of corpses and banners, hailed their triumphant king as "emperor". Sure enough, within seven years, he was crowned by the Pope in Rome. The line of emperors that began with him would continue unbroken for centuries, and only finally come to an end in 1806.

The battle of the Lech was decisive in another way too, though. The Hungarians had ranked as merely the latest in a whole succession of nomadic peoples who, possessed of such speed as to seem barely human and the devilish ability to fire arrows even while at full gallop, had repeatedly menaced the settled realms of Europe. Back in the 5th century, the onslaught of a steppe people named the Huns had overwhelmed the defences of the Roman Empire, and helped to precipitate the implosion of its entire western half. Now, by laying claim to the title of Caesar, Otto was declaring that the age of such invasions was past, that the frontiers of Christendom were stable, and that never again would the ululations of horse archers be permitted to chill the souls of decent Christians. A line had been drawn under the age of mass migrations. And so, astonishingly, it proved. Those Hungarians who had survived the killing fields of the Lech withdrew to the Carpathian Basin, to lick their wounds and to start putting down roots themselves. Fifty years on from the great battle, and their chieftain, graced with the name of Stephen, could be welcomed publicly into the ranks of Christian kings. Sent a diadem by the Pope, he was also presented by Otto's grandson with a replica of that most awesome of all the weapons in the possession of the German monarchy: the Holy Lance itself.

Elsewhere too Christendom was rallying against its foes. Both the Slavs, whom Otto had been fighting when first informed of the Hungarian invasion, and the pagans of Viking Scandinavia, whose depredations had set Britain, Ireland and northern France to bleed, were increasingly being brought to Christ. Meanwhile, along the southern flank of Christendom, the enduring menace of Arab slavers, which had prompted one pope in the 9th century to lament that the whole of Italy was being "stripped bare of its inhabitants,"[*] had likewise begun to be tamed. Not that the warriors charged with the securing of Christendom's frontiers were content to confine themselves merely to defence. A hundred years on from the battle of the Lech, and the tramping of their heavy warhorses was becoming a thing of dread to Muslim and pagan leaders alike. Over the centuries that followed, a great wave of conquest, colonisation and evangelisation saw them reclaim territory lost to Islam in southern Italy and Spain, and expand deep into Eastern Europe. Mosques were converted into churches; pagan shrines put to the torch. Nowhere else in Eurasia was there a civilisation quite so religiously monocultural; nowhere else in Eurasia was there one quite so secure against the armies of mounted archers who tended otherwise to dominate the medieval battlefield. Even the Mongols, who in the 13th century put much of Eastern Europe in their shadow, failed to penetrate the heartlands of Latin Christendom. Only with the expansion of Ottoman power, which saw Muslim rule established over the Balkans and much of Hungary, did the civilisation of Christian Europe face a serious menace from adversaries who did not subscribe to its own faith. Even that, though, after the failure in 1683 of a second Ottoman attempt to capture Vienna, ended up in palpable retreat. By the 18th century, with their fleets sweeping distant oceans, their flags fluttering over distant colonies, and their emigrants settling across the world, Europeans could take for granted the impregnability of their own continent. Mass migration, so it had come to be assumed, was something that they inflicted upon the lands of non-Europeans – not the other way round.

It went without saying, of course, that the lethal talent displayed by Europeans for war and empire-building in the world beyond Europe did not remotely preclude them from unleashing it against one another as well. The ambitions and capabilities of Christian warlords had invariably been honed within the frontiers of Christendom itself. The same Normans who wrested Sicily from Muslim rule had only a few years previously conquered the thoroughly Christian kingdom of England. Otto, despite the greatness of his achievements and the splendour of his coronation, had failed to mould his empire into a simulacrum of that of the Caesars. The dream of a pan-European imperium, far from joining the peoples of the continent within a single political order such as had been forged at the opposite end of Eurasia, in China, served only to perpetuate the hatreds and rivalries that divided them. The termination in 1806 of the line of emperors founded by Otto the Great came amidst the convulsions of Napoleon's own attempt to found a great empire, and which, despite the astonishing sweep of his conquests, ultimately left Europe more fatefully riven than ever. The fracture line between France and Germany, one of the oldest in the continent, was entrenched as its most dangerous as well. In 1870, and then again in 1914, hostility between the two powers exploded into war. The second conflict, by dragging in other countries as well, and by harnessing the full capabilities that decades of industrialisation had bestowed upon its generals, engulfed Europe in a war more ruinous and terrible than any in its history.

"For a moment the water below him looked like some window, glazed with grimy glass, through which he was peering. Wrenching his hands out of the bog, he sprang back with a cry. 'There are dead things, dead faces in the water,' he said with horror. 'Dead faces!'"[5] This terrifying vision, of corpses in the mud of a battlefield, and left to float for all eternity, appeared in the novel that has probably done more to define a particular vision of European history than any other published in the last century. Its author, who had joined the British army in 1915 and fought in the battle of the Somme, was one of numerous writers and artists who sought, in the wake of the Great War, to make sense of the calamity that had engulfed Europe. Like others, he recognised in the mechanised slaughter that had left over 10 million Europeans dead a distinctive darkness bred of the age. In 1917, recuperating in a military hospital, he composed a fantastical tale, 'The Fall of Gondolin', in which monstrous machines of metal, powered by "hearts and spirits of blazing fire"[6], were portrayed as bringing ruin to a beauteous city. The echo of the tanks, which only the previous year had made their first appearance in combat, rumbling across the Western front, was palpable. Yet the wellsprings of J.R.R. Tolkien's imagination did not ultimately lie in the present. Twenty years on from the Great War, as hopes that conflict had been banished for good from Europe grew ever more delusory, the mirror that he held up to humanity's capacity for good and evil was one forged from the very beginnings of Germanic culture. *The Lord of the Rings*, which Tolkien began in 1937 and continued to write over the course of Europe's second great civil war of the 20th century, drew heavily for its inspiration on the early literature and history of the country with which Tolkien's own was locked in mortal combat. Conversely, no matter how hard he might subsequently deny the influence of contemporary events "upon either the plot or the manner of its unfolding"[7], his fiction was not shaped exclusively by ancient song. By 1946, while Hans Fallada was writing *Jeder Stirbt für sich Allein*, Albert Camus *La Peste* and George Orwell *Nineteen Eighty-Four*, Tolkien was working on a narrative that, though it might feature elves and wizards, was no less for that a portrait of total war, existential doubt and totalitarian ambition.

"The plain was dark with their marching companies, and as far as eyes could strain in the mirk there sprouted, like a foul fungus growth, all about the beleaguered city great camps of tents, black or sombre red."[8] So Tolkien, writing in the year that followed the liberation of Auschwitz and the suicide of Hitler, described the opening of the great military engagements that were to provide *The Lord of the Rings* with its narrative climax. Minas Tirith, bulwark of the free lands of the West, is invested by an invasion force sent from the East by the Dark Lord, Sauron, whose stronghold of Mordor constitutes a hellish wasteland of prisons, furnaces and blackened industrial squalor. Attempts by readers to see in this an allegory of the Battle of Britain or the Cold War would be dismissed by Tolkien with gruff disdain – and reasonably so. While there are certainly echoes of European history in his novel, they derive from the ancient past, not the 20th century. Minas Tirith, vast and beautiful, yet "falling year by year into decay",[9] is menaced by land and sea as Constantinople was in 716 by Arab task forces. The armies of Sauron repeat the strategy of Attila, the King of the Huns, on the Catalaunian plains – and suffer a similar fate. Above all, though, the narrative of the siege of Minas Tirith and its ultimate defeat derive from the momentous events of 955: the attack on Augsburg and the battle of the Lech. A wise and battle-seasoned scholar, consecrated in his mission by a supernatural power, stands in the gateway of the breached city, and blocks the enemy's advance. An army of heavily armoured horsemen arrives to contend the battlefield just as the invaders seem to have victory in their grasp. A king armed with an ancient and potent weapon wins such glory for himself that in time, once the war is successfully concluded, he is able to lay claim to a venerable but vanished monarchy. The roots of *The Lord of the Rings* in the early Middle Ages, a period when Christendom was repeatedly battling for survival against invaders from the East, could hardly be more evident.

Naturally, though, when Tolkien drew on the records of attacks by Huns, or Arabs, or Hungarians, he did not mean to equate any of them with the monstrous evil embodied by Mordor. The age of migrations was sufficiently remote, he believed, that there was little prospect of his readers believing that. He had no wish to demonise entire peoples – ancient or modern. "I'm very anti that kind of thing."[10] Instead, the darkness embodied by Sauron and his teeming hordes of orcs was of an altogether more universal order. "One has indeed personally to come under the shadow of war to feel fully its oppression," Tolkien wrote in his introduction to the second edition of *The Lord of the Rings*; "but as the years to go by it seems now often forgotten that to be caught in youth by 1914 was no less hideous an experience than to be involved in 1939 and the following years."[11] He knew what it was to stare into the heart of Europe's 20th-century darkness. The blasted desecration of tree and flower that had run like a scar across Belgium and France during the Great War features in *The Lord of the Rings* as the invariable marker of Sauron's rule. The orcs, twisted simulacra of the free peoples of Middle Earth, represent neither Hungarians nor Germans, but are emblematic instead of the capacity for murderousness that Tolkien had witnessed for himself in the trenches – British as well as German. Beauty throughout the novel is menaced by ugliness and pollution, and freedom by the dread that an acceptance of servitude might provide the surest way to stay alive. The gaze of Sauron himself, a lidless eye of fire, can penetrate even into the minds of his foes, and either seduce them into collaboration, or else drive them to despair. "The West has failed," laments the Steward of Minas Tirith, Denethor, who has been rendered suicidal by his adversary's propaganda, and the revelation of the teeming numbers under Sauron's power. "Go back and burn!"[12]

That horrors conjured up from both the distant past and the age of fascism should meet and merge in the narrative of *The Lord of the Rings* marks it out as no less recognisably a product of Europe's mid-century agony than are, say, *Guernica* or *Doktor Faustus*. What did render Tolkien exceptional, though – and indeed, perhaps, the last of a kind – was the degree to which he took literally notions that were already venerable in the age of Otto the Great. "We will burn like heathen kings,"[13] says Denethor, as he prepares to immolate himself and his unconscious son on a pyre. It is one of the few moments in the novel where its profoundly Christian character is rendered overt. Tolkien, devout Catholic that he was, believed in evil, not as an allegory or as a metaphor, but as something literal: a satanic force. The character of his faith was of a kind that Bishop Ulrich of Augsburg might have recognised: one that took literally the intervention of angels in human affairs, the legitimacy of sacral kingship, and the potency of sanctified weapons. *The Return of the King*, Tolkien titled the last volume of *The Lord of the Rings*; and when Aragorn, claimant to the throne of Minas Tirith, appears before the walls of the city at the head of a great host, and leads the slaughter of those besieging it, he is armed – just as Otto had been at the battle of the Lech – with a token of his supernatural mandate. "But before all," Tolkien writes, "went Aragorn with the Flame of the West, Andúril like a new fire kindled, Narsil re-forged as deadly as of old..."[14] The ideal is that of the Christian warrior, dressed in the armour of God's favour; and sure enough, when Sauron is finally overthrown, and Aragorn's return as king thereby rendered certain, Tolkien made sure to confirm for his readers the precise theological context for this dramatic climax. The fall of Mordor, so he specified, occurred on the twenty-fifth of March: the very date on which, back in the age of Otto the Great, it was conventionally believed that Christ had been crucified.

Such subtleties, it is true, have rarely been noted by the millions around the globe who have helped to make *The Lord of the Rings* the single best-selling European novel of the past century. For all that its seedbed lay in Tolkien's incomparable knowledge of the languages, literature and history of early medieval Europe, its bloom required no specialist knowledge to be enjoyed. As a result, and by an irony that would doubtless have appalled Tolkien himself, its principal impact has been to inspire a repackaging of the culture of the early Middle Ages in a form that has been largely drained of historical specificities. Magical weapons and warlocks with staffs have become the common currency of an entire new global genre. The very word used to describe it, 'fantasy', suggests just how severed from the moorings so treasured by Tolkien it has become. When Peter Jackson, a New Zealander working for an American studio, made a three-film adaptation of *The Lord of the Rings*, its massive global success demonstrated just how universal was the appeal of narratives garbed in the armour and samite of Europe's medieval past; but demonstrated as well just how deracinated even those directly inspired by Tolkien had become.

It is hardly surprising, in a continent that has witnessed as many social and ideological upheavals as Europe has over the past millennium, that the world of Otto the Great should now in many ways appear as fantastical as that of Aragorn. We are separated from the ideals and convictions that inspired him at the battle of the Lech by the Reformation and the Enlightenment, and by both the French and the Industrial Revolutions. Nothing, though, has done more to prevent Europeans – and Germans in particular – from eulogising the martial exploits of Otto and his ilk than the calamitous events of the past century. In 1946, even as Tolkien was writing his account of the siege of Minas Tirith, the trial opened in Nuremberg of the most prominent surviving members of the Nazi leadership. A year on from the liberation of Belsen and Auschwitz, details of the proceedings made clear to the world the full genocidal scale of the Third Reich's crimes. The image of the First Reich, founded by Otto the Great in the wake of the battle of the Lech, could not help but be contaminated by the uses to which it had been put by Nazi propagandists. Himmler had enshrined Otto's father, a famed warrior-king by the name of Heinrich, as the supreme model of Germanic heroism, and was darkly rumoured to have believed himself the king's reincarnation. Hitler, although privately contemptuous of Himmler's more mystical leanings, had himself been obsessed by Wagner's opera *Parsifal*, which gave a prominent role to the Holy Lance. The wellsprings of German history could hardly have been more poisoned. The warrior traditions of the First Reich, which had long provided Germans with a source of patriotic pride, were fatally tarnished. Only if recast as fantasy could their enduring glamour still be enjoyed without the risk of triggering baneful associations with Nazism. In the mythology of post-war Europe, it is no longer the kings of the First Reich who are associated with the Holy Lance, but Hitler.

The guilt, though, was not the Germans' alone. "To write poetry after Auschwitz," Theodor Adorno famously wrote, "is barbarism."[15] It was the history and culture of Europe as a whole that had helped lead to the Holocaust, and so it was the history and culture of Europe as a whole that stood on trial. European self-loathing was then compounded by two further momentous developments: the collapse of the British, French and Dutch empires, and the arrival in Western Europe of large numbers of immigrants from non-European countries. Britain's painting of the globe red and France's *mission civilisatrice* were transformed in the course of only a couple of generations from causes for widespread national self-congratulation to embarrassments. In particular, as Western Europe – for the first time since the expulsion of Spain's Moors in 1492 – came to play host to large numbers of Muslims, it was the history of the West's interactions with Islam that provided scope for particular revisionism. The involvement of numerous European countries in the US-led invasion of Iraq in 2003 was placed firmly and understandably by its critics in the context of two centuries of British and French weight-throwing in the Muslim world. The *Reconquista*, long celebrated by Spaniards as the redemption of the country from alien conquerors, came increasingly to be recast as the destruction of an oasis of sophistication and tolerance, in which Jews, Christians and Muslims had all happily sat next to tinkling fountains, snacking on oranges and discussing Aristotle. National heroes such as Godfroi de Bouillon, Richard the Lionheart and Don John of Austria were all quietly retired, and 'crusader' rendered a dirty word. The assumption that the conflict between medieval Christendom and its Arab and Turkish adversaries was merely an expression of inveterate European racism, rather than what it truly was – a desperate, see-sawing struggle for survival – was enshrined as a new orthodoxy. Elites who had once delighted in proclaiming the supremacy of their own culture were now more likely to pat themselves on the back for scorning it. A continent that had come to pride itself on transcending history had no wish to dwell on the more embarrassing aspects of its own past. In 2003, when the first draft of a putative EU constitution was drawn up, its authors were happy to acknowledge Europe's debt to ancient Greece and Rome, and to salute the achievements of the Enlightenment – but of the Christian roots of European civilisation not a mention was made. The implication was obvious: everything between Marcus Aurelius and Voltaire ranked as mere backwardness and superstition. Europe's values had to be reckoned, not sectarian, but universal – or they were nothing.

That the European Union owed nothing to Christianity would, of course, have come as news to men such as Konrad Adenauer or Robert Schumann: founding fathers of the European project who were at the same time devoutly Catholic. Even today, with pews across Europe increasingly empty, the attempt to fashion an inclusive and multi-faith future for the continent remains shadowed by a paradox: that it has patently been grounded in Christian doctrines. The inheritance of Christendom, even when most assertively repudiated, has proven a hard one to buck. The Bible, for all that it might be deployed to mandate the violence of warrior kings and crusaders, was not merely a tool of the mighty. It served as well to endow the weak, the poor and the needy with a value that they had never before possessed. "You have heard that it was said, 'You shall love your neighbour and hate your enemy.' But I say to you, 'Love your enemies . . .'"[6] Such a command, like many that Jesus gave, might seem so counter-intuitive as to appear impossible to fulfil; and yet for all that, and however little many may have paused to contemplate its ultimate derivation, it has tended to provide elites across Europe, in their efforts to accommodate immigrants from outside the Christian tradition, with their moral lodestar. In the wake of Nazism, and the traumatic demonstration of just what depths the peoples of Europe might be led to by their capacity for hatred, no text has done more to underpin the construction of a new and multicultural identity for the continent than the Sermon on the Mount. It is not enough for Europeans merely to tolerate different cultures: they must learn to respect and embrace them as well. "We don't have too much Islam," as Angela Merkel, Germany's Chancellor, put it last November, "we have too little Christianity."[7]

A striking suggestion for Europe's most powerful leader to float. Merkel made it as she sought to win her party's support for her policy towards the thousands upon thousands of migrants and refugees from Muslim countries who, over the course of the summer, had been moving through the Balkans and into Hungary. Merkel had not summoned the heavy cavalry; she had not played at being Otto the Great. Instead, on 4 September 2015, she had opened up Germany's borders. Syrians, Afghans and Pakistanis had immediately begun crossing into Bavaria.

Soon, upwards of 10,000 a day were entering Germany. Crowds gathered at railway stations to cheer them; football fans raised banners at matches to proclaim them welcome. The scenes, Merkel declared, "painted a picture of Germany which can make us proud of our country".[18] The exorcism of the Nazi years, when minorities had been bundled onto trains as part of a programme of extermination, appeared complete. Yet Merkel, although all too painfully conscious of the shadow cast by her country's history, was inspired as well by her upbringing as the daughter of a pastor, and of a mother no less devout. Rainer Eppelmann, an old political associate of the Chancellor's, and a pastor himself, has emphasised the influence on her as a girl of the Sermon on the Mount. "The daily message was: Love thy neighbour as yourself. Not just German people. God loves everybody."[19]

Yet, inevitably, not all Merkel's compatriots have been enthusiasts for her open-doors policy, nor her acknowledgement that a huge influx of people from very different cultures to that of Germany will inevitably change the country. "That is then a different society." So the Bavarian leader, Horst Seehofer, has complained. "People don't want Germany or Bavaria to become a different society."[20] The particular irony that German Christians who do their duty towards Muslim refugees may thereby be expediting a transformation of Europe's Christian character has not gone un-noted. By a further irony, the man who has pointed this out most intemperately, and thereby invoked something of the martial spirit of Otto the Great, is none other than Viktor Orbán, the Prime Minister of Hungary. That Orbán himself was until recently a self-avowed atheist has not prevented him from publicly doubting – much as Otto might have done over a millennium ago – whether unbaptised migrants can ever truly be integrated. "This is an important question, because Europe and European culture have Christian roots." In countries like Orbán's, where folk memories of the Ottoman occupation remain strong, or Poland, where the population's religious complexion retains something of Christendom's old homogeneity, Muslim immigrants are now openly described by government ministers as a menace. In Germany too, where street campaigns against 'the islamisation of the Occident' have swelled over recent months, and in the ranks of nationalist parties from Finland to France, and in angry chatrooms, and on websites much adorned with images of magical swords, there is no lack of people to play the role of Denethor, and warn, "All the East is moving".[21]

The abiding potency of such a dread, bred as it is of the marrow of European culture, is hardly surprising. If the imagery of knights manning the battlements of a beleaguered city against orcs can be used to sell video games, then why not a political narrative? It is, after all, a multiplayer edition. Europeans were not the only ones in the Middle Ages to sacralise violence. The Muslim forces who, shortly after the death of Otto the Great, sacked the cathedral of Santiago de Compostela in northern Spain and harvested the heads of its defenders were no less convinced of their divinely authored mandate than was Bishop Ulrich as he stood in the breached gate of Augsburg. Muslim corsairs, as they descended on an unsuspecting Italian town, would hunt out slaves in the certainty that they were licensed to do so by God. To Muhammad, and to all who followed him, had been granted the "spoils of war"[22] – and a constituent part of this plunder was human livestock. So, at any rate, Muslims tended to believe back in the 10th century. That most no longer believe it today demonstrates the degree to which ethical standards in Islam, as in Christianity, have evolved over the centuries. Yet just as the Norwegian mass-murderer, Anders Breivik, when he denounced Labour Party members as representatives of a "multiculturalist regime" deserving of execution, invoked the Knights Templar to justify his rampage, so are there Muslims living in Europe now convinced that decapitations and slavery can readily be justified by the example of Muhammad. "We estimate", declared the EU Commissioner for Justice last spring, "that 5,000 to 6,000 individuals have left for Syria"[23] – there to join an organisation that openly exults in the beheading of prisoners and the enslavement of 'pagans'. The past, it turns out, is a nightmare from which Europeans have not woken up, after all.

The conceit that secular liberal democracy embodies an ideal that can transcend its origins in the specific cultural and religious traditions of Europe, and lay claim to a universal legitimacy, is one that has served the continent well. It has helped the grievous wounds inflicted by the calamities of the first half of the 20th century to heal; to integrate large numbers of people from beyond the borders of Europe; and to provide a degree of equality for women and sexual minorities that has rendered untold numbers happier. What do the sanguinary fantasies of either Breivik or of the jihadis who twice in 2015 brought carnage to the streets of Paris have that can compare? Only one thing, perhaps – a capacity to excite those who find the pieties of Europe's liberal society boring. The more of these there are, the more – inevitably – the framework for behaviour and governance that has prevailed in Western Europe since the end of the Second World War will come under strain. At stake is whether the large numbers of migrants into the Continent who have no familiarity with the norms of a secular and liberal society such as have evolved in a country like Germany will find them appealing enough to adopt; and whether native Europeans, confronted by a vast influx of people from a very different cultural background, will themselves be tempted to abandon liberal values, and reach, perhaps, for a Holy Lance.

Otto the Great, despite the brutality with which he trampled down the Hungarians on the plain of the Lech, and torched the villages in which the fugitives from his onslaught had taken refuge, never doubted that migrants from beyond the limits of Christendom could be integrated into his realm. Baptism, a rite of such awesome potency that it was believed to wash away all the sins of those who received it, offered any pagans who wished to take their place among the ranks of the Christian people a ready entry visa. The defeated Hungarians were not alone in accepting it. So too, in France and England, did Viking chieftains cornered by their adversaries, and offered lands if they would only bow their necks to Christ. The forefathers of those same Normans who conquered Sicily back from Islam had been worshippers of

Odin. Today, though, in a Europe that has long ceased to rank as Christendom, no ritual comparable to baptism exists – nor could it possibly exist. The nearest equivalents, perhaps, are the classes given in Norway to refugees about the principle of sexual consent, or the cards issued by the Austrian government to migrants advising them that it is perfectly permissible for two men to kiss. Whether these rituals will inspire new arrivals to do as the Hungarians and Vikings did, and abandon the convictions and conventions of their homelands, only time will tell. About one thing, though, there can hardly be any doubt: the conceit that European values are somehow universal is about to be put to its severest test.

Notes

1. Gerhard, *Vita Sancti Uodalrici Episcopi Augustani*: cap. 12. Translation by Charles R. Bowlus, in *The Battle of Lechfeld and its Aftermath, August 955: The End of the Age of Migrations in the Latin West* (Aldershot: Ashgate, 2006), p. 176.
2. *Ibid*, p. 177
3. Liudprand, *Antapodosis*, 4.25, in *The Works of Liudprand of Cremona*. Translation by F.A. Wright (London: Everyman Library, 1930).
4. John VIII. Quoted by Michael McCormick in *Origins of the European Economy: Communications and Commerce, A.D. 300-900* (Cambridge: Cambridge University Press, 2001), p. 736.
5. J.R.R. Tolkien, *The Two Towers* (London: Allen & Unwin, [1954] 2005), p. 820.
6. J.R.R. Tolkien, *The Book of Lost Tales, Part One*, ed. Christopher Tolkien (London: Allen & Unwin, 1983), p. 176.
7. Forward to the second edition of *The Lord of the Rings* (London: Allen & Unwin, 1966), p. xvii.
8. J.R.R. Tolkien, *The Return of the King* (London: Allen & Unwin, [1955] 2005), p. 1075.
9. *Ibid*, p. 984.
10. Quoted by John Garth in *Tolkien and the Great War: The Threshold of Middle-earth* (London: Harper Collins, 2003), p. 219.

11. *Op. cit*, p. xvii.
12. *The Return of the King*, p. 1079.
13. *Ibid.*
14. *Ibid*, p. 1110.
15. 'Cultural Criticism and Society', in *Prisms*, 17-34 (Cambridge, MA: MIT Press, 1983), p. 34.
16. Matthew: 5.43-4.
17. In her speech to the CDU annual conference in Karlsruhe, 14 November 2015.
18. http://www.bbc.co.uk/news/world-europe-34173720.
19. http://www.spiegel.de/international/germany/why-has-angela-merkel-staked-her-legacy-on-the-refugees-a-1073705.html.
20. http://www.bbc.co.uk/news/world-europe-35405896.
21. *The Return of the King*, p. 1117.
22. Qur'an: 33.50.
23. https://www.middleeastmonitor.com/news/europe/18031-thousands-of-europeans-have-joined-isis-in-syria.

On the Identity of the West

Larry Siedentop

Early in what we call the "modern" era in Europe – in the 17th and 18th centuries – three distinct points of view emerged and contended for ascendancy over minds. They were views laying down different principles for the governance and development of European society. One made the assertion and protection of "natural rights" crucial, another focused on the satisfaction of individual preferences or "utility", while a third held up the banner of "citizenship".

By the end of the 18th century the first viewpoint had been asserted in the American Declaration of Independence and revolutionary France's proclamation of the Rights of Man.

The second had been espoused by the English philosopher Bentham, whose "happiness principle" provided the basis for what became widespread movements for legal and penal reform, while the third, associated especially with Jean-Jacques Rousseau, transformed the ancient conception of citizenship into a notion of public morality expressed as a "social contract".

Not one of these viewpoints prevailed to the exclusion of the others. Instead, they all contributed to what is probably best described as a broad movement of reform directed at the church and state of the ancien régime, in order to create what we would now call a liberal secular order.

Despite important differences between these points of view, on closer inspection they shared one fundamental assumption: the belief in an underlying equality of humans, their "moral" equality. All three took it for granted that the basic, organising social role should be "the individual" rather than the family, tribe or caste. They understood society as essentially an association of individuals. And it is that belief which provided, in turn, the radical, subversive edge of the doctrines they defended – leading those who espoused them into changes which they did not always foresee or welcome. Thus, the assertion of "natural rights" contributed to the later emancipation of women and other minorities and Bentham's insistence that "everyone counts for one and no one for more than one" could become a "populist" majority principle, while invoking Rousseau's "general will" might involve the confusion of freedom and virtue.

Despite these differences and their implications, it is important to remember what they nonetheless shared, the assumption of human equality – of a moral potential inherent in individual agency. But here important questions arise. Where did this assumption come from? What are its origins? How did it emerge to shape the modern identity of the West? Was it created ex-nihilo at the end of the middle ages – a capricious turning of the human mind that became in time a threat to inherited social statuses and forms of "community"? Or is there a longer story to tell?

These are important questions. For most human societies have understood themselves differently. They have understood themselves essentially as associations of families, tribes or castes rather than as associations of individuals endowed with rights. Of course, there have long been some Western intellectuals who deplored what they considered an a priori "mistake" – an arrogant rationalism – which threatens important values such as community and sociability, by dissolving social bonds and justifying a "privatising" of life. Recently, moreover, that "communitarian" critique has acquired an ally in the form of multiculturalism – with its insistence that sensitivity to cultural differences raises serious doubts about the ideal of individual freedom ("an equal liberty") as a universal goal.

These criticisms – reinforced by pressures arising from massive immigration and shifts in the balance of worldwide economic power – are today subjecting Western beliefs and values to quite unprecedented challenges. But inadequate self-understanding – our failure to understand the moral depth of the liberal tradition – has made these challenges even more formidable. For it is striking how in recent decades the term "liberal" has become a term of opprobrium in parts of the West. In Europe, the influence of economics and partisan conflicts have led to its identification with a laissez-faire form of capitalism (neo-liberalism), while in some regions of the United States, the term has come to stand for a kind of immorality – for permissiveness, if not decadence.

These recent developments reveal a failure to understand the origins and nature of liberal beliefs, their moral foundation and content.

Understanding our own tradition better therefore seems to me a matter not just for our leisure moments, but a kind of duty. For if we are to continue defending liberal values, we owe it to ourselves and others to provide an adequate account of their foundation. If, as I say in my book *Inventing the Individual*, we fail to understand the moral depth of our own tradition, how can be hope to shape the conversation of mankind?

So where should we start in order to understand the Western tradition better? How did belief in the moral equality of humans generate an unprecedented social role? How did the "individual" become the organising social role in the West?

We must start by looking critically at the categories we rely on when identifying the chief stages of our history: the "ancient world", the "middle ages" and the "modern era". What is striking about these categories is that they introduce a radical discontinuity into our history. For while the first and the third periods are associated with secularism, rationality and (at least in some respects) progress, the second period is conventionally associated with regression – with ignorance, superstition, social inequality and clerical oppression. Even now "medieval" is used as a term of denigration.

I believe these categories stand in the way of understanding the development of Western values and beliefs. We can understand why if we look at the period during which they became established, the 17th and 18th century "Enlightenment". This was a period when revulsion against the religious wars following the Reformation – in which states sought to enforce religious uniformity – created a powerful surge of anti-clericalism. Reaching its peak during the second half of the 18th century (you may remember Voltaire's ecrasez l'infame!) this anti-clericalism had an important effect on Enlightenment writers' approach to Western history.

Anti-clericalism created a great temptation. Enlightenment thinkers were tempted to minimise the moral and intellectual distance between modern Europe and Graeco-Roman antiquity, while maximising the distance between modern Europe and the middle ages. They liked to contrast the "dark" middle ages with the "light" of their own age, while identifying the same light in the ancient world. For them, the absence of anything like the Christian church and its dogmas in the ancient world provided a lesson in secularism and rationality. Unfettered rational enquiry should again become the agency of human progress. The liberation of the human mind from self-serving clerical dogmas – as well as the liberation of the individual from feudal social hierarchies – represented the birth of "modernity" in their eyes. 18th-century intellectuals (led by the philosophes) saw themselves as retrieving from antiquity the torch of reason which had been extinguished during the middle ages.

While it is easy to sympathise with the motives of the philosophes (who faced a privileged church making coercive claims) when championing antiquity, their accounts of both antiquity and the middle ages are, I think, misleading and prevent us from understanding the sources and early development of a moral tradition which gave birth to Western liberalism.

So let us begin by looking closely at their account of antiquity as "secular". The problem with this account is that it looks in the wrong place for religion. The religion of the Greeks and Romans did not speak to the individual conscience. Rather, it spoke to and through the family. And it is to the family that we have to look to find religion and priesthood in antiquity.

The ancient family was itself a religious cult, with the father as its high priest tending the family altar and its "sacred flame", the flame that made his ancestors visible. Ancient religion consisted in worship of divine ancestors through the paterfamilias, a radical inequality of roles within the family and a series of elaborate ritual requirements. The family was, at least originally, a self-contained moral universe. It did not seek or welcome any deep or "moral" connection with humans outside.

To be sure, this kind of hermetic family cult was altered by the emergence of the polis or city state. But it was altered only to the extent that the bond of association constituting the city was itself a religious bond. The city was an association of families and tribes, each defined by a shared worship of ancestors. Little wonder, then, that the formation of a city required the emergence of a new cult or worship, through discovery of a "hero" as founder of the city. As the family had its gods, and the tribe its gods, so the city had to become the domain of gods, its "protecting deities".

So instead of an antiquity free of religion, priesthood and superstition – a "secular" inspiration for modern Europe – we find on closer examination that the family, tribe and city were each a kind of church. Each had its own rites, a worship with elaborate requirements. As Fustel de Coulanges noticed, "faith and purity of intention counted for very little, and the religion consisted in the minute practice of innumerable rules..." Fear of failing to observe those rules led to elaborate rites of purification.

In Greek and Roman antiquity the limits of personal identity were established by the limits of physical association and inherited, unequal social roles. The Greeks described anyone who sought to live outside such associations and such roles as an "idiot".

Thus, the assumption which dominated the ancient world was the assumption of natural inequality. Everything and everyone was assumed to have a fixed, prescribed place in a "great chain of being". Inequality reigned even in Athenian "democracy", which excluded women, slaves and the foreign-born categorically from citizenship. There was no liberalism as we understand the word.

What began to change that world? The spread of Roman power until it created an empire surrounding the Mediterranean undoubtedly undermined localism and the elites it had fostered. That mixing of peoples and cultures created the foundation for a more "universalist" culture. But one movement, more than any other, exploited the opportunity it provided – the early Christian movement.

Christianity changed the ground of human identity. For it overturned the assumption of natural inequality that had permeated Greek and Roman antiquity. It was able to do this by combining Jewish monotheism with an abstract universalism which had roots in later Greek philosophy. By asserting the moral equality of humans – quite apart from any social roles they might occupy – Christianity changed "the name of the game". Social rules became secondary. They followed and had to be understood as subordinate to a God-given human identity, something which all humans share equally.

We can see this merger of Judaism and Greek philosophy especially in Paul's letters – in his conception of the Christ, which is remarkable for its universalism. The love of God he celebrates imposes opportunities and obligations on the individual as such, that is, on conscience. In his vision of Jesus, Paul discovered a moral reality which laid the foundation for a new, universal social role. The atmosphere of the New Testament is one of exhilarating detachment from the unthinking constraints of inherited social roles. That emerges in Paul's references to "Christian liberty".

Individual liberty is celebrated in the writings of early Christian apologists. In the 2nd century Origen argued that God had created "rational creatures endowed with the faculty of free choice", who were led "each by his own free will either to imitate God and so to advance or to ignore him and so to fall". Tertullian, writing at the end of that century insisted that "one mighty deed alone was sufficient for our God – to bring freedom to the human person". He went on to insist on freedom of conscience. For "...it is a basic human right that everyone should be free to worship according to his own convictions". Was this perhaps the earliest assertion of "human rights"?

These apologists' emphasis on human freedom made them equally sensitive to human weakness. The weakness of the will – when subject to temptations which, reinforced by memory, lead us to lose our freedom in compulsions – was explored by Saint

Augustine in his incomparably subtle and influential account of human agency. "Often I do not do what I want, but the very thing I hate."

That equal emphasis on human freedom and human fallibility – our moral equality – laid the foundation for a moral tradition that would create modern liberalism, with its commitment to individual rights and the dispersal of power by constitutional arrangements. This tradition slowly undermined earlier conceptions of society, whether as an association of families, tribes or castes. The story of the West can therefore be understood as the story of how a moral revolution slowly gave rise to a social revolution, to a new organising social role, the "individual".

We should not be surprised that this process was slow, fitful and difficult. For the new assumption had to struggle against beliefs and statuses sometimes as old as the social division of labour.

I shall try to describe briefly what seem to me major steps in the process leading to the emergence of basic principles of liberal secularism. The first is the period from the 1st century to the fall of the Western Roman Empire, the second is the period often described as the "dark ages", while the third extends from the 11th to the 15th century, beginning with what has been described as the "papal revolution". In each of these periods I shall point to a few notable developments.

The inclusiveness of the early church is striking. It was as individuals that the rich and the poor, including those previously outside the citizen class, approached the sacraments of the church. They were baptised and received the Eucharist as individuals seeking salvation rather than as members of a group. By the 3rd century the belief in moral equality and a sense of being "outside" established society generated a remarkable ascetic movement of individuals (who became known as anchorites or monks) leaving cities and withdrawing into the "wilderness" in Egypt and Syria. They withdrew as individuals rather than as organised groups. When their numbers grew to such an extent that they began to organise (becoming cenobites), they created a new form of human association: voluntary association. Monasticism introduced a form association based on individual choice rather than merely on birth, custom or force. It gave an institutional form to the belief in moral equality.

Is it mere accident that the 4th and 5th centuries also saw women begin to emerge from the subordinations of the ancient family – patrician women for the most part, who sought education and travel in a way unknown to previous centuries? I don't think so. The institution of slavery also came under moral scrutiny in a new way. While the early church was cautious about challenging such a fundamental ancient institution, it emphasised enfranchisement as a virtue – and by the 5th century slaves could be freed in ceremonies before bishops as well as before civil magistrates.

To be sure, the association of Christianity and individual liberty was compromised after the conversion of Constantine. Becoming the official religion of the empire, the church acquired influence over the exercise of state power. It developed some very bad habits, involving attempts, at times, to coerce belief. Yet that development was itself cut short in the 5th century by the Germanic invasions and fall of the Western Roman Empire.

Here we enter the second period of development. Christian bishops often found themselves the de facto, popular leaders of cities, trying to prevent pillage and defending urban autonomy as much as possible. How could they protect themselves from invaders who had a virtual monopoly of force? They fell back on the only sword they possessed, that is, their beliefs. So they increasingly insisted on the difference between temporal and spiritual power. The clergy defended a realm to which they alone had access, the "eternal" or spiritual realm. Thus, the law of an invisible king – the Christ who offered the hope of "salvation" to individuals – became a moral sword wielded with dramatic effect by the hard-pressed clergy. Columbanus, a 6th-century Irish missionary to the continent, conjures up their frame of mind: "I am coming from the end of the world, where I have seen spiritual leaders truly fighting the Lord's battles."

During the next centuries – often called the "dark ages" – the clergy's efforts began to distinguish spiritual from temporal power. As the great French historian Francois Guizot long ago argued "the separation of temporal and spiritual power is based on the idea that physical force has neither right nor influence over souls, over conviction, over truth". To make that point, better educated members of the clergy drew on the writings of Pope Gregory the Great. Gregory sought to impress on secular rulers their duty to respect and promote the "care of souls". It became an influential rhetoric.

To be sure, "barbarian" customs and manners made this an uphill task. Yet church councils in 6th-century Gaul did introduce a concern for "charity" into public deliberations. The influence of the clergy also began to undermine paterfamilias. Thus, in the late 6th century a Frankish king, Chilperic, declared: "A long-standing and wicked custom of our people denies sisters a share with their brothers in their father's land; but I consider this wrong, since my children came equally from God...." The church also struggled to introduce greater equality into marital obligations.

Deployed by bishops and missionaries, the rhetoric of "the care of souls" began to amount to an alternative vision of social order – "another world" which provided sharp contrast to the real world of violence and inequality. It remained a vision of heaven rather than of earth. Yet by the 8th century and the emergence of Charlemagne's empire it began to impinge on temporal affairs. For Charlemagne tried to combine two visions of social order. On the one hand, he continued to believe that lordship and aristocratic subordination remained the necessary condition of social order. Yet, influenced by clerical advisors such as Alcuin, Charlemagne had another vision of the foundations of his power. He wanted consent. So he asked for all his subjects (eventually including slaves and women as well as serfs) to swear an oath of allegiance! It was a step inconceivable in antiquity.

A respect for conscience – with the touch of equality that suggested – entered public life with Charlemagne's oaths. At times his advisor Alcuin rebuked his master for neglecting the role of conscience. When Charlemagne ordered the mass "conversion" of thousands of Saxons at the end of a campaign, Alcuin protested: "Faith must be voluntary not coerced. Converts must be drawn to the faith not forced. A person can be compelled to be baptised yet not believe".

The belief in moral equality thus continued to have a subversive role in the so-called "dark" ages. And it played some part in the decline of ancient slavery and development of serfdom under the Carolingians. These amounted to further steps in the process of "individuating" society.

The collapse of the Carolingian empire in the 10th century left the Frankish church once again without protection. Fears for the "liberty of the church", now exposed to the depredations of local lords, created a reform movement led by the Abbey of Cluny in the 10th century. This monastic movement of reform sought to defend the freedom of the church from secular interference. The movement spread so rapidly and became so influential that by the mid-11th century it came to dominate the papacy itself.

Under Gregory VII the papacy began to promote reform by centralising authority within the church. It did so with an ambitious programme to create a system of church law, drawing on Roman law but "correcting" it with Christian moral intuitions. The claim of papal "sovereignty" over the church turned on its responsibility for "the care of souls". The jurisdiction it claimed rested on individual souls – their equal moral status – rather than on unequal social distinctions and roles. This assertion of papal "sovereignty" over the church soon led not only to the development of a sophisticated system of "canon law", but also a hierarchy of church courts to administer that law.

An unintended consequence of the "papal revolution" was the development of a clearer distinction between the religious and the secular spheres. For it was not long before secular rulers glimpsed the advantages of developing a legal system "in their own sphere", which would bypass feudal intermediaries and paterfamilias, enabling them to rest their authority on their individual "subjects". This was a move that led to the emergence of the modern "sovereign" state.

But the influence of canon law did not stop there.

It has long been supposed that the earliest form of natural rights theory – the assertion of what we now call "human rights" – was an achievement of the 17th and 18th centuries, the Enlightenment. Yet recent research has demonstrated that in fact the earliest form of natural rights theory was put forward by canon lawyers from the 12th to the 14th century. These lawyers transformed the ancient conception of natural law. No longer would it rest on the assumption of natural inequality. It became instead a theory of fundamental rights springing from the nature of human agency. Where the Stoics had understood natural law to refer to a cosmic order of things, the canonists of the 12th century construed it to mean free will or power, an "area of choice" for individuals justified by the nature of human agency. Trained in Christian theology, they reasoned on the basis of the Golden Rule, with its postulates of equality and reciprocity.

By the 14th century canon lawyers moved beyond laying down a fundamental equality of status and identifying a series of natural rights. They began to work out the implications of these postulates for the nature and governance of associations or "corporations". They soon turned the traditional idea of a corporation – which derived both its nature and its proper governance from higher authority – upside down. Corporations were no longer understood as having a reality apart from and superior to their members. When reflecting on the relations of a bishop to his diocese, the canonists interpreted episcopal authority as a "delegated" authority, that is, limited by the purposes for which it was delegated and always subject to the best interests of those whom it represented.

This development was nothing less than the emergence of a theory of representative government. Traditional claims to authority, even those made by the pope, could no longer be taken for granted. It is hardly an accident that schism in the church at the end of the 14th century – with three rival "popes" contending for ascendancy – saw the emergence of a powerful "conciliar" movement. It was in effect a struggle for a more representative and collegiate form of government in the church. Conciliarists sought to establish that general councils, meeting at regular intervals, should be recognised as the ultimate authority in the church.

That reform movement failed. But the ideas persisted, and doubtless contributed to the outbreak of the Reformation.

So what have we found? We have found that by the 15th century some basic moral intuitions generated by Christianity were being turned against some claims and practices of the church itself. The conviction that the ultimate source of authority in the church lay in the consciences of believers and hence the importance of voluntary association had developed from the conviction – always important within the Christian movement, even if at times only as a minority opinion – that "enforced belief" is a contradiction in terms.

But we have discovered more than that. This account explains how Christian moral intuitions played a pivotal role in shaping the discourse that gave rise to modern liberalism and secularism. Indeed, the pattern by which liberalism and secularism developed from the 16th to the 19th century resembles nothing so much as the stages through which canon law developed from the 12th to the 15th century. The sequence of argument is extraordinarily similar.

The sequence began with insistence on equality of status, moved to the assertion of a range of basic human rights, and concluded with the case for representative government. Thus, from Hobbes' insistence on basic human equality, in preparation for defining "sovereignty" in terms of "equal subjection", through Locke's defence of human freedom by identifying a range of natural rights, to Rousseau's making the case for the sovereignty of the people and self-government, each of these steps in modern political thought had its counterpart in the evolution of medieval canon law.

The canonists, so to speak, "got there first".

To be sure, there remain important differences between the two traditions of thought. The Pauline moral source is frequently asserted in canon law, whereas developing liberal thought often conflated assumptions about God and nature. As the historian Carl Becker once remarked, the 18th century "denatured God and deified nature". The foundation for the claim to liberty became "human nature" and personal conscience. Yet the conception of human nature relied upon – and elaborated by the great philosopher Immanuel Kant at the end of the 18th century – continued to have a markedly Christian impress.

Understanding this deep continuity makes the idea of a "war" between Christianity and secularism seem unnecessary and tragic. In view of their shared moral roots, such a struggle would be better described as a pointless "civil war". Yet Europe endured such a "civil war" for several centuries. And now, alas, that war seems to be developing in the United States, where in the past the civil liberty provided by secularism was understood as the necessary condition of "authentic" belief.

Yet the genealogy of Western liberalism I have outlined has implications for another contemporary problem: the problem of state-building. For the individuation of society (carried by the very idea of a state's "sovereignty" over individuals) was a difficult, centuries-long process in the Christian West. So is it surprising that Western attempts to build new states in societies where the organising social principle has long been the family, tribe or caste – and where a different religious tradition makes the goal of an "equal liberty" problematic – have met with so many reverses? I think not.

The liberal commitment to creating a society of autonomous moral agents is both more valuable and more fragile than some contemporary versions of Western liberalism suggest. These versions of the liberal project can reduce society to little more than a market place, with the privatising of life at the expense of citizenship. And that, in turn, can reduce the scope of public policy decisions to a rather simplistic cost-benefit analysis, whereas the proper object of liberal government is to foster and protect the attitudes and habits of a free people.

So I return to the question I raised earlier. If we in the West do not understand the moral depth of our own tradition, how can we hope to shape the conversation of mankind?

The Cowardly Lion in Quest of Peace

The EU and Its Fear of Power

Stella Ghervas

In a novel written at the turn of the 20th century entitled *The Wonderful Wizard of Oz*, L. Frank Baum introduced a thought-provoking character: the Cowardly Lion, whose despondent image was immortalised in the film of 1939. The feline joins the quest of the heroine for a mysterious wizard, in the hope of retrieving his lost courage. Could it be that the European Union fits this archetype of the reluctant hero, who is required to face the present by first coming to grips with his own past?

This metaphor comes to mind for the European Union, because in addition to its explicit value of peace, it also has an unexpressed *anti-value*: a shyness about anything that resembles either power or brilliance, which borders on self-denial. This can be observed in many of its exterior signs: from the carefully cultivated absence of charismatic leaders (apparently, some unwritten rule requires them to look like sun-deprived bookworms), to the punctilious equal weight that it gives to its twenty-four languages (even though it is public knowledge that an Anglo-European pidgin is used for most conversations and internal memos). Not to mention the European anthem, a splendid composition by Beethoven played against type, turned into a pompous lullaby that would make a football player cringe; and finally the Euro banknotes, uncannily lifeless because they are forbidden to feature a human being. Another characteristic of the current European Union is its obsession with its own sickness and the imminence of its death – especially today with the accumulated onslaught of the sovereign debts, Brexit, the refugee crisis, and terrorist attacks.

Why Peace?

But first of all, why peace? In fact, Title I of the Treaty on European Union (Art. 3) gives it an even higher status than a value, since it is stated as the *aim* of this institution ("The Union's aim is to promote peace, its values and the well-being of its peoples.")[1] There is good reason, since the European construction was hardly born on a bed of roses. In May 1945, the criminal Nazi Reich had been crushed, and Germany militarily occupied by the Allies of the Second World War. But at what cost for the Old Continent! History books, particularly in France, like to extol the three decades after the Liberation as the "Trente Glorieuses", as if the continent had miraculously tipped overnight from war privations into the post-war boom of the 1960s. In truth, the decade that led to the founding of the European Economic Community (EEC) at the Treaty of Rome in 1957 had little glory about it. As Winston Churchill aptly said in a speech at the University of Zurich, over a year after the end of the hostilities: "Over wide areas are a vast, quivering mass of tormented, hungry, careworn and bewildered human beings, who wait in the ruins of their cities and homes and scan the dark horizons for the approach of some new form of tyranny or terror. Among the victors there is a Babel of voices, among the vanquished the sullen silence of despair."[2]

The European Communities, and today the European Union, cannot be understood outside of what Churchill aptly called, on that day, the *Tragedy of Europe*. It went beyond the war atrocities, the immense devastation and even the endless food rationing that continued until 1954 in Britain – while it became a permanent fixture of Poland until the fall of the Iron Curtain. The degradation of Europe was first and foremost moral. That this civilisation, which had so far claimed its superiority on all others, could have given birth to a monster like the Third Reich was a stain that drowned Germany in shame, but that had also spilled over to the rest of the continent. Other countries had their share in the atrocities of the Nazi regime. Even liberated France had to come to terms with its humiliating defeat of 1940 and worse, the *collaboration* of its ruling class with the invader. Beyond the Iron Curtain, speaking of "liberation" took more and more the connotation of a grim joke, after thousands of tanks from the Red Army and the Warsaw Pact rushed into Budapest in 1956. As for Britain, though it unquestionably had (in Churchill's terms) its "finest hour" when its fighter pilots stood in 1940 as the last fighting bastion of democracy in Europe, and the whole country went on to win the war, it had completely consumed itself in the process. Churchill, the man of victory, summarised the unpalatable fault of Europe in one sentence, in his Zurich speech: "That is all that Europeans, grouped in so many ancient states and nations, and that is all that the Germanic races have got by tearing each other to pieces and spreading havoc far and wide." To which he added: "Indeed, but for the fact that the great republic across the Atlantic realised that the ruin or enslavement of Europe would involve her own fate as well, and stretched out hands of succour and guidance, the Dark Ages would have returned in all their cruelty and squalor. They may still return."[3]

That was exactly so: on the global scale, the great powers of the Old Continent had almost reduced themselves to insignificance and world leadership was transferred to two superpowers, the United States and the Soviet Union. The European countries had built for themselves a future of vassalage – or *alignment*, to use the neologism in vogue during the Cold War, quite liveable and soon very comfortable in the West, decidedly less so in the East. Germany, partitioned, technically still at war (for lack of a peace treaty), continued to exist as a broken pawn, in two pieces divided by the walls and barbed wires of the Cold War. Indeed, wherever there was economic recovery in Europe, it was because the United States of America had extended the substantial financial resources of the Marshall Plan. All in all, the mood of the European ruling classes in the immediate post-war period was not festive at all. It more resembled that of a seriously crippled patient who had woken up in a rehabilitation facility, after a failed suicide attempt; and who found a benevolent nurse spoon-feeding him with a nutritious broth: groggy, grateful, but painfully aware of what he had done to himself. The European nation state had disqualified itself as a credible international actor, in front of the US and the Soviet Union, which had already taken the important step of becoming large federations. The explanation of Europe's collapse at the end of the Second World War and the simultaneous rise of the two superpowers lies in the failure of the European countries to create a continental alliance after the First World War.

Antidotes to Empire

It is however, necessary to go further back in time in order to understand why Europe has had these periods of intensely suicidal behaviour: in other words, why great continental wars (of which the Second World War was only the last) kept recurring. One of the worst threats to Europe and mankind in general – outside of pandemics and natural catastrophes – was the periodic rise of a new continental empire that would destroy the liberties of one and all. One archetype was the Ottoman Empire, which had reached its apogee during the 16th century. In truth, its prodigious expansion in the Balkans was due to the pathological inability of the European states to put up a common front; worse, they made a habit of betraying each other to court short-term advantages from the Sultan. Paradoxically, the person who changed that attitude was the Habsburg Emperor Charles V, even though it was through no will of his own. This monarch, who had inherited half of Western Europe by some freak of genealogy, suddenly conceived the project of establishing a pan-European empire that would rival the Ottomans in the East. His attempt not only failed, but it accidentally managed what the Turkish menace had not: to crystallise the resolve of the French, the English and soon the Dutch, to create an alliance to defend their independence at all costs. From the 16th to the 20th century, all states of Europe found a defining moment for their identity, in a struggle against an empire: France, Britain and the Netherlands against Spain, Spain against France, Germany against France, Italy against Austria, Russia against Poland, Poland against Russia, Greece against the Ottoman Empire... The novelty, however, was that nation states found their long-term survival against new empires by creating defensive alliances. It is unquestionable that this was a very successful procedure: in 1814-15, a grand European coalition of Britain, Russia, Prussia, and Austria managed to defeat the Empire of Napoleon, after a strenuous effort. In 1918, the Allies dealt a fatal blow to the Central Empires of the First World War and overwhelmed the Axis in the Second World War. Every single empire that sought to conquer Europe during modern history was crushed.

The problem is that while strong military alliances did preserve the liberties of Europe, empires still kept rising again and again, like bramble bushes, causing new wars. In the long term, this state of affairs threatened to compromise the influence of Europe on the world. Already after the First World War, the realisation dawned on a group of European statesmen (among them the French Aristide Briand, the German Gustav Stresemann and the British Austen Chamberlain) that something had to be done to prevent wars once and for all. They tried to achieve it in 1925 with the Locarno Treaties, as well as the Kellogg-Briand Pact of 1928, also known as the "General Treaty for Renunciation of War as an Instrument of National Policy", which France and the United States of America were the first to sign. In those same years the Austrian count Richard Coudenhove-Kalergi pointed out in his book *Pan-Europa* (1923) that the states of the continent would be in mortal danger if ever there were a new continental war. He argued that the saving grace in the previous centuries had been that no power outside of Europe had been in a position to challenge the world supremacy of its great powers.[4] Yet the situation had changed with the rise of new federations. The great powers of the time, notably the US, Great Britain and the Soviet Union, had economic markets of bigger size than the puny national markets in Europe. They were in a position, with the League of Nations, to actively intervene in European affairs – while the European states had more difficulty to express themselves about the rest of the word. Indeed, the speed of communications having shrunk distances, the European states of the 20th century, now too small, were no better than the Italian city-states of the Renaissance had been in front of Spain or France. This was, of course, without counting the rise of two totalitarian empires, Nazi Germany and Stalinist Russia; they entered the Second World War as accomplices in order to achieve a new partition of Poland, before turning against each other in a hideous war of attrition. After the senseless carnage of Europe was over, it is highly symbolic that Churchill, who had led the fight of Britain in the war, paid homage to two men of the interwar period, Aristide Briand and Coundenhove-Kalergi. In the apocalyptic prophecy that the latter had made in the 1920s about a new war in Europe, there was one aspect that he had only marginally contemplated: that Britain, after having fought gallantly to save the common liberties, would bankrupt itself. By the end of the war, it was clear that Britain was also in the process of losing its status of world power and its colonial empire was doomed – at which point its lot was the same as any other European country. The *coup de grâce* was the Suez crisis of 1956, when both the US and the USSR easily called off an attempted coup by France and Britain to recover this strategic canal leading from the Mediterranean to the Red Sea.

From the above, it should be clear why peace – and in the first place, reconciliation between France and Germany – had become an aim of the European Communities after the Second World War. It was not a mawkish call for brotherly love, but a last-ditch attempt from these two diminished countries, as well as the Benelux and Italy, to still amount to something on the grand stage of the world. And it is not a coincidence that crestfallen Britain first applied to join the EEC in 1961, only four years after the Treaty of Rome.

The Courage to Dare

The above may lead us to a diagnosis of the *malaise of Europe*, of why the Cowardly Lion refuses to be what he should be. It could be that the European Union is afraid of becoming itself the problem it has sought to solve: an empire that will cause new wars. This is not an idle joke. Vladimir Bukovsky, a former Soviet dissident, expressed in 2006 his fear that the EU could become a dictatorship.[5] In 2011, the former President of the European Commission, José Manuel Barroso, stated that the EU is a "non-imperial empire".[6] Today, the generally unspoken anxiety (but openly expressed in Britain) is that the EU – if allowed to become a federation – could become a new superstate that would suppress the liberties of the Old Continent and possibly start bullying its neighbours, in order to create a new colonial empire outside of Europe.

Clearly, the suffering caused by Nazi Germany from 1939 to 1945, as well as that caused by the communist regimes in Eastern Europe goes a long way to explain this anti-value of the EU. This abhorrence for empires had, perhaps, a positive side effect: the evolution of mentalities on the continent toward a renunciation of colonialism. In essence it led to the general realisation, among the political personnel of European countries, that at a time when Europe was struggling to safeguard its own liberties, it had become materially impossible (as well as contradictory) to continue to deny those of non-Europeans. Today, however, this legitimate distrust has turned into the syndrome of the Cowardly Lion: it is the apparently insurmountable barrier for both the European Council and the European Commission, between the current status quo of the Treaty of Lisbon and the last practical steps necessary to achieve a European federation: a European budget (and thus a majority rule in tax matters) as well as a European army under a single command. On that condition alone, Coudenhove-Kalergi's slogan "Europe to the Europeans" – in other words a principle of non-interference analogous to Switzerland's armed neutrality – could become something other than a utopia.

As a cure for the Lion's phobia, the risk that the European bloc could become an empire should be considered carefully: what would it really take? To use a powerful metaphor from filmmaker

George Lucas that made its way into public culture, the EU would have to select the path to the *dark side of the force*. If European history is any indication, it would take three steps in addition to the suppression of civil liberties: first, to define "Europeans" as an exceptional people, with some "duty" to impose their will on other peoples; the second would be to glorify the army as a chief instrument of foreign policy; the third would be a messianic leader who would stir up hatred in the populace and lead soldiers to achieve those aims. This is undoubtedly a frightening prospect. Intellectual courage lies in facing it and discerning how likely this is. Would the living memory of the Tragedy of Europe not be a deterrent, and the value of peace a good guide? Furthermore, the Eurobarometer surveys show that interventions of European troops outside of Europe are distressing for public opinion.[7] And in matters of human rights and civil liberties, the European Court of Justice has proven a powerful tool against violations by member states. Far from being the apex *predator* that a lion is supposed to be, the EU has so far acted more as a *protector* and its enlargement occurred by states voluntarily joining, rather than military conquest. And since the lack of negotiation was the cause of conflicts that brought about the demise of France, Germany, and Britain as great powers, this would also be the cause of the dissolution of the European bloc.

From a logical viewpoint, it should thus become obvious that the alternative to the dark side (empire) is not necessarily *no force at all* for the EU; it could also be a chivalrous *light side*, willing to use (military) force "for knowledge and defence". To keep it in check, political Europe would have to use its treasures of political experience. Having committed many errors in the past, having acknowledged them, and having paid for them dearly, it also has more maturity to avoid them in the future. Hence it may be understandable, but not necessarily rational, that intellectuals, political leaders and public opinions should find refuge in a weak EU and the past glory of nation states. The European state has been clinically dead for several decades as a significant international actor, because it is too small – economically and militarily – to be seriously considered in international negotiations. The Most Serene Republic of Venice, a maritime power that was too proud of its ancient and glorious past to enter an alliance with other European states, committed the same mistake of wanting to keep to itself; its penalty was cancellation from the political map of Europe in 1815, as a result of a secret appendix in a peace treaty. When obstinate attachment to *sovereignty* of the state has been consistently failing to ensure *freedom*, has it not become a self-deception?

It is unfortunate that the myth of the international significance of nation states, particularly France and Britain, has been artificially kept alive in political speeches and schoolbooks, as well as token military interventions overseas. Yet is it not a fact that any military operations these two countries have participated in since the Suez crisis of 1956 had to be requested or at least approved by the "great transatlantic power", the US? And by contrast, is it not also clear that the refusal by France to participate in the Iraqi war of 2004 earned it a vibrant rebuke and was a lesson that later governments had to keep in mind? This persistent denial of their subordinate status is proof that the mortification of the Tragedy of Europe is still difficult to accept. Furthermore, could it be that a strongly emancipated Europe (out of the cosy and reassuring cocoon of NATO), behaving as a responsible buffer between the antagonisms of US and Russia, would be in a better position to calm the waters in Eastern Ukraine and in the Middle East?

To uphold that stance, the EU would have to re-exhume the project of a European Defence Community. That would be in the event it should have to defend itself against another power – Russia – whose leaders have not yet been able to fully face the logical conclusion of their own recent tragedy, which they aptly call the *smuta* ("trouble", or chaos): that the Soviet Union caused its own collapse, because it relied on military force as the chief instrument for solving international disputes. In Europe, the only sensible use of military force is as an instrument of defence in case of aggression, not for annexations.

All this is arguably a tall order and is not yet on the agenda of political leaders and parties. Hence, as is traditional in European unification, it is the task of intellectuals and artists to act as the vanguard. Until this becomes reality, the EU might have to do what it has done very well until now: surviving crisis with some half-hearted compromise and bumbling along despondently until the next in the hope of a better outcome, but always persuaded that any new day might be the last one. Between the two attitudes lies the virtue of courage. Just as the Cowardly Lion of the *Wizard of Oz* had to get out of his comfort zone and come to grips with his true nature, the members of the European Council might become more at peace *with* themselves, and *between* themselves, if they stopped trying to prevent the EU from being what it cannot help but be: a significant great power. The proud and fiercely independent nation states of Europe (and thus still in a somewhat uncivilised state) would have to realise the advantage of living together under a stable social contract, and thus the reason *why* they should delegate some of their own force to the European Union. Indeed, this moment of crisis might be a good opportunity for pointing this out.

Peace, to express itself as an aim or "gut value" of political Europe, would have to be backed up by a deeper quality: the courage of the European political classes to face the errors of the past and the threats of the present. The anti-value of a weak EU should belong in an intellectual cemetery, as does the shyness to face a proportionate usage of rational force for freedom and the common good. Just as the Cowardly Lion had to face his past failings before facing the here and now, the leaders of political Europe might have to get over the fact that the paradigm of the obsessively independent ("Westphalian") state as a strong international actor has outlived its usefulness. Such a state would have to overcome its qualms of joining a strong continental alliance, in order to continue to exist as a free and self-determined actor on the world stage, so that Europeans could again be their own masters. Because in the end, is it not better to have a proud citizen's voice in Brussels, than to be supplicants in Washington or Moscow?

For more information on the arguments and ideas in this essay, see:

Ghervas, Stella, "Antidotes to Empire: From the Congress System to the European Union", in *EUtROPEs. The Paradox of European Empire*, ed. John W. Boyer and Berthold Molden (Chicago: University of Chicago Press, 2014) *Parisian Notebooks*, 7, pp. 49-81.

Ghervas, Stella, "Ten Lessons for Peace in Europe: From the Congress of Vienna and WWI, to the Failure of the G8", in *Multilateral Security Governance*, ed. Felix Dane and Gregory John Ryan (Rio de Janeiro: Konrad-Adenauer-Stiftung, 2014), pp. 212-227.

Ghervas, Stella, "'L'Europe élargie' d'après 1989: comment se réorienter dans la pensée?", *Questions Internationales* 68 (2014), pp. 94-101.

Ghervas, Stella, "La paix par le droit, ciment de la civilisation en Europe? La perspective du siècle des Lumières", in *Penser l'Europe au XVIIIe siècle: Commerce, Civilisation, Empire*, ed. Antoine Lilti and Céline Spector (Oxford: Voltaire Foundation, 2014), pp. 47-70.

Ghervas, Stella, "Les valeurs de l'Europe: entre l'idéal, le discours et la réalité", in *Rethinking Democracy* (Kiev, 2012). Article in French, Russian, and Ukrainian. https://www.academia.edu/1477500/Les_valeurs_de_lEurope_entre_lid%C3%A9al_le_discours_et_la_r%C3%A9alit%C3%A9_European_Values_Between_Ideal_Speech-making_and_Reality

Notes

1. Treaty on European Union (Consolidated version 2012), Title I, Article 3 (ex Article 2 TEU).
2. Winston Churchill, 'Speech at Zurich', 19 September 1946, in *Blood, Toil, Tears and Sweat: The Speeches of Winston Churchill*, ed. David Cannadine (Boston: Houghton Mifflin Company, 1989), p. 309.

3. Winston Churchill, 'Speech at Zurich', p. 310.
4. Richard N. Coudenhove-Kalergi, *Pan-Europe* (New York: Alfred A. Knopf, 1926), pp. 4-9.
5. Vladimir Bukovsky, 'The European Union: The New Soviet Union?' http://www.youtube.com/watch?v=js4oQG3UEE8
6. José Manuel Barroso: "Sometimes I like to compare the European Union, as a creation, to the organization of empires. Empires! Because we have [the] dimension of empires," Video press conference EUX.TV, 2007, http://www.youtube.com/watch?v=c2Ralocq9uE
7. Special Eurobarometer 146: Europe of Defence (December 2014): http://ec.europa.eu/public_opinion/archives/eb_special_160_140_en.htm#146

Afterglow of a Dead World

Memories of the future

Benno Barnard

Would you allow me to begin by sketching my background.

I am a child of Protestant parents; indeed, my father was a minister. Looking back from this century, I have the feeling that the simple Latin vocative of the word "mister" may sound to you, reader, as though it alludes to an exotic species at the zoo, a rock from space, or an artefact in a display case with objects from the Humanist Christian Civilisation...

Anyway, my father was the child of the petite bourgeoisie, and as such he harboured sympathies for the social-democrats who, in his youth, continued to preach the elevation of the people, but whose overwhelming banality instilled in him, from the 1970s onwards, an ever greater distaste. When he died in 2010, he considered himself to be non-partisan.

I am digressing a little, but digressing is the only way to get to the point, at least if you're me.

Around the time that my father grew estranged from "the left", I travelled to Prague as a student with a couple of friends, spurred on by curiosity and armed with notions about the true, or at least less untrue, communism.

Little mother Prague disclosed herself to me on a grey February day in the year 1976, if memory serves. We'd headed off on the hoof, poorly prepared but in possession of a visa, and leaving head-shaking parents in our wake: no one travelled behind the Iron Curtain of their own accord, where the world was cold and cruel. We'd seen their anxiety in our early puberty, when the Russians crushed the Czechs' desire for freedom beneath their boot heels, but at the same time, we felt that right-wing propaganda in the West was greatly exaggerated.

It was already growing dark – it had been growing dark all day – and my two friends and I drove through the dimly lit centre of the city in search of a hotel. There was snow on the ground; and above, in my recollection, a thin mousseline mist to provide a dash of atmosphere, the forms and colours of the houses were new to us; a modest pile of canned goods rose behind an all-but-bare shop window; the streets were as tangled as rope, and before we knew it we were driving in the wrong direction, which wasn't too bad because there were hardly any cars driving around in this romantic underworld, but which was too bad because a police car immediately appeared from some ambush point or other.

Hotels? But communication with the police was impossible, bank notes had to be handed over. This was the first lesson: in non-Capitalist countries, money played an all-pervasive role.

The next day, we traipsed through the city. On a street corner, we fell into a conversation with a man of about thirty. Whether he could point us in the direction of the Castle. He had a reddish beard and was funny in a nervous kind of way. In laboured English he said: "If only I knew!"

This is how I remember our first meeting with Slávek. In some way or another, he became our friend, then, at the bottom of the 1970s, there, in the heart of a Europe torn in two. He invited us to his home, in the charming bourgeois apartment where his widow still lives, in a side street off Wenceslaus Square.

From that moment on, everything was marvellous.

He showed us naive students Prague: the wretched overground city of the communists and their cronies, the elegant historical city of the Habsburgs and the brilliant first president, Tomás Masaryk, the literary-historical city of Franz Kafka and Bohumil Hrabal; but most of all the underground, dissident Prague of him and his friends, who by night typed out entire books on antediluvian machines – three sheets of paper, with two carbons tucked between them – which today my children would look at wide eyed. Also part of that rebellious Prague was a framed photo of the Polish pope that graced a wall in his apartment. This rather surprised us, but he was Catholic, and as a Catholic, a dissident too because he was a "pink Catholic"; he had leftist sympathies…

We discussed all this in our common variant of English. Slávek had a wide vocabulary in that language on paper and used Latin as an aid because he often didn't know how to pronounce a word: living English was something underground too. I spoke German with his mother (or was it his mother-in-law), but that language – which had been the *lingua franca* of Central Europe for centuries – had been all but phased out by our century.

This first visit was unforgettable and transformed my life. I returned many times later with the same, and other, friends. "Extra Bohemia non est vita et si est vita non est ita!" How many times did the cheerful, vital, fundamentally melancholy Slávek quote that? Life outside Bohemia certainly wasn't the same as life inside Bohemia, whether it was ruled by communists or not…

We ate excellent sauerkraut and sausage in a dark bar, setting the tankards of Urquell on display around us. A day later, the same waiter announced with his papier-mâché face that there was no sauerkraut on the menu. Yesterday, there was no sauerkraut on the menu either, actually. What's more, not a single tendril of sauerkraut had ever been cooked in his establishment. We visited other melancholy cafés. Whispering moneychangers appeared and disappeared again. We met dissidents, writers, artists, including the later president Havel, of whom I still have a photograph in my study, with a personal inscription. One of us wheedled an authentic Samizdat book out of our host. It was always fun – for us, at least, because after a week we'd again leave the Iron Curtain behind us, heading west.

Both Prague and Slávek had more experience of life than me, which meant I learned a lot on every trip. For instance, that Communism was no good. Yes, Prague was like a lye bath, in which ill-considered red sympathies were dissolved.

Years passed. Prague was liberated. Free Prague was less enchanting than occupied Prague. The West, with all its good and objectionable traits grew to be a banal commonplace to Slávek and his countrymen.

When my son, Christopher, was baptised, in 1999, Slávek was present as a godfather. It was the last time I saw him. Something dark occurred that finally dissolved our conversations, those hundreds of conversations, into total silence. I still don't know what it was. Maybe some demon had decided enough was enough, that friendship and freedom were a combination that no one of this world deserved.

When Christopher was bigger, he sometimes asked about his unknown godfather in Prague. We had just decided to go to Prague together "in the summer", he and I, when the telephone rang, and from the one moment to the next Slávek could never be visited again.

Slávek! More than anyone, he was old Europe to me – no, Europe *tout court*.

I placed a cross beside his name in my address book, plunged into a deep sorrow for our existence.

My mother derived from an entirely different milieu than my sire. Her father was a factory owner. German maids cleaned the house – these days, they would be Polish or Ukrainian – and the family spent six weeks of the summer holidays at the coast. In my imagination, they grew up in *Een zomerzotheid (A Summer Folly)*, a famous Dutch novel from the 1930s, in which a rich girl falls in love with the chauffeur who, thank God, turns out to be the son of rich folk, incognito. If you peek between the lines, you can still just about see the class struggle.

I'm digressing again and in so doing again come to the point, as will become evident.

Towards the end of my mother's life, her favourite children's book for adults was Kazuo Ishiguro's novel *The Remains of the Day*. She recognised the world sketched in it as the bygone age of her young girlhood.

The story is narrated in 1956 by Mr Stevens, the butler of Darlington Hall, and predominantly takes place immediately before the war. An extremely characteristic scene is the one in which Stevens has the silverware polished to such a degree of perfection that would seem impossible. The silver reflects the dedication of the staff like a precise measuring instrument, and proves that the social system, in which everyone knows their place, is still intact. Only revolutionaries – and both the communists and the Nazis are revolutionaries – do not understand that the world can only be made worse.

His employer at the time, the last Lord Darlington, organises international conferences at his home, in a naive but noble attempt to preserve the peace. He has grave concerns about the consequences of the Treaty of Versailles because he has a German friend and knows of the terrible poverty in the Weimar Republic. He's right. But peace cannot be preserved. Lord Darlington allows himself to be used like a child by Joachim von Ribbentrop, Hitler's ambassador in London at the time.

But the silverware gleams all the same, which delights Lord Halifax and will certainly be a great help in the discussions with von Ribbentrop...

Yes, Mr Stevens, give the truth its due: if only the Nazis had been gentlemen, you would have helped to prevent the Second World War. And then the British Empire would have collapsed much later. And perhaps my parents wouldn't have been such incurable Anglophiles.

In his and my year of 1956, four decades before Google, I move to England with them and learn to speak. My first word is "mummy", my second "peanuts" because that's what our cat was called. From 1956, I turn into me, even if we do move back to the Netherlands. And Stevens, meanwhile, enters the service of the American millionaire who buys Darlington Hall after the war: a romantic American Anglophile, like my American wife, who is rather ecstatic that she, Christopher and I finally moved to England again last year...

In the English hierarchy that survives posthumously to this day, Stevens is the lord of the serving staff. He is Mr Stevens. Even the American gentleman addresses him by his surname, although he *does* omit the "Mr". Perhaps Stevens does not have a Christian name, at least I can't remember one. He has his position. He is his position. He is contours. His interior world is irrelevant. Modern narcissistic caprice! He, and my mother, would want to have nothing to do with it! Etiquette, that's something else – etiquette makes the entire field of psychology redundant...

No, I wouldn't be able to employ Mr Stevens, despite my mother's past. As the child of the tennis playing, telephoning interbellum, scrubbed spic-and-span by two maids, she'd have got along with him excellently. Me, on the contrary... I'm no employer. The times have driven me in the direction of egalitarianism. Even though this is, of course, the year 42 Before Google, from which he and I can no longer escape.

You may wonder now how my parents ever managed to get engaged with the warm consent of my four grandparents in the Netherlands of the interbellum. The answer is astonishingly simple: it was thanks to Christianity. They attended the same run-of-the-mill Protestant church; and in one way or another, the realisation that Christianity viewed them as brothers and sisters transcended the not inconsiderable class differences between the two sets of parents.

The consequence was a happy mésalliance, if I can put it that way. My parents certainly doted on each other but, in a curious way, the difference in milieu continued to play a role in the backdrop of their individual lives. My mother did her best to maintain leftish sympathies, but these remained the sympathies of a lady. If I were to say that she and Stevens would have understood each other, I chiefly mean that they shared the notions of a deceptively stable world, which was held together by one's position, role, duty, respect and good manners. Naturally, these things were not impervious to the violence of the Nazis and the Communists.

I am one of those mythical creatures that doesn't even appear in Harry Potter: a left-wing liberal, Christian conservative, because I was bred from social antitheses, and a deeply spiritual and physical unity between two Europeans from shortly after Versailles, and raised in the afterglow of a dead world.

And now for my European credo.

I believe in the old-fashioned elevation of the people, and the social and intellectual emancipation of women. But I also believe in patience. After every attempt to give the wheel of history a twirl in the name of "progress" and the "engineerable society", we only get lumbered with problems. Dreaming of systems so perfect that no one will need to be good, as T.S. Eliot put it, is the most dangerous thing that exists. Such systems make their hecatombs by the thousands. It is much more sensible to change things cautiously. For our social happiness and world peace, we have to remember that man is a dark creature, inclined to self-destruction. On this point, I am in agreement with Calvin, whose doctrine of predestination I, in imitation of my father, view as sadistic nonsense. Nothing is dumber than overthrowing a hierarchical equilibrium, the laborious result of gradual developments. That porcelain is always shattered.

I also believe in the Western notion of freedom and I am of the opinion that this freedom is undermined by forms of politically-correct thought that bury us beneath the ash of a paralysing sense of historical guilt.

I believe, furthermore, in a continuum of knowledge, culture, education and science, and more generally in the superiority of European civilisation. You'd be better off studying Shakespeare, Kant and Flaubert than the products of non-western cultures. I'm sorry that this conflicts with the zeitgeist.

And finally, I believe in the values of Christianity...

Ah, Christianity! Does Europe still have any use for that? This is undoubtedly the point you, reader, will stumble over, certainly if you've been extracted from the great continuum of European history with a size 68 shoehorn...

The great English essayist and Catholic convert G.K. Chesterton explains in his book *Orthodoxy*, which I strongly recommend, that religion is something monstrous, but also something ineradicable, and that of all things, the Church has tamed these dark forces the best. It is 1908, and this visionary writes the following about the consequences of estrangement from Christianity in Europe:

When a religious scheme is shattered, it is not merely the vices that are let loose. The vices are, indeed, let loose, and they wander and do damage. But the virtues are let loose also; and the virtues wander more wildly, and the virtues do more terrible damage. The modern world is full of the old Christian virtues gone mad. The virtues have gone mad because they have been isolated from each other and are wandering alone. Thus some scientists care for truth; and their truth is pitiless. Thus some humanitarians only care for pity; and their pity (I am sorry to say) is often untruthful.

Do you understand this? Do you recognise this?...

It comes down to the fact that the new narrative of the post-revolutionary secular world has alienated man from the history and narratives of his forebears, and in place of consolation, offers him a paid vacation and unemployment benefit, at least for as long as that lasts – and afterwards, when it has run out, he will not receive a thing. The dismantling of the Christian world will be followed by the dismantling of the welfare state.

It comes down to the fact that unbridled goodness is much worse than ego-inspired badness. No thief, no murderous robber can cause as much misery as the real idealist. Because the robber will cease to murder when he's filled his pockets, but the idealist will only stop when paradise has been established on earth.

Oh, in the past Christianity has wreaked frightful havoc, as you say, unquestionably. But why not stop harping on about it. The most awful barbarism in western history has been perpetrated by the great atheist systems of the Twentieth Century – systems that dispensed with the ethical criteria of Christianity and replaced them with the *principle of the interchangeability* of individual human lives. I'm not stating anything original here, although it is astonishing how easily everyone continues to forget the unoriginal. Even though this is, of course, a logical consequence of dispensing with historical consciousness as the leading criterion in education.

Even in its dispensed-with state, Christianity still seems to be functioning, for the time being – but in intellectual circles, it is functioning in the way that Chesterton describes. Most intellectuals proceed via several hobbyhorses, of which The Engineerability Ideology, Climate Panic and Unthinking Pity are the most widely known. These ideas have a Christian pedigree: they are a substitute for the City of God, the Four Horsemen of the Apocalypse (even the notion of destructibility is part of man's overestimation of himself) and the "Let the Little Children Come to Me". Because western society is permeated with notions like forgiveness, meekness and peace, to the point of self-destruction. And so, for now, the Christian faith continues to have its effect, but beware, it has gone mad, one might say it is God forsaken...

What insights will the above lead to for the *future* of our poor continent?

My view is that art and the intellect must declare war on imposed egalitarianism. This means too – oh, bitter news for the adherents of that vile strand of the postmodern left that facilitates every possible unacceptable, fundamentally extreme right-wing notion about women, homosexuals, Jews and atheists – that an emphatic European *Leitkultur* is utterly indispensable. How can an immigrant integrate into European civilisation if he or she is told that it doesn't make any difference what he or she thinks, given that all cultural traditions are, in principle, equal? For heaven's sake, stimulate emancipation!

And defend freedom. I mean both individually and collectively. When I became embroiled in a political debate a couple of years ago, a fellow writer who had never completely been cured of Trotskyism snarled that I should keep my mouth shut for a year. I didn't do that. And as far as the collective is concerned: I have rejected the pacifist ideas of my parents with a bleeding heart. There are quite a number of rulers who only comprehend a discussion partner with a gun.

Continue to propagate the tradition, the continuum, and a knowledge of art, literature and history that is as broad as possible.

The matrix of our civilisation no longer covers reality: studies demonstrate that most children from respectable middle-class families have no idea what we celebrate at Christmas. So prevent the non-thinking from occupying the department of education because knowledge must be accessible to every receptive mind, irrespective of the milieu that that mind derives from – which is something quite different than making a gift of a meaningless diploma to everyone.

And, above all, accept the fact that you are a product of western culture, before criticising that culture. Improve your position, if possible, through diligent work and making the most of all your talents. The New Jerusalem descends from heaven, or not, of course, but you can never build it yourself; at best, an imperfect approximation of that transcendental promise is possible.

Translated from Dutch by Paul Evans

Anatomy of Resentment

Ivan Krastev

As it stands now, Europe has lost its self-confidence, its energy and its hope that the next century will be the "European century". From Beijing to Washington – and even in Brussels itself – the Old Continent is widely viewed as a spent geopolitical force, as a great place to live but not a great place to dream. These days the European Union is less a declining power than a "retired power" – wise but inactive, prosperous but elastically accommodating. The perversity of the situation is that the European model has fallen victim not to its failure but to its success. The shock that Europeans experience today recalls the shock of the Japanese technology companies of a decade ago when they suddenly realised that although they manufactured the world's most advanced cell phones, they could not sell them abroad. Consumers elsewhere simply weren't ready, since Japanese devices relied on advanced technologies, such as third-generation e-commerce platforms, that were not widely used in other countries. Japanese cell phones, in other words, were too perfect to succeed.

Some dubbed this phenomenon Japan's "Galápagos syndrome", referring to Charles Darwin's observation that animals living in the remote Galápagos Islands, with their unique flora and fauna, had developed special characteristics not replicable elsewhere. Much the same could be said of today's Europe, which evolved in an ecosystem shielded from the wider world's rougher realities – and has consequently become too advanced and too particular for others to follow. So, is Europe's attractiveness rooted in the universal appeal of its culture and institutions or in its unique nature? The current refugee crisis in Europe suggests an interesting answer to this question.

A decade ago, the Hungarian philosopher and former dissident Gaspar Miklos Tamas[1] observed that the Enlightenment, in which the idea of the European Union is intellectually rooted, demands universal citizenship. But universal citizenship requires one of two things to happen: Either poor and dysfunctional countries become places in which it is worthwhile to become a citizen, or Europe opens its borders to everybody. Not one of these two is going to happen soon, if ever. Today the world is populated by many failed states nobody wants to be a citizen of and Europe neither has the capacity to keep its borders open nor will its citizens-voters ever allow it. So, the real debate in Europe is not whether the European Union should make its borders harder to cross, it is clear that it should, the split is on whether we should feel morally right doing so and how we should best help the most vulnerable people in the world.

In 1981, when the researchers of the University of Michigan conducted the first world value survey[2] they were surprised to find that nations' happiness was not determined by material well-being. Back then Nigerians were as happy as West Germans. But now, 35 years later, the situation has changed. According to the latest surveys in most of the places in the world people are as happy as their GDP will predict. What has happened meanwhile is that Nigerians got TV sets and the spread of Internet made it possible that young Africans or Afghans with one click of the mouse can see how Europeans live and what their schools and hospitals look like. Globalisation made the world a village but this village lives in dictatorship – a dictatorship of global comparisons. People do not compare their lives to the lives of their neighbours any more: they compare themselves to the most prosperous inhabitants of the planet.

In this connected world of ours migration is the new revolution – not the 20th-century revolution of the masses, but the 21st-century exit-driven revolution performed by individuals and families and inspired not by the ideologues' painted pictures of the future but by the Google maps-inspired photos of life on the other side of the border. It offers radical change now. In order to succeed, this new revolution does not require ideology, a political movement or political leaders. So, we should not be surprised that for many of the wretched on earth crossing the

European Union's border is more attractive than any utopia. For a growing number of people the idea of change means to change your country, not your government.

The problem with a migrants' revolution is that it has a worrying capacity to inspire a counter-revolution in Europe.

The myriad acts of solidarity toward refugees fleeing war and persecution that we saw months ago are today overshadowed by their inverse: a raging anxiety that these same foreigners will compromise Europe's welfare model and historic culture and that they will destroy our liberal societies. Fear of Islam, terrorism, rising criminality and a general anxiety over the unfamiliar are at the core of Europe's moral panic. Europeans are overwhelmed, not by those more than one million refugees that have asked for asylum, but by the perspective of a future in which the European Union's borders are constantly stormed by refugees or migrants.

Even before Cologne, the majority of Germans had started to doubt the government's open door policy. Chancellor Angela Merkel, who until recently was the symbol of the European Union's self-confidence and resilience, is now portrayed as a Gorbachev-like figure, noble but naïve, somebody whose – "We can do it" – policy has put Europe at risk.

The refugee crisis has confronted the EU with the question of its borders and it signalled that the threatened majorities that have emerged as the major force in European politics fear and loath a "world without borders" and they demand from the European Union clearly defined and well-protected borders. The threatened majorities fear that foreigners are overtaking their countries and threatening their way of life and they are convinced that the current crisis is brought on them by a conspiracy between cosmopolitan-minded elites and tribal-minded immigrants.

In short, the refugee crisis is changing European politics and threatening the European project in a way that neither the financial crisis nor the conflict with Russia does.

If the financial crisis divided the EU on creditors and debtors, opening a gap between the North and the South, the refugee crisis reopened the gap between East and the West. What we witness today is not what Brussels describes as a lack of solidarity, but a clash of solidarities: national, ethnic and religious solidarity chafing against our obligations as human beings. In the 1920s the number of refugees who came to Bulgaria, amounted to ¼ of its population. At that time Bulgaria looked like Jordan and Lebanon today and Bulgarians are rightly proud that in a very short time they succeeded to integrate these people. They did it because then the refugees were of similar origin. But East Europeans do not agree that the solidarity they owe their own folks is also owed to those others running from war and persecution. The refugee crisis made it clear that the European East views the very cosmopolitan values on which the European Union is based as a threat, while for many in the West it is precisely these cosmopolitan values that are the core of the new European identity.

"I can comprehend it only with difficulty," German president Joachim Gauck confessed, "when precisely those nations whose citizens, once themselves politically oppressed and who experienced solidarity, in turn withdraw their solidarity for the oppressed."[3]

Three decades ago "solidarity" was the symbol of Central Europe. Dissident intellectuals claimed that the difference between the East and the West was that the East truly believes in the European Union while the West only belongs to it. So why is it that today Central Europeans have become so estranged from the fundamental values that underpin the European Union and are so unwilling to show solidarity with the sufferings of the others now?

The scandal in East Europeans' behaviour as viewed from the West is not its readiness to build fences against refugees in the very places where walls were destroyed only 25 years ago, but the claim that "we do not owe anything to these people". While in Germany almost 10 per cent of the population took part in various voluntary activities aimed to help the asylum seekers in Eastern Europe, the public in Eastern Europe remains unmoved by the tragedy of the refugees, and leaders there have lambasted

Brussels's decision to redistribute refugees among European Union member states. Prime Minister Robert Fico of Slovakia asserts that his country would be ready to accept only Christians (there are no mosques in Slovakia, he argued, so Muslims have nothing to do in his country). The leader of the governing Law and Justice party in Poland Jaroslaw Kaczynski warned that accepting refugees is a health risk because they would bring unknown and dangerous diseases. Hungary's Viktor Orbán argues that the European Union's moral duty is not to help the refugees, but to guarantee the security of its own citizens. In most West European countries the refugee crisis polarised societies, setting advocates of open-door policies up against its critics, confronting those who open their houses to the refugees and those who are setting fire to refugee camps. Meanwhile, in Central and Eastern Europe, the crisis united the otherwise fragmented societies in their almost anonymous hostility towards the refugees. It is one of the few times in recent years when governments say what the overwhelming majority of people think. While Germans were trying to make sense of East Europeans' compassion deficit, East Europeans were puzzled why Germans who were not ready to pay for the Greeks are eager to help Syrians and Afghans.

The Central European refugee resentment looks odd if we take into account two aspects: first, that for the most part of the 20th century people in Central and Eastern Europe were busy either emigrating or taking care of immigrants. Second, that at present there are simply no Syrian refugees in most of the Central and East European countries. The number of refugees who entered, for example, Slovakia in 2015 was 169 people and only 8 of them asked to stay.

The return of the East-West divide in Europe is not an accident or bad luck. It has its roots in history, demography and the twists of post-communist transition, while at the same time representing a Central European version of people's revolt against globalisation.

History matters in Central and Eastern Europe and very often the region's historical experience contradicts some of the promises of globalisation. Central Europe, more so than any other place in Europe, is aware of both the advantages and the dark sides of multiculturalism. East European states and nations came late in the 19th century and nearly instantaneously. While in the Western half of Europe it was the legacy of the colonial empires that shaped the encounters with the non-European world, Central European states were born of the disintegration of empires and the processes of ethnic cleansing that followed. While in the pre-war period Poland was a multicultural society where more than a third of the population was German, Ukrainian, or Jewish, today Poland is one of the most ethnically homogeneous societies in the world with 98 per cent of the population being ethnic Poles. For many of them the return to ethnic diversity is a return to the troubled times of the interwar period. The 19th-century ethnic landscape of Western Europe was harmonious like a Caspar David Friedrich landscape, whereas the one of Central Europe was more like a Kokoschka one. And while the European Union is founded on the French notion of the nation (where belonging is defined as loyalty to the institutions of the Republic) and the German notion of the state (powerful *Länder* and relatively weak federal centre), Central European states were built on the German notion of the nation and the French idea of the state. Central Europe combines the admiration of the centralised and all-powerful state of the French with the idea that citizenship means common descent and shared culture, as adopted by the Germans.

In the view of French political scientist Jacques Rupnik, Central Europeans were particularly outraged by Germany's criticism directed against them in the course of the refugee crisis, because it was precisely from 19th-century Germans that Central Europeans borrowed the idea of the nation as cultural unity.

But Central Europe's resentment against the refugees is rooted not only in its long history but also in the experiences of the post-communist transition. What came after Communism and liberal reforms was pervasive cynicism. Central Europe is a world champion in mistrust in institutions. Brecht is not in the school curriculum anymore but many East Europeans will be ready to subscribe that "For this world we live in/ None of us is bad enough". Faced with an influx of migrants and haunted by economic insecurity, many Eastern Europeans feel betrayed in their hope that joining the European Union would mean the beginning of prosperity and life without crises.

Being poorer than Western Europeans, they point out, how can anyone expect solidarity from us? We were promised tourists, not refugees. The tourist and the refugee have become symbols of the two faces of globalisation. Tourism is the globalisation we like. Attracting tourists and rejecting migrants is the short summary of Eastern Europe's view of the desired world. The tourist is the benevolent foreign. He comes, spends, smiles, admires and leaves. He makes us feel connected to the bigger world, without imposing its problems on us. The refugee, who could have been yesterday's tourist, in contrast is the symbol of the threatening nature of globalisation. He comes bringing with him all the misery and trouble of the bigger world. He is among us but he is not one of us, and on top of that is often critical to our culture.

Curiously, demographic panic is one of the least discussed factors shaping Eastern Europeans' behaviour towards refugees. But it is a critical one. Nations and states have the habit of disappearing in the recent history of Eastern and Central Europe. In the last 25 years, around 10 per cent of Bulgarians have left the country in order to live and work abroad. According to United Nations projections, Bulgaria's population is expected to shrink by 27 per cent till 2050. The alarm of "ethnic disappearance" could be felt in many of the small nations of Eastern Europe. For them the coming of the migrants signals their exit from history, and the popular argument that aging Europe needs migrants only strengthens the growing sense of existential melancholy. When you watch on television the scenes of elderly locals protesting the settling of refugees in their depopulated villages where no child was born in the last decades, your heart breaks for both sides – the refugees, but also the old, lonely people who have seen their worlds melt away. Is there going to be anyone left to read

Bulgarian poetry in 100 years? Communism-imposed secularism made Central and East-Europeans very sensitive to the risk of destruction of their Christian identity. One does not need to be a believer to be worried about the future of Christianity and its culture in Central and Eastern Europe today. It is also to be remembered that Central and Eastern Europe is the part of Europe that has probably the most complex relations with the Islam. There you have two types of countries. You have countries like Bulgaria, which has the biggest Muslim minority in Europe and is on the border with the Muslim world, and you have countries like Slovakia, a country without a single mosque. For opposite reasons, both Bulgaria and Slovakia feel very nervous about the idea that most of the refugees are Muslims.

The failed integration of the Roma also contributes to Eastern Europe's compassion deficit. Eastern Europeans fear foreigners because they mistrust the capacity of their society and state to integrate the "others" already in their midst. In many of the East European countries Roma are not simply unemployed but unemployable because they drop out of school at a young age and they fail to acquire the skills needed for the 21st-century job market. It was the failure of the Roma integration that makes East Europeans believe that their countries "cannot do it". And the fact that East Europeans and refugees coming from Asia or the Middle East quite often end up as their competitors on the Western job market do not make East Europeans more open to the politics of integrating them. Citizens of the Western Balkan countries are probably the most powerful example of the collateral damage of the current crisis – according to the plan to deal with the growing influx of refugees entering Germany by sending them back home without hope that they can go back to the EU.

But at the end of the day, it is Central Europe's deeply rooted mistrust of the cosmopolitan mindset that divides the East and West. The current resentment against cosmopolitanism that in many aspects reminds us of the successes of the anti-cosmopolitan campaigns in Stalin-dominated Europe, is well captured by the growing eagerness of the voters to support nativist political leaders whose major advantage is that they are not interested in the world, do not speak foreign languages, do not have an interest in foreign cultures and avoid visiting Brussels.

The attitude divide between Europe's West and East on the issues of diversity and migration strongly resembles the divide between the big cosmopolitan capital cities and the countryside within Western societies themselves, two worlds – deeply mistrustful of each other.

Writer Joseph Roth was spending most of the interwar years wandering around Europe and taking refuge in the lobbies of the big hotels because for him hotels were the last remnants of the old Habsburg empire, a postcard from a vanished world, a place he felt at home. Some Central European intellectuals share Roth's nostalgia for the cosmopolitan spirit of the empire, but ordinary citizens of Central Europe do not. They feel comfortable in their ethnic states and they deeply mistrust those whose hearts are in Paris or London, whose money is in New York or Cyprus and whose loyalty is towards Brussels. In Tony Judt's words, "from the outset Eastern and 'Central' Europeans, whose identity consisted largely in a series of negatives – not Russian, not Orthodox, not Turkish, not German, not Hungarian and so forth – had provinciality forced upon them as an act of state making. Their elites were obliged to choose between cosmopolitan allegiance to an extraterritorial unit or idea – the Church, an empire, communism, or, most recently 'Europe' – or else the constricting horizon of nationalism and local interest". Being cosmopolitan and at the same time a "good Pole", "good Czech" or "good Bulgarian" is not in the cards. And it is this historically rooted suspicion towards anything cosmopolitan and the direct connection between communism and internationalism that is part of the explanation of Central Europe's sensitivities when it comes to the refugee crisis. In this respect the legacies of Nazism and communism significantly differ. Germans' drive for cosmopolitanism was also their way to run away from the xenophobic legacy of Nazism, while it could be argued that

Central Europe's anti-cosmopolitanism is partially rooted in the aversion to communism-imposed internationalism.

So, how important will the West-East divide in Europe caused by the responses to the refugee crisis be for the future of the European Union? Is it going to fade away in the way the division between Donald Rumsfeld's "old Europe" and "new Europe" faded away at the very moment Central Europeans turned against George W. Bush's war in Iraq, or will it lead to the emergence of a two-tier European Union? Is European solidarity possible in the absence of solidarity with the most vulnerable people in the world?

Many in Central Europe today point to the hardening of anti-refugee sentiments in Western Europe arguing that Europe is not divided anymore and that European unity is only one election away (the election that Chancellor Merkel will lose). Now, when Germans have got disillusioned with the policy of open doors, the differences will be easily bridged. Many Central Europeans celebrate that change of mood in the West as a victory of East Europe's hard-nosed realism over the hypocritical moralism of the West. You can sense evil pleasure when reading Central Europeans commenting on the "jewellery law" consensually adopted by the Danish Parliament. According to that law the government will confiscate any valuables of the refugees exceeding slightly more than 1000 euro. Is this West Europeans' compassion?

But the paradox of the refugee-crisis split in the EU is that the convergence of the anti-immigrant sentiments will not bring Western Europe and Central Europe any closer. It separated them even more. Unlike "Germany for the Germans" or "Bulgaria for Bulgarians", the slogan "Europe for Europeans" cannot fly politically. For many conservative Germans who oppose the direction in which German society is heading Romanians or Bulgarians are not less alien than the Syrians, while for the cosmopolitan-minded Germans who embraced Chancellor Merkel's culture of integration of the refugees, tribal-minded Central Europeans are perceived as the major obstacle for an open-society European

Union. In a sad way the split over refugees reconfirmed all the prejudices that East and West held against each other.

This crisis also demonstrates that European solidarity cannot be divorced from its Enlightenment roots. At the moment when East Europeans made the claim "we do not owe the refugees anything", many in the West realised that they do not owe Eastern Europe anything either.

The East-West split in the course of the refugee crisis teaches Europe a valuable lesson when it comes to its influence in the world. What the European Union can offer to the others is not a set of institutions that others should imitate but a centuries-long struggle to reconcile the universal and the local in its culture. It is the experience of cosmopolitanism as an ideal and as a crisis that makes Europe attractive to others and defines the world of today as a Europe-made world.

Notes

1. Gaspar Miklos Tamas, 'What is Post-fascism?', openDemocracy. net, 13 September 2001, https://www.opendemocracy.net/people -newright/article_306.jsp
2. European Values Study, 1981. http://www.worldvaluessurvey.org/ WVSContents.jsp?CMSID=History
3. Andrew Rettman, 'Austria imposes asylum cap to "shake up" Europe', Euobserver, 20 January 2016, https://euobserver.com/ justice/131928

Thinking Europe – No Future?

A Continent Torn Between Two Dreams

Philipp Blom

Europe is a continent without a future. Not because of the structural fault lines and increasing dysfunctionality of the EU – the crisis of its currency, the influx of refugees or the threat of a European break-up – it has no future because its societies and leaders have chosen not to have one. Future means change, and change, we have learned, is mostly negative: climate change, collapsing social systems, threats to social cohesion, the likely loss of Europe's global position, the problems of demography, and the limits of growth. European societies have therefore decided not to have a future, but to drag out the present as long as possible. Our civilisatory goal appears to be to retreat into an oasis of wellness and conspicuous consumption.

We have to accept a considerable degree of cognitive dissonance to maintain this blessed state. We are the first generation in history to have a good idea of what the consequences of our actions will be. Scientific models and analyses have been applied to crucial scenarios, most significantly linked to global warming, the rise of global populations and the decline of European ones, to the automatisation of work, the consequences of unsustainable consumption, and the extremes of reckless capitalism, and while there is a range of interpretations, the general direction of the developments affecting our future is clear. It is also transparent that our room for action is narrowing with every passing day, but instead of imagining and constructing the societies we want to live in thirty years hence, we are closing our eyes to the necessity of change. We allow change only where there is an immediate threat of being overwhelmed by current events. We have, to all intents and purposes, abolished our future in order to cling to the status quo of unsustainable wealth and artificial social peace.

The Little Ice Age

There can be no doubt that the European model has been extremely successful, and this success was based not on Christianity, but on an economic and social model which emerged from what historians term the great crisis of the 17th century, when the Little Ice Age cooled down the northern hemisphere by some two degrees Celsius. This incident of global climate change, which reached its apex roughly between 1570 and 1650, had a devastating effect on Europe's post-feudal economies during the late 16th century.

Before the Columbian exchange which brought crops such as potatoes, tomatoes and rice to the old world, the diet of most Europeans consisted mostly of wheat and other cereals. Famine occurred roughly once per decade as harvests were spoiled by bad weather. Beginning with the cooling during the 1570s, the rate of disastrous harvests and famines increased significantly as late springs, cool and rainy summers and brutal winters destroyed crops, broke up communities and caused rebellions. In the German-speaking countries there is a strong correlation between years with bad harvests and epidemics of witch hunts, during which the accused, mostly older, marginal women, were charged with being in league with the devil, casting evil spells on the weather and ruining harvests. A rash of millennial sects preached that the series of disasters was an expression of God's wrath and the end of days.

European societies emerged from this crisis through large-scale transformation. Four generations after the onset of the Little Ice Age, societies still bearing the imprint of feudalism, social hierarchies based on aristocratic lineage and landownership and economies depending almost exclusively on local grain production, had changed into a continent of trade and manufacturing, as well as a diversified and intensified agriculture.

The protagonists of this change were a new breed of social actors: members of an educated middle class, experts, entrepreneurs, engineers, and merchants. Scholars renewed agricultural practices, educated officers revolutionised the military in a century of savage wars, schools and universities were founded throughout the continent, merchants engaged in lucrative international trade with territories which were being conquered and turned into colonies not by trade, but by the force of arms and the relentless efforts of missionaries. Bolstered by diversified risk through stock exchanges (the first being founded in Amsterdam in 1602) the resulting unequal trading relationship made Europe rich and globally powerful.

The largely static societies of Europe were transformed in this process. The entrepreneurial model and the newly powerful middle class made societies more fluent, allowed for the accumulation of capital and a more dynamic social model - at least in the large cities. Many of the main exponents of the Enlightenment belong to this class: Descartes was trained as an artillery officer, Spinoza was an import-export merchant, Hobbes worked as a private tutor, and a hundred years later Rousseau hailed from a watchmaker's shop, Diderot's father was a master cutler, Adam Smith's father was a customs officer, and Kant was born into a saddler's workshop.

The economic model developed in Europe during this period made the continent wealthy. It is based on a simple mechanism: economic growth based on exploitation. Of course, there had always been exploitation, but its proceeds were not used for growth and investment, but were largely employed to finance the life and wars of Church and aristocracy. Now the exploitation of colonial peoples, of the landless poor in Europe, and of natural resources was turned into a dynamic process bringing Europe, and increasingly also the colonial settlements in the Americas, vast wealth and political power.

Growth and Exploitation

We are still operating within this 17th-century model. We are still fetishising growth, which is now almost exclusively dependent on stimulating artificial domestic consumption and aggressive promotion of export without regard for environmental or social impacts. We are still exploiting workers on other continents toiling in conditions tantamount to slavery, irreplaceable natural resources, as well as the imagination of our own citizens, caught in a rat race of getting ahead and fixated on a gospel of happiness through consumption.

It has long become clear that this model is unsustainable, but the status-quo bias of societies owing their unprecedented wealth to this practice is overwhelming. Postponement is the name of the game. Even the recent Paris climate summit, hailed as a historic success, will not come into force for another five years, after which there will no doubt be defaulters, disputes, dissimulation - and disasters. While the window for action is closing further by the day we appear to be determined to continue enjoying ourselves as long as the going is good, or as long as we can block out or export the negative effects and environmental fallout. An everlasting present. No future.

The Price of Transformation

The French-American anthropologist Scott Atran has pointed out that every society needs transcendence, a common goal, a dream that defines objectives, motivates restraint and morality, and transforms a conglomeration of individuals into a single social organism. After the waning of religions and the disastrous collapse of political ideologies in the twentieth centuries, the transcendence of the West has been economised. Our transcendence is commercialised, our icons are not saints but stars and models, our ambitions are largely defined in economic terms. While it is clear that we are living on time borrowed from our children, there is still no political conversation about radical social and economic transformation.

We are not alone in this. Throughout history, societies have tended to cling to existing structures and to suppress calls for change. The result is a historical phenomenon which tends to manifest itself with alarming regularity: almost all social transformations which we might consider as progress are preceded by mass murder, slaughtering a maximum of people according to the technological possibilities of the period. Freedom of religion and nation states are results of the Thirty Years War, the welfare state was put in place to care for the widows and invalids left by the First World War, human rights and international organisations such as the UN emerged out of the shadows of the Second World War. We appear not to learn from history, but from collective trauma.

Can we be sufficiently rational and, perhaps more importantly, sufficiently imaginative to break this rule and create real transformation before another catastrophe of our own making occurs? Psychologists occasionally employ the German word *Leidensdruck*, the burden of suffering necessary to make a patient realise that change is inevitable, to describe the point at which a patient decides to act. They also recognise that in many cases patients wait until their suffering has become crushing before they resolve to change.

Europe's unwillingness to imagine and confront a future worth living in seems overwhelming. Surrounded by historic wealth and living with unprecedented security at home and in spite of (perhaps because of) knowing what is to come, our *Leidensdruck* has obviously not yet reached proportions sufficient to motivate us. This phenomenon is exacerbated by what appears to be a fundamental error of Enlightenment thought.

Most, if not all, Enlighteners and most 19th-century socialists and communists were convinced that ending unjust oppression and religious tyranny would result in human flourishing. Workers would educate themselves and flock to concerts and libraries, the electorate would become informed, egalitarian, and rational. They apparently did not foresee that granting people the right to shape their own lives and set their own priorities might result in the fact that a majority of them would opt for sitting on their sofa and watching TV. In spite of the spread of literacy and human rights, the educated, politically informed and socially aware societies envisaged by the Enlightenment seem to be little closer than they were during the Little Ice Age.

This design flaw in Enlightenment thinking does not invalidate its ideas, but it makes them more difficult, if not impossible, to realise. Growth based on exploitation has been the lynchpin of the West's dominance for more than three centuries, but is rapidly becoming its most existential threat. Not only has our preoccupation with growth begun to overwhelm our societies by focusing them on the purely imaginary riches created on the world's financial markets and on economic success rather than social wellbeing, it has also begun to undermine the purely physical conditions necessary for our survival as a species - let alone that of thousands of others.

A Fragile Dream

But while some aspects of the Enlightenment heritage have proved highly problematic, others have enabled us to formulate values and rights which are representative of what is best in the human animal. The dream of human rights, of equality before the law, of the dignity of every life, of access to education and opportunity is the most beautiful dream ever dreamt by our species.

It is a fragile dream, and we must realise that as the environmental pressures of global warming, overpopulation, and mass migration increase, it may evaporate as quickly as it came into being. Human rights and freedoms are just as fictional as any religion. They do not exist in nature. Nature only knows the hunters and the hunted, as well as collaboration with members of the pack (very occasionally also clearly defined and limited inter-species cooperation). There is nothing more radical in history than the idea to extend the idea of the rights of individuals in the pack to all members of a species.

The idea of these rights may reach back to human history beyond Christianity to its earliest philosophical sources, but as a social movement, carried by a growing middle class in part as a defence of its own interests, it is barely three hundred years old, and as a widely recognised political principle it exists for no more than eighty years or so.

Human rights are a story which our civilisation tells itself, and they live only as long as they are kept alive by the retelling of the story, and as long as we support institutions which make them a reality by making them enforceable. Other societies are operating successfully without them, and these rights will vanish from our lives if we allow them to atrophy through indifference, greed, or in the name of short-term gain.

There can be no doubt that we are facing another Great Transformation as the economist Karl Polanyi called the revolution of the 17th century, but this time more drastic and pervasive than the changes Europe experienced during the Little Ice Age. The current scientific consensus is that the climate change we have initiated by releasing the carbon deposits laid down over millions of years back into the atmosphere in less than a century will result in a likely increase of temperatures of not two, but of three or four degrees, leading to a heating up of our oceans and to chaotic and unmanageable changes in weather patterns. This will result in large-scale flooding and desertification, extreme weather events, and consequently historic mass migration, as well as wars and famines, fanned by the explosive population growth especially in regions in which states are weak, corrupt, and unable to confront the challenges ahead.

We have one single asset in facing this future. Like all other organisms, like mosses and roaches and songbirds, we must adapt, move away, or die out, but unlike other organisms our capacity for intellectual and cultural adaptation allows us not just to wait for biological evolution to take its course but to short-circuit this process by changing our societies. That will be the challenge of the decades ahead, and it is quite uncertain how or even whether we will navigate it successfully.

Can abstract ideas be a part of the solution in this struggle for survival which will intensify during our near future? How do our changing physical circumstances interact with our unique evo-lutionary asset, the formulation and implementation of ideals?

Two Dreams

Perhaps the key to understanding this process lies in the fact that we are symbolic animals, and that we negotiate present challenges by projecting values and ambitions into a future, by operating with cultural metaphors. During the 16th century, these metaphors were magical or religious: witches, divine anger. As the crisis of the 17th century took its course, the metaphors were adapted and were now increasingly expressed as ideas of freedom, human rights, and the fight of light against darkness.

Today, our cultural metaphors have changed yet again and it appears that our future will be negotiated in different terms. Just as 17th-century Europeans cast their transformation and the emerging social conflicts between the aristocracy and the emerging middle class and working class in theological and philosophical metaphors, we have already formulated our own cultural lens through which we view the transformations that are taking place around us. This lens refracts our social realities and casts them in two images, two dreams which frame our visions of a future.

The first of these might be called a liberal dream. It traces its origins to the Enlightenment. It speaks of human rights and of individuals, of self-determination and of freedom. It has created Western societies and their moral framework, and has spread around the world not only through colonialism, but also through post-colonial liberation movements. In recent decades it has been found that it is by no means unequivocally positive. It can express itself as a morally anarchic, libertarian or neo-liberal dream, abandoning the weak to the greed and superior resources of the strong. Philosophically speaking, it also forces a particular kind of freedom on people, which may rob them of a sense of purpose, a universal meaning, a sense of place.

The moral ambivalence of this liberal dream is the central point of criticism from its opponents, which one might call adherents of an authoritarian dream. It restores the sense of place by fighting the liberal dream as morally bankrupt, arrogant, decadent, and culturally doomed. It sees people not as individuals but as part of historical or religious collectives, of cultures with fixed historical identities and destinies.

This authoritarian dream is often born out of humiliation and a sense that the experience of modernity has derailed humanity from the course ordained by providence. It unites such seemingly disparate actors and movements as Vladimir Putin and European right-wing populists, Evangelicals in the USA and the terrorists of the so-called Islamic State, Hindu nationalists in India and President Erdogan in Turkey, the murderous Sharia courts of Saudi Arabia and the neo-fascist mobs in Western capitals. It also resists a scientific approach to the world in the name of preordained destiny and frequently denies not only climate change but also individual rights, focusing on sexual identities (feminism, homosexuality) and practices as a problem far greater than rising ocean levels.

These two dreams, liberal and authoritarian, have become the cultural metaphors we use to describe the world, as well as the ideological poles between which we will have to find a path to a liveable future. They confront each other in debates, as well as on the battlefield, and they create deep rifts not only between countries, but within societies. This confrontation has the potential not only to destroy the Enlightenment dream, but also to lead to a future in which an aging, authoritarian, rich Fortress Europe suppresses dissent at home and sinks refugee boats in the Mediterranean, while accommodating itself with an Orthodox Greater Russia and an Islamic Caliphate in the Middle East.

The authoritarian dream promises a retreat from modernity, simple truths, traditional values, and ruthlessness against enemies, real or imagined. The tragedy of the liberal dream is that its answers will always be couched in social and theoretical complexity, relative values, historical entanglements, and political compromise.

In all their ambivalence, the liberal dream and the dream of the Enlightenment describe similar hopes and ambitions. Its values are not set in stone – they have been hotly debated and fought over since the 17th century, and they will continue to be contentious, precisely because they do not appeal to a single revelation, but to reason and solidarity. In recent decades these values have been cast mainly in the language of economics, but the debate doesn't rest there; it must be intensified.

Human Rights - Indivisible?

After centuries of growth based on exploitation there can be little doubt that the only possibility of successfully navigating humanity's greatest challenge in its known history is through furthering sustainability and solidarity, even if this may mean losing the wealth we have accumulated on the backs of others, and compromising the security we paid for by collaborating with dictators.

The transformation of our natural environment and its cultural consequences can be bought off and denied for a little while, but they will assert themselves eventually, and if we only react by building dams against it, they will burst and submerge what is left of the liberal dream. We can ride this wave of change by undermining the Enlightenment values which created our world for a limited time, but only if we accept this Great Transformation and adapt to its conditions will we be able to create societies and cultural metaphors which do not only allow us to survive physically, but to thrive.

Let us return to Europe and its immediate future. There can be no doubt that the post-war world belongs to the past and that even the period since 1989 has come to an end. We are heading for a new and possibly cataclysmic era which will, I believe, be imagined and described in terms of the confrontation between a liberal and an authoritarian dream in various guises and permutations.

One central challenge to the liberal dream is that it is in danger of being overwhelmed by its own promises. If Western values are, at least in terms of empirical outcomes, superior to others which have less regard for the life and dignity of individuals, if human rights are universal and indivisible, then how can we pay authoritarian rulers such as Erdogan (and before him Gaddafi) to keep refugees from crossing our borders, no matter how brutally? How can we continue to profit from exploitation? The problem is not just ethical, but also practical: if one divides human rights into a two-class system with first-class rights for the West and second-class rights for the rest it is only a question of time before one finds oneself at the wrong end of this definition. If the fiction of human rights is not maintained intact it becomes a simple apology for privilege.

Torn between a liberal and an increasingly aggressive authoritarian dream, Europe will have to decide between simply defending its privileged status quo as long as possible, or allowing and encouraging a social, political, economic, and environmental transformation which will result in vastly different societies, and very possibly in less security, less wealth, and a less predictable social reality.

Europe's transformation during the Little Ice Age is a lesson in cultural resilience and imaginative adaptation. It is also a warning. Then as now, there are no easy solutions, no clear decisions. Change did not come from above but bubbled up chaotically and marked by improvisation, experiment, and conflict. "There are crises which cannot be solved but only survived," writes the Bulgarian political scientist Ivan Krastev.

At the same time, the historic turning point we have reached also harbours a chance: the confrontation between liberals and authoritarians shatters the illusion of living in a consumer paradise outside of history and forces us to politicise our discussion, to imagine the kind of Europe we want to be living in in twenty or thirty years. If Europe's liberals do not have the will and the determination to formulate and implement this vision and to navigate the resulting uncertainty, the dream of the Enlightenment and of human rights might soon dwindle to a footnote in the history of the West, an episode of decadence that was finally overcome.

My EUtopia

Empathy in a Union of Others

Kalypso Nicolaïdis

There are stories one remembers till the end. Stanley Hoffmann, renowned Franco-American political scientist and a friend, died recently. He passed on many stories but one stands out in my memory that serves as a retrospective beacon, a story illuminating our future in spite of our present European predicament. In the story, Stanley is fifteen and hiding with his mother in Lamalou-les-Bains, a charming village at the foot of rolling hills in the south of France. The village is occupied by German soldiers, most of whom are barely older than him by the end of the war. In the story, Stanley and his mother, originally Austrian Jews and the only ones in the village to understand German, manage to listen to their occupants as they open letters from home, letters full of catastrophic news of bombardments and death. And so Stanley and his mother pass on the message to the villagers, that in truth the boys in Nazi uniforms are *malheureux comme des pierres* (as sad as stones), and the villagers in turn send instructions to their sons in the *maquis* of the surrounding hills not to shoot. When the village was liberated in 1945, he recalls, not one drop of blood was shed. It was not like this everywhere.

Can this testimony inspire new generations who witness their own wars and atrocities, to believe in the possibility of a more ethical world – *malgré tout*? Can we not together project ourselves back to the numerous pockets of deep humanity that were left even at the end of such an atrocious war (are they not all?!) and to these ineffable attitudes that made reconciliation possible after the war? And if we do, can we not share Stanley's gaze and suppose that the European Union was made possible, at least initially, from sparks like these? Ripples of empathy in the mist of Inferno.

Like other intellectuals who grew up in wartime, Stanley spent his life trying to understand a century which witnessed in its first half a collapse of all the restraints put on war in previous centuries, and in its second half a frantic search for new more drastic restraints. This search may have led *inter alia* to the birth of the UN and the EU, but alas war could only be kept at bay by some peoples in some places some of the time. As they edged closer to the Kantian ceiling and away from the Hobbesian floor, Europeans were lulled in the illusion that they had collectively transcended self-inflicted disaster.

Fast forward to 2016 and the doom besetting our European continent, a continent torn apart by a tsunami of crises, ranging from the Eurozone's multiple debt wounds to the tragic moral tale of refugees dying across borders, a project of union from which a greater number than ever want out, whose open-society values are mocked from within by leaders who prefer to look up to Putin than to Mandela, and all this against the backdrop of terror in our cities inflicted by our own children, kids from the suburbs who, in another universe, could have been the friends of their lifeless victims. Many now say that the question is no longer "more or less Europe" but "Europe still"? Will Europe be reborn like the phoenix or crash like Icarus for daring to fly too close to the sun?

There are countless ways of asking, or not asking, or even mocking these questions. Indeed there are countless European stories, ways of thinking through what Europe does for me and what I should do for Europe, ways of dreaming or rejecting Europe, endowing it with all sorts of goods and evils, all sorts of pasts, pedigrees and prejudices. No doubt the book in which I write these pages offers an equally attractive European narrative. Our task is not to find one best story but simply to amplify the echoes between European stories in the firm knowledge that it is their tapestry of contrasting textures and colours which will continue to constitute the European project for decades to come.[1]

For my part, I focus on one story – the story of the echoes of what happened in Lamalou-les-Bains 70 years ago, a moment pregnant with the promise of reconciliation, for there and then, empathy had become contagious against all odds. I ask what to make of the fact that the rest of the world sees us as a "European civilization" without empathy, turning its back on its credo, forgetting the lessons it had so painfully learned.[2] And in doing so, I attempt to sketch a realist EUtopia, that of a Community of "others", peoples who while holding on to their differences somehow manage to recover and nurture that original spark and translate their simply human empathic instincts into a sustainable form of institutionalised togetherness.

I do so under three labels: Promise, Trial and Hope. The promise has lived in many minds over the centuries. One version of it can be called post-Holocaust humanism, and can be inspired *inter alia* as this book is by Isaiah Berlin's musings captured in his November 1959 speech to the Fondation Européenne de la Culture in Vienna, *European Unity and its Vissicitudes,* grounded in Europe's history, pathologies and aspirations.[3] And it can be found in a missing albeit implicit ingredient of his philosophy, namely the role of empathy, recognition and solidarity in the cooperative promise. We must however, reckon with the fact that neither in Europe nor elsewhere can we rely on the better angels of our nature to translate the empathic impulse into lasting peace nor can we rely on institutions to compensate for our empathic deficits. Today's European Union may be on trial precisely because it cannot sustain the institutions that were meant to foster it. Finally, then, our hope rests with the politics of empathy and the related praxis of recognition and solidarity. Perhaps paradoxically, one of the most solid grounds to entrench such a praxis will be found in all the forms of art and education which encourage flights of imagination and thus help us inhabit each other's worlds.

I.   Promise: Isaiah Berlin's Humanist Tradition

Like Stanley Hoffmann, Isaiah Berlin spent most of his life trying to understand the follies of his century and their historical roots in order to extract fragments of wisdom from the still smothering fire of history. He made one of Kant's dicta his own – that "out of the crooked timber of humanity, no straight thing was ever made" – in the firm belief that trying to fit humanity into any kind of straitjacket is bound to fail.[4] Never mind that this was not really what Kant meant, referring as he did not to human beings in general but to the fallibility of individuals who pretend to incarnate the sovereign.[5] Never mind that Kant did believe that the collective destiny of humanity, working through the deficiencies of its individual members and the progressive force of competition, reveals what he called "the hidden plan of nature to bring into existence an internally and externally perfected political constitution". Why else offer posterity a blueprint for Eternal Peace?

If Isaiah Berlin, in contrast, passionately rejected any perfectionist utopia, this does not mean that he gave up on the belief in an ideal, one that could still be possible in a post-Holocaust world.

In this spirit, if we may still dare today to speak of an EUtopia, it is precisely in this non-teleological sense, to refer to a posture-driving action, a belief in a Union as we would want others to see it and whose never fulfilled promise we would like to remain faithful to.[6] In such a EUtopia, it is the manner in which we trace our course which matters, guided by an ever receding horizon and our normative compass. It is because this EUtopia was born from *aporia* – impossible situations from which there seems no way out – that Europe is a political existentialism justified by the doing rather than the being, whose existence as a project must always take precedence over some essence of "Europeanness", where experience must trump ideology, and experiment bypass grand designs. There is an answer to *aporia*. In the words of the French philosopher Sarah Kofman, "to say that a *poros* is a way to be found across an expanse of liquid is to stress that a *poros* is never traced in advance, that it can always be obliterated, that it must always be traced anew, in unprecedented fashion".[7]

Can we read Isaiah Berlin's European narrative in this spirit? In particular his reading of European history as a dialectic between the craving for public order and for individual liberty, a history where resources lay vibrant to sustain the tilt towards the kind of liberty which we must still thrive for, crooked timber of humanity that we may be.[8] The search for these resources takes the historian of ideas back to our forefathers' simple enlightenment belief that "although there existed obvious differences between individuals, cultures and nations, the similarities between them were more extensive and important, above all the faculty called reason". Upon this foundation lay the possibility for social life through human attempts to communicate and "try to persuade each other of the truth of what they believe".

Henceforth, with the enlightenment, we were able to move beyond the fundamental assumption by which men lived for more than 2,000 years, "that all questions have their answers, and that there exists a perfect pattern of life, compounded of all the true answers to all the agonising questions". We came to understand that tragedy in this world is born from the incompatibility of equally justified human actions, and that heretics, dissidents and minorities of all hues did deserve at least to be seen as dying for their own truth, for there was no such thing as one truth. And this, while hierarchy and subjugation between peoples increasingly came to be exported from an intra-European scene to the global in the imperial frenzy of the 19th century. In this regard, Great Britain's schizophrenia may have been the most egregious.

Isaiah Berlin's dilemma however takes us back to the relationship between France and Germany as he agonises about the road taken when 200 years ago, the liberal enlightenment intuition underwent its romantic transmutation. We must try to take in what happened to this powerful story of rising individuation and tolerance, when by the early 19th century romantic humanism took over and with it the idea that the noblest task for a man has become "to fight for his own inner ideals which cannot be tested as true or false but simply as goals whose design do not pre-exist anyone else's thought of them". Yes, here was the long shadow of the call for liberty, the assertion of Protestant renaissance against the old order dominated by the French and King Louis XIV whose arc of resistance stretched from the Holy Roman Emperor to Spain, Sweden, Saxony and Bavaria. Germany's counter-attack against the French, the praise of variety, the wild and the spirit may have elevated art and literature to an exalting pinnacle. But, alas, the tidal wave of feelings "rose above its banks and overflowed into the neighbouring provinces of politics and social life with literally devastating effects".

From this, Isaiah Berlin expresses a general warning against "great imaginative analogies from one sphere, where a particular principle is applicable and valid, to other provinces, where its effect may be exciting and transforming but where its consequences may be fallacious in theory and ruinous in practice". By inspiring leaders of men and nations, the chaotic rebellion of the romantic artist on the hill, the heroic free creator haranguing the universe, somehow can be connected to the sinister descent into totalitarianism and nationalism of the 20th century. As Heinrich Heine warned the French already in the 1830s, "one fine day their German neighbours, fired by a terrible combination of absolutist metaphysics, historical memories and resentments, fanaticism and savage strength and fury, would fall upon them, and would destroy the great monuments of Western civilisation".[9]

If Napoleon had been the first great romantic political demiurge making his creation the transformation of the world, the creation of states and the bending of wills, it is in Germany that totalitarian destruction would find its most inspired agents. In Isaiah Berlin's history, the romantic worship of art as inviolable and absolute led in the end to the extreme of nationalism and Fascism where all limits were trespassed, even the assumption from a prior age of inter-religious hatred that the other should be converted rather than liquidated.

Yet, it would be simplistic to see the last 150 years as solely the scene of conflict between the older universal ideal founded on reason and the new romantic idea founded on self-assertion where the former finally and thankfully returned with the advent of our technocratic Union, a small island at the end of history in a Hobbesian world. If we believe in the irrevocable plurality of *European Stories*, Isaiah Berlin's story is not that straightforward. We must be relieved that "the conception of man inherited from the romantics remains in us to this day", that political pluralism can successfully tame the exaltation of singularities ushered in by the 19th-century romantic declaration that man is independent and free. It is this spirit of "indestructible regard for what a man himself believes to be true" that led countless human beings to give up their life in the resistance to Nazism, to rise in the name of ideals that might have been universal or local, collective or personal, but ultimately ideals that did not belong to some grand overarching truth but to each one's inner calling, romantic as that may sound. There cannot be a single path to history, *notwithstanding* Marx or Hegel "metaphysical intimidation". But there may be a different kind of a "cunning of history", a cunning which recovers the force of multiplicity, diversity, pluralism, tolerance, and creativity from the clutches of its nationalist perversions. Ultimately both ideals, the many and the one are but abstract poles between which we seek the flourishing of individual human beings.

With Isaiah Berlin, we may now hope to ground our *living together* in the idea that the essence of man is the power of choice and the history of mankind the play in which all men improvise their parts, searching for a *poros* in a vast expanse of liquid, knowing full well that every choice sacrifices a path not taken. And we can now finally live together with the complementary idea that the improvisation is not random, for the essence of humanhood is also what keeps the great majority from acting outside the bounds of decency for "we know of no court, no authority, which could, by means of some recognised process, allow men to bear false witness, or torture freely, or slaughter fellow men for pleasure".

How do we bring this story to bear on Europe's current predicament? We could repeat like others that in the EU today, the forces of selfish retrenchment and fragmentation, parochialism, and indeed nationalism, have again gained the upper hand over the forces of reason and unity of mankind. But we know that such a story is too black-and-white. And we should know in fact that living together in this overcrowded continent of ours requires more than an abstract yearning for unity that after all has inspired the most destructive of aspiring pan-European sovereigns, the all too crooked Napoleons, Bismarks, Stalins, and Hitlers.

Instead, we need to continue down the road sketched by Berlin, and see the promise of Europe's unity in diversity as predicated on the most universal of human traits, a trait at least as powerful as the will to power and the yearning for freedom, that is the trait of empathy or the ability and even the desire to imagine oneself, as separate as one may be, in the skin of another. If much of international political thought, including Isaiah Berlin's, is about drawing the line between the universal and the particular, empathy rather than competition stands at the interface. It explains how the common moral foundation of our conduct or "universal ethical laws" *a la* Berlin can coexist with realms "where we actively expect wide differences – customs, conventions, manners, taste, etiquette". Empathy connects the many without merging them into one.

Empathy of course is not *per se* a European story. But we can ask ourselves how this universal trait has been brought into play in the project of European integration and when and how it has failed us. And in the process, we can venture that the world of art and politics could still be linked in ways more profitable for humanity than the unfortunate echoes of German romanticism in the 20th century.

Empathy has of late become a buzzword in both public media and scientific discourse and is increasingly studied in social, political, and cultural contexts.[9] We have come to understand that it is because early humans developed the capacity to internalise their mutual goals so well that they were able to coordinate complex activities leading to leaps in evolution unattainable by other species. Without this capacity scientists tell us, our brain volume would not have grown along with our capacity for cooperation. While in sympathy, pity or compassion we remain apart, in empathy we enter the world of others, not just our family or friends or community, but others who have no relation to us, aliens who are not like us but whose reality we recognise and act upon. And it is not enough to put oneself in the other's shoes, what is equally essential to complete the cycle of empathy is a "return to self", a self transformed by that projection and yet still capable of acting from its own standpoint, its own goals amended but not dissolved in the encounter with the other.

In the global village where the range of our mediated vicarious experiences has grown exponentially, we have not automatically become global citizens or digital nomads, but we have become neighbours of sorts. Which is why the likes of Sen, Nussbaum or Rifkin call for all of us to become "empathetic actors".[11]

To be sure, applying insights from our understanding of human development and face-to-face relations to organisations or entire complex systems like the EU is not a straightforward story.[12] We need to consider how empathy applies to groups, crowds or even more abstractly "publics". In doing so, the related concept of recognition can be considered not only as a form of empathy writ large, but the expression of empathy in action, since from empathy to recognition we move from inhabiting other individuals' personal experiences, to considering what is universal about them, from "taking in" a uniquely particular viewpoint to acknowledging each other's more abstract social identity, and we move from asymmetric to fundamentally reciprocal relations. Some would argue that what is at stake in recognition is not simply empowering, but literally constituting the other, while others would counter that this is attributing too much power to recognition as opposed to self-understanding.[13] Nevertheless, the part we each play in the larger worlds we inhabit, as citizens for instance, can only exist in its recognition by others. Yet, recognition may even express the opposite of empathy, that is, the necessity that we establish a distance in order to live with our differences.

In a similar vein, empathy is closely linked yet not equal to solidarity which is also a *hybrid* concept, used to describe both an observable *empirical* behaviour amongst people, an affect, and the normative grounds on which there *ought* to be such behaviour.[14] In this distinction also lies a cogent *critique* of relying on empathy for social change for this overlooks the structural barriers to social change and the normative need to pursue justice irrespective of affect. But the kind of empathy we are concerned with here is not simply *affective* but also *cognitive*, a capacity for perspective taking grounded on reason as much as passion.[15] But of course, that empathy "cracks open the door of moral concern" does not mean that it suffice in the toolkit that motivates justice – we need and rights and laws wedge that door wide open which in turn requires a collective purpose.[16]

Analysing the effect of social boundaries, including national boundaries on dynamics of empathy, recognition and solidarity is a complex task, beyond the scope of this essay. But we can say in general that the purpose of institutions as fields of empathy and recognition is to make an affect and an idea real. Institutions can enter, reflect, magnify or deflect struggles for recognition which may use the human capacity for empathy but also take account of the limits of such capacity.

We can see the EU project as seeking to channel the empathetic instinct across borders through democratic political, legal and economic institutions. It may seem like a stretch to ground such complex institutional structures on empathy, which is after all an individual human affect. Yet, if there are so many of us on this small cramped space at the tip of the Asian continent we have no choice but to reinvent the code of empathy across borders. How then do we aggregate empathy in the European Union?

II. Trial: The Elusiveness of Empathic Transnationalism

European integration seems to have little to do to with empathy. It has been about fulfilling functional needs, accommodating differences in interests and power through political narratives often disguised as clashes over ideas. But let us entertain the notion that empathy has been both its secret weapon and its Achilles heel.

We can start with the observation that the European Union was built by bringing together nation states, which at their best can be thought of as clusters of "organised empathy", the training schools of empathy for neighbours-as-strangers. The bet: that the perversions of nationalism and racialism were indeed that – perversions, and that the version of the national consciousness which had also been the well of resistance during the war was still worth rescuing. The European Union was constructed as an anti-hegemonic not anti-national project. Three hundred years after Westphalia, while the idea of Union in Europe could prevail as an alternative to the closure of sovereignty, it was to remain complementary to the idea of European nations.

To the extent that these peoples do not merge into one single European people, this is a Union of others.[17] Others, not in the sense of perfect strangers, or the essentialist understanding of other ethnic nationals (although, alas, this remained and remains a widely shared perception of what other nationals are within Europe). Others rather as simply the recognition that different political communities forge their own "overlapping consensus" through their own political ways and languages, their own political bargaining mode, their own notions of what the role of the state should be etc. The challenge for the EU has been to build an overlapping consensus of existing overlapping consensus, rather than a single overarching political order. Such a focus on horizontality best helps us understand European institutions as they are, as well as the dangers faced by the EU when its leaders forget this foundational truth.

Arguably, the edifice that was being built could only work properly if the peoples of Europe were to adopt a posture of radical openness to each other's realities. This is what I call the idea (or ideal) of European demoicracy, the idea that the EU is best conceived as connecting separate but interdependent sovereign peoples, "a Union of peoples who govern together but not as one".

This necessity of radical intermingling is best expressed by the term Union as opposed to Unity (although I suspect this is also what Isaiah Berlin means when he contrasts Unity with Uniformity: "indeed we do not look on variety as being itself disruptive of our basic unity: it is uniformity that we consider to be the product of a lack of imagination, or of philistinism, an in extreme cases a form of slavery"). Whether we refer to it as unity or uniformity, the message remains the same, that is, that there is nothing grand or ideal or beautiful in the merger of the many into one, the Europe of "one size fits all". "The worst of all sins," says Berlin, "is to degrade or humiliate human beings for the sake of some Procrustean pattern into which they are to be forced against their wills, a pattern that has some objective authority irrespective of human aspirations."

This is not an easy proposition and one that alas the EU has only approximated very imperfectly over the years. To some extent, the kind of intense and continuous negotiating mode in which European elites have been engaged requires a certain degree of empathy, if only to better identify potential "trades" over issues that are relatively more crucial to the other side than to mine, and vice versa. Political negotiations in Europe cannot be grounded on such continuous compromise building bolstered by consensus, without a modicum of empathy between national negotiators as to the hierarchy of their preferences.

But with the increased sensitivity and visibility of the issues dealt at European level, this logic has run against that of democratic interdependence: decisions need to be vetted by the peoples of Europe and these vetting processes are not amenable to the same bargaining dynamics. If addressing issues of burden sharing when the burdens are large (whether in financial or human form) requires the active involvement of Europe's respective "publics", we can no longer ignore the need to play out the dynamics of empathy, recognition and solidarity among the peoples of Europe and not only their leaders and lawmakers.

We could argue that the EU's legal order is both made possible by and conducive to a kind of legalised empathy across borders, predicated as it is on turning the laws of individual states into other-regarding laws, under the principle of mutual recognition. The boundaries of mutual recognition are drawn by relational calculations involving a complex mix of trust and expediency: if one side observes that the other side's laws are not good enough, it will not arrest someone and extradite her there. Although, EU institutions sometimes pretend otherwise, other-regarding law in the EU calls not for blind trust but binding trust – trust that must be merited including in the eyes of publics.

The refugee regime is *par excellence* a global institutionalisation of empathy. But what we have learned from the current so-called refugee crisis in Europe is that this regime rests on the capacity of European states to deal with the way in which each state is dealing with its own bit of the problem, its own bit of the responsibility owed to strangers fleeing death in their own country. And in doing so a kind of hierarchy of empathy is instituted, with empathy for the most vulnerable from without (refugees) vying for the kind of empathy dictated by the ties that bind neighbours within (European citizens). In making this nexus between internal and external "institutions of empathy" highly visible, the crisis has revealed the limits encountered by Europe's heroic attempt at institutionalising empathy. The spectacle of refugees hurdled behind Europe's fences does not seem to speak to those sitting around the EU decision table. In the great game of politics, individual impulses seem lost in translation, disregarded as a piece of inconvenient DNA. Do European leaders reflect popular sentiment? Following their lead, we turn a blind eye, shroud ourselves in indifference, don't want to know, hear or see. But against this cynical appraisal, witness the splendid *elan* across Germany and witness crisis-stricken old pensioners in Greece sharing their loaf of bread with a refugee. And witness Germany's support for Greece's plight, now that its plight is about helping others rather than itself.

We are left with three observations that may be at the root of our current disillusionment and may point to what may be the way forward.

First, *Europe's legal and constitutional order is but the thin superstructure of institutionalised empathy.* The history of law has long demonstrated that law cannot be sustained if it is not in phase with social change. Of course, judges have allowed themselves sometimes to supersede politics. But that only happens when the social terrain is ripe. As for politicians, they have failed to realise that given the EU's involvement with increasingly sensitive policy domains, their intergovernmental bargains and implementing law need to be embedded in bargains between societies. An elite-driven EU may have been a necessary sin in the first few decades, but the EU must now operate under the full force of democratic anchoring. And while the cracks started to open with early debates about the Euro, Polish plumbers, and benefit tourism, they have become schisms with the management of the Euro- and Schengenland. Structural reform in Eurozone countries or refugee resettlement across Schengen cannot happen without the engagement of citizens. The EU must now become a genuine demoicracy, that is, a polity which involves relations between "peoples" rather than simply states or their official representatives, relations underpinned by the various ways in which the peoples accept and practice their interdependency, including the way they open their own house under the ultimate Kantian requirement of hospitality.

Second, transnationalism in Europe has moved from the grounds of sympathy to empathy, *from a focus on transnational basic transfers to a focus on the need to change one's own politics when it produces dramatic externalities.* In this context, it can be counterproductive to speak of compulsion and coercion. In the EU, like in any modern marriage, nothing is irreversible. We are together by choice if we are a federal Union, not a federal state like the United States. One can be against both Grexit and Brexit and yet argue for a Europe where both are possible. Short of this nuclear option, as the issue has become increasingly sensitive, *integration through law* must be supplemented by each country's increased capacity to internalise through its parliament, fiscal councils or civil society organisations the consideration of the impact of its action on other countries, peoples, communities. And in turn, radical openness within the EU space can prepare its peoples for the ways in which they manage openness on their external frontiers.

Third, *altering one's own life, or at least one's political stance, on empathic grounds is strongly conditioned on perceptions of fairness.* Publics may be generous to each other, but not if it is taken for granted or if burdens are not shared at all.

III.   Hope: Cultivating Empathy through the Art of Translation

What are the requirements and tensions associated with the quest for a politics of empathy in the EU today? Can empathy be cultivated, and moulded to fit our collective ambitions? How can we better achieve what Ulrich Preuss calls the necessary cognitive and moral learning for democratic institutions – starting with the presumption that peoples, cultures, language groups do not have the right to be ignorant of each other?[18] This is a vast agenda for which I can only offer a few fragments here.

Poetic Empathy

The European Union may not have started with culture, as in the regret expressed by the apocryphal Monnet quote, but education and culture is probably where we must start if we are to explore the sources and resources of empathic demoicracy. What better way to overcome mutual ignorance than to cultivate the flights of imagination made possible by reading poetry and novels from other countries and languages, the guided tours of the mind of others, the romantic thrill of hearing another mind in a foreign accent, stories of strangers whom we can inhabit for a while and might inhabit us for the rest of our lives. Much of the creative literary process after all relies on what the great English Romantic poet John Keats saw as the ability to negate oneself, which he called *negative capability,* explaining to his friend Woodhouse: "A poet is the most unpoetical of anything in existence, because he has no identity, he is continually in for – and filling – some other body."[19] Or, as Hazlitt, Keat's mentor, remarked on Shakespeare "(he) throws his imagination out of himself". Schools are at their best when they tell our kids stories of the "sympathetic imagination" as it used to be called and inspire them on their own journey of translation between self and other.

In fact, isn't translation the generic name for universality?[20] Schools throughout Europe could do well to make compulsory the reading of several novels a year translated from another European language. An adolescent who reads Larsson's *Millennium,* Ferrante's *Brilliant Friend,* or Mulisch's *Discovery of Heaven* may be more in tune with Swedish, Italian or Dutch sensitivies than a political scientist who knows every twist of their political system. It may even be the case that English can only play its role as Europe's *lingua franca* if its generalised use is conditioned on universal access to Europe's singular voices (warranting for instance a radical increase in EU support for literary translation).[21] If they are to play their part, so-called "European schools" need to stop isolating language sections in their silos and start being about their intermingling. And Erasmus students may surely learn a lot about other countries in pubs and cafés but how about also asking them to write their own little novels, novellas or blogs as instantaneous translations between their home and host institutions?

Intrusive Empathy

Amidst pronouncements of retrenchment within the safe havens of our parochial identities, something else has happened in Europe in these crisis years which may give us hope. Never before have Europeans known so much about each other's politics, each other's hang-ups, flaws, and insecurities. To be sure, this increased mutual awareness has often been put to bad use, simply feeding prejudices and attacks. But it is nevertheless what is needed if we are to avert EU drift towards blind interventionism within national democratic dynamics. If we consider for instance that in a world of uncertainty, the EU is a vast insurance project and that making good on that promise requires a combination of rule obedience and solidarity, intrusive intervention might only be justified if filtered through empathic lenses. Consider for instance that a disproportionate share of the cost of adjustment from the Greek debt saga has fallen on the poor and created a whole new class of *nouveaux pauvres* in the country. It seems that many officials in European capitals among the creditors fail to be concerned about the distributive impact of their requirements, as if the country could be considered a black box in social terms. Would it not be preferable for them to worry about these differential impacts? And for their publics to lead the way? Calls for justice across borders must recognise the tension, the aporia between democratic autonomy, which requires less interventionism, and just intervention which means peaking inside the black box of other countries. And for European peoples to accept, or better wish, to open their democratic choices to each other in this way, we will need more transnational politics where cleavages emerge across countries and not only between them, among those for instance who across borders are most exposed to collective risks and less to opportunities. Uniting across borders is an old but fragile process which does not happen in a vacuum.

Theatres of Empathy

Youth activism can be the first school of empathy. In fact, it is often a live *theatre of empathy*. Take the "I am" movement: *Je suis Charlie*, or perhaps better: *Je suis Ahmet*. It has a long historical shadow: "We are all Palestinians" and all "children of the Holocaust" at the same time. Just as in the spring of 1968 we were all "German Jews" with Dany Cohn Bendit (including six-year old me!), and later all "Jan Palach" setting himself on fire in Prague's Wenceslas Square. But what did we mean then? And what do we mean now? For sure, that we commit, deeply and truly to the victims of violence and oppression everywhere. But are we asking any kind of political authority to do something about their oppression? Are we organising to intervene ourselves as civil society? Or do we prefer to stay on the side of contestation?

In our epoch, it seems that it is no longer enough to simply "unite" in "solidarity" with our brothers and sisters as in the good old days of international unions and parties. Today's moving force is to *be* the other, to feel her pain, inhabit her suffering. The web connects the "je suis" everywhere and them with that which they claim to be. But how many of those who "are" *Charlie* get the jokes in its pages and share the last laugh? And does it matter? What kind of conversation are they ready to engage in with those who shout back: *Je ne suis pas Charlie?*[22] Or what does it mean for activists to enact a "die-in" during the Gaza bombardment or for Ai Weiwei to re-enact the drowned infant Alan Kurdi on a Lesbos beach? While such acts may constitute a step beyond solidarity in the scale of other-regarding-ness, the theatre of empathy may become a regression when disconnected with a sense of responsibility for the ultimate outcome which this empathy implicitly calls for: do not confiscate my dignity, do not maim me, do not kill me. And should we not prefer calls for a solidarity which is not predicated on pretending to be equal but on acknowledging our inequality and privilege (as white, middle class, young, men, ...). This is not about you.[23] Empathetic actors can turn rebels into victims and rob them of their own voice with the good intention of lending theirs. Why do I need to imagine that it could be me in order to act, when the real problem is that people like me will never *know* what it means to be on the other side? Should my appeal for justice be grounded on affect, an affect presumably demanded from those who are supposed to deliver the goods, or should it be grounded in struggle and *rapport de force?* The theatre of empathy too often ignores question marks.

Mimetic Empathy

Helping the helpless may be the most basic universal value, but empathy for the plight of refugees seeking to cross European boundaries has exhibited many different hues. In Britain for instance, the vision of scores of Germans lifting "Welcome" placards in a football stadium did more to trigger empathy than countless pictures of refugees in life boats on our TV screens. Somehow, here as elsewhere empathy is not only contagious but has taken on mimetic qualities. Publics empathise all the more with refugees when their neighbours do, as if some sort of vindication was needed. Is this wisdom of the crowds? Statesmen are supposed to know that theirs is the burden of putting burdens on everyone else. Never was Angela Merkel more of a statesman than when she did. But it would be wrong to believe that what is urgently needed is democratically virtually impossible to do. In fact, polls show that a majority of European citizens are in favour of taking in significant numbers of refugees in their own countries, especially if other countries do the same. Empathy does not trump demands for fairness. But conversely, taking in refugees is preferred over the closing off of borders as long as there is to be a "fair" allocation of refugees – of course the meaning of fairness is hotly contested although per capita measures can be a pretty good start as argued by the European Commission. This demonstrates how misplaced can be our politicians' fear of "the blind fear of their electorate". Perhaps they might start believing in the empathetic intelligence of their citizens who do not in their great majority subscribe to the pronouncements of Marine Le Pen or Jarosław Kaczyński against "bacterial immigration", threatening the import of "protozoa and parasites". The countless cities and towns around Europe organising refuge testify to that effect.

Virtual Empathy

Is life on social media and the continuous navigation among virtual worlds which defines the new generations changing the parameters of empathy in our transnational community? In a world of Facebook, WhatsApp and Twitter our children learn to inhabit seamlessly many parallel lives at once, learn to recognise the many cues that facilitate empathy, juggle with the multiple lives of others, and enter them in a heartbeat. But they also tend to interact with like-minded groups to the detriment of those who might really require empathy rather than simple connection. We have only started to explore the huge potential of e-democracy and how these virtual networks might be expanded into shared political lives full of new modes of virtual exposure and radical transparency as well as ubiquitous resistance to injustice. Europe *must* be part of this adventure.

Conclusion

We should certainly fear the technocratisation, banalisation and marginalisation of empathy bred by the complexity of today's globalisation. If empathy is about staying oneself while entering the other's mind and dreams, it is ultimately a call to action. A call for action by Europeans in the world ought to be based in part on our capacity to understand the perceptions that others have of the EU, including their perception of the EU as a post-colonial power. But more fundamentally, a global empathetic actor must find ways of empowering actors for change elsewhere by co-inhabiting their worlds if and when they will let us.

In our own neck of the woods, we Europe must rediscover and cultivate empathy for those left behind – left behind by the dignified Greek old man who killed himself not to be a burden for his family, left behind by the lifeless corpses at the bottom of the Mediterranean, left behind by all those who died in greater numbers in Paris' Bataclan because they did not want to leave their mates behind.

We are also those left behind. So let us not forget these young German occupants in the village of Lamalou-Les-Bains whose despair echoing through the hills of the *maquis* protected them and ultimately won the European peace. It is in their name, and in the name of all those who fought in the past for a cause other than themselves, that we should continue to build, painstakingly, step by step, the institutions of empathy in a community of others.

Notes

1. Justine Lacroix and Kalypso Nicolaïdis (eds.), *European Stories* (Oxford: Oxford University Press, 2010).
2. Ramin Jahangegloo, A Europe Without Empathy, *The Indian Express*. September 16, 2015.
3. Justine Lacroix and Kalypso Nicolaïdis (eds.), *European Stories* (Oxford: Oxford University Press, 2010).
4. Isaiah Berlin, *The Crooked Timber of Humanity: Chapters in the History of Ideas* (London: Murray, 1990).
5. Perry Anderson, 'England's Isaiah'. Review of *The Crooked Timber of Humanity*, op cit. *London Review of Books* (20 December 1990); Berlin, *The Crooked Timber of Humanity* (1990).
6. Kalypso Nicolaïdis and Robert Howse, 'This is my EUtopia: Narrative as Power', *Journal of Common Market Studies*, Special Anniversary issue, (40)4 (2002), pp. 767-92.
7. Sarah Kofman, 'Beyond Aporia?', in Andrew Benjamin (ed.), *Post-structuralist Classics* (London & New York: Routledge, 1988).
8. Berlin, *The Crooked Timber of Humanity*.
9. Heinrich Heine, *On the History of Religion and Philosophy in Germany* (1834).

10. The literature on empathy in neurobiology and psychology is vast. For a recent application to humanities and social science see, Aleida Assmann and Ines Detmers, *Empathy and its Limits* (London: Palgrave MacMillan, 2016).

11. Jeremy Rifkin, *The Empathic Civilization: The Race to Global Consciousness in a World in Crisis* (New York: Penguin, 2009).

12. See for instance: David Levine, 'Keeping track of the self: Empathy, recognition and the problem of emotional attunement in organizations', *Journal of Organizational Psychodynamics* (1)1 (2007).

13. Contra: Nancy Fraser and Axel Honneth, *Redistribution or Recognition? A Political-Philosophical Exchange*. Translation by Joel Golb, James Ingram, and Christiane Wilke (London and New York: Verso, 2003).

14. Juri Viehoff and Kalypso Nicolaïdis, 'Social Justice in the European Union: The Puzzles of Solidarity, Reciprocity and Choice', in Dimitry Kochenov, Grainne de Burca and Andrew Williams (eds.) *Europe's Justice Deficit* (Oxford: Hart Publishing, 2015).

15. See series of contributions on the "empathy wars" published openDemocracy.net in the course of 2015-16. See in particular, Laura Cram, 'Empathy, Belonging and the EU-UK Question', 9 March 2016.

16. Roman Krznaric, 'Welcome to the empathy wars', openDemocracy.net, 29 June 2015.

17. For an early formulation, see Joseph Weiler, *The Constitution of Europe: "Do the New Clothes Have an Emperor?" and Other Essays on European Integration* (Cambridge: Cambridge University Press, 1999).

18. Claus Offfe and Ulrich Preuß, *Citizens in Europe: Essays on Democracy, Constitutionalism and European Integration* (ECPR Press, 2016).

19. John Keats, Samuel West, and Matthew Marsh, *Realms of Gold: Letters and Poems of John Keats* (Naxos Audio Books, 1999).

20. Dipesh Chakrabarty, *Provincializing Europe: Postcolonial thought and historical difference* (Princeton: Princeton University Press, 2009).

21. Phillipe van Parijs, *Linguistic Justice for Europe and for the World* (Oxford: Oxford University Press, 2011).

22. Kalypso Nicolaïdis, 'Charlie Hebdo numero 1178: All is forgiven?', openDemocracy.net, 28 January 2015.

23. Mathijs van de Sande, 'Don't confuse solidarity with empathy', *Doorbraak.eu* 23 February 2015.

Culture and the EU's Struggle for Legitimacy

Claudia Sternberg

Europe's current crises seem to have true potential of splitting the Union apart. The Euro crisis, the looming threat of Brexit, and the refugee crisis have put the legitimacy of the EU and the integration project into serious question in the eyes of many. The EU's multiple crisis has once again shifted the question to the fore of why we are in this together to begin with. What are the ideas, commonalities, and aspirations that unite us? What differences divide us, are they dooming integration to failure, and do they have to be divisive? Might shared ideas, values, and goals help in overcoming Europe's present discontents, or is all lost in the face of clashing interests and incompatible identities? What role might culture play in this?

It is important to see today's crisis of EU legitimacy in historical context. This is what I will try to do in this essay, moving from the foundation of the European Communities in the 1950s to Europe's present discontents. I shall tell a story of how our ideas and standards of what it would *mean* for the EU to be legitimate have evolved over time – and of the roles that culture has played in these ideas. My story is a tale of how the European institutions, political leaders, opinion-making elites (what I shall refer to as "EU official" discourses) and the wider public in the members states fought over what the point of integration was, what form it should take – and on what grounds it could be claimed to be legitimate. I trace processes of meaning making, by which some ideas become more important than others in how we make sense of the EU and its legitimacy. Culture has played key parts in various of these competing ideas around EU legitimacy, not least in many claims that the Europeans form a community, and not only because they share a joint project,[1] but also because they share common values and ideological commitments – and that, therefore, integration and a common European polity are justifiable.

My underlying philosophical notion of legitimacy is that something is legitimate not to the extent that it meets some abstract ideal criteria, nor to the extent that people believe that it is – but rather to the extent that it can be justified in terms of their beliefs about what constitutes legitimacy, in terms of what seems plausible to them.[2] But what are people's beliefs about legitimacy? They change over time, are essentially contested, and embedded in deeper cultural, ideological, or cognitive conditions that circumscribe what it is plausible to say in a given context.

A Discursive History of Struggles over EU Legitimacy

A central discursive foundational legitimation technique of the 1950s, but still robust today, was to focus on common grounds, and gloss over potentially contentious issues. Central in this discursive culture of *depoliticisation* was the storyline that European integration was the only way to secure peace and prosperity across Europe. In this picture, integration was indispensable to achieving security, economic stability, and improved living conditions for Europe in an increasingly interdependent world, and, given the absolute necessity of securing these aims, a matter of no alternative as such. Note how this line of argument projected that there was such a thing as a European common interest, the lure of which belittled any clash of ideas regarding what it may consist in, or any disagreements over how to pursue it and how to distribute costs and benefits of doing so. A related narrative was that that everyone agreed on this European "common good", and what it consisted in. Cultural or ideological differences had no particular place in these discourses. Another technique of placing certain rules, actions, and institutional features beyond contestation appealed to "the law", and the constitutionalisation of Community law, as a source of legitimacy for the Communities. More fundamentally though, these peace and prosperity, indispensability, and common good storylines were underpinned by a general emphasis on harmony and agreement on universally shared goals. This rested on a discourse of hope, progress, and rising above circumstance, not least through enlightened planning and expert knowledge.

Notwithstanding, and counter to all harmonising efforts, rivalling ideas and understandings did exist, and were gathering force. The 1960s and 1970s were marked not least by demands for European elections, first held in 1979. This campaign actively politicised what the Communities should be doing, and how they should be doing it. The stakes of integration, was the rallying cry, were "too important" to be decided on without the people. Rather, demands for European elections insisted on *democracy* as a condition of the Communities' legitimacy, reflecting a deeper cultural shift in hegemonic legitimacy understandings. Immediately after the Second World War, it had not been so clear that democracy was what rendered the post-war regimes of Europe legitimate in the eyes of their populations. Given the experience of authoritarianism, many people's ideas on democracy were marked by a certain distrust in unobstructed mass politics. Only gradually, over the course of the 15 years following the Second World War, did democracy emerge as the key element of political legitimacy in post-war Western Europe.[3]

The disputes of the 1960s over how supranational the Communities should be, culminating in the French boycott of Council meetings, dealt another deadly blow to the narrative that largely everyone agreed on what they should be doing and how. The oil crises of the 1970s, finally, entailed severe financial and economic turmoil. This, in turn, undermined any claim that the Communities were guaranteed to bring Europe prosperity. It also undercut arguments turning on efficient governance on the basis of expert rationalities, and on overcoming clashing ideas, interests, and identities through the provision of competent problem-solving that benefited everyone.

To these existential challenges, the European Institutions responded with a turn to "the citizens", and a pledge to "listen to what they wanted" in their official legitimation discourses and strategies. This new paradigm was anchored even more firmly when, in the early 1980s, the "peace-and-prosperity" storyline came under even greater fire. East-West relations were fraught once again, and the economies were in recession once again. Now the European institutions started a concerted campaign, aimed at reimagining the European (Economic, Atomic Energy, and Coal and Steel) Communities, holistically, as a "People's Europe". This appealed to people no longer as "market citizens" or consumers of energy and security: but as culturally embedded human beings, and as political citizens ("Union citizens") who had rights (participation and protection rights) that were specific to the European Community. The idea was to make Europe present and tangible in their everyday lives: through symbols and material benefits, through actively forging a European identity, by solemn declaration as well as by multiplying budgets in the cultural and communication policies.

Appeals to culture (and that was European as well as diverse national or subnational cultures, all "united in diversity") made their grand entry to the landscape of arguments about EU legitimacy. People were to associate Europe with culture, and this culture with themselves. The Commission in particular promoted production, consumption, and collaboration across member states, in music, fine arts, popular culture, as well as the field of the information media. This was to "bring the peoples of Europe together", and make them get to know, identify, and sympathise with each other. An underlying hope was that citizens would come to associate the practices of both consuming and producing culture with Community Europe. The gradual transnational intertwining of cultural production and consumption was to make Europeans identify with each other, with "Europe", and with the European Community as generous patron of culture.

Such legitimation efforts became all the more necessary as integration picked up speed towards the goal of completing the Single Market by 1992. And then came Maastricht. The Maastricht Treaty, in the early 1990s, was a watershed. Its difficult ratification changed the landscape of what could plausibly be claimed about EU legitimacy. Fierce popular and political resistance, combined with plummeting public support rates, caused commentators as well as politicians to declare the "permissive consensus" dead, whereby the public had supported European integration enough not to interfere, or was at least indifferent enough about it. It became impossible to maintain that the EU reflected what the Europeans wanted. It was widely agreed then, too, that the EU's legitimacy was in crisis, and in many ways this is the crisis that has lasted ever since.

The Maastricht debates in the member states turned centrally around Economic and Monetary Union, and around concerns for economic and price stability. Yet, these concerns tended to have deeper cultural foundations. The French, for instance, dreaded subjecting their monetary action range to an independent European Central Bank and to the reunited Germany, whereas the Germans feared for their beloved national currency, stylised as a symbol of German wealth, power, and national identity – basically all that was good about Germany – and all now threatened by the Euro. Another central point in the ratification debates was whether democracy was possible at all on a European scale. An important French discourse in particular confined the practice of democracy and citizenship, or simply "the political", to the nation state. And a prominent German critique questioned whether meaningful EU-wide democracy was conceivable at all, given the lack of a European *demos* or people.

Together, these discursive developments rebuffed not only the peace-and-prosperity promise, but also the official focus on the "human dimension" of the EU, the promotion of "European culture", the fledgling efforts at EU-wide identity building, and the introduction of Union citizenship. In discursively managing the Maastricht crisis and the EU's ensuing general legitimacy crisis, the European institutions framed the EU's legitimacy gap almost exclusively in term of its "democratic deficit". This did take up national wider public critiques of EU democracy. But official rhetoric focused so much on this issue that it shifted much more urgent public concerns with the monetary union, or with the power balance in post-cold war Europe, to the background. About the Euro, one communication strategy was silence.

In addition, official discursive usage effectively stretched the meaning of "democracy" in three ways. During and immediately after the ratification crisis, it often equated democracy with transparency or openness, and "closeness to the citizens" with subsidiarity. In the medium term, the paradigm of governance claimed to offer (Romano Prodi) a more "genuine" and "authentic" alternative to traditional representative democracy, with which citizens had anyway become increasingly disillusioned. "Governance" focused attention on the consultation of civil society organisations as opposed to individual citizens or "the people". It prioritised responsiveness to citizen expectations over democratic control, representation, or accountability. Finally, institutional discourses and policies projected Union citizenship, and identity building, as solutions to the EU's democratic deficit.

If there wasn't a European demos, the challenge was to forge one, complete with constitutional patriotism. These discourses, policies, and reform attempts culminated in the project of the EU "constitution". The very name of the constitutional convention, and the eventual constitutional draft treaty was emblematic of the fact that the onus had now shifted, from a focus on culture and deliberate identity making of the essentialist kind, to the instigation of a constitutional "We, the people(s)" moment. The subsequent fate of these attempts is well known.

Perhaps at the end of the day, the official emphasis on democracy of the 1990s and early 2000s backfired. In national debates on the constitutional treaty, for example, democracy did play a key role – but not in the senses advanced by official rhetoric. Across the member states, the reading was pervasive that citizens resisted the EU constitution so as finally to throw a spanner into the works of the integration process – which otherwise would continue to proceed entirely beyond their influence or control. The French No-vote, in particular, was a statement of popular sovereignty – in a rather traditional, majoritarian-electoral sense of democracy.[4] In other words, the innovative ways in which official discourses had employed terms like citizenship or democracy had failed to turn around the member state's public spheres – they held on to French national-republican tendencies, or the traditional democratic ideals implicit in British or German EU-democracy critiques. Even more importantly perhaps, the constitutional debates constituted powerful assertions of the will of the peoples to influence their country's future, and Europe's future.

The Euro crisis and the national debt crises in a number of member states, or now the current Brexit debate, have brought this message home with even greater urgency. Greek or Spanish resistance to externally imposed austerity measures, or the refugee crisis and the way in which the EU and Europe's leaders have addressed it, have seen forceful assertions not only of a popular will to be involved in the will formation about what is to be done. Even more importantly, on all these occasions it is now there for all to see how widely visions diverged of what was to be done, and of the social and economic future of Europe and its individual member states' social and economic future. Everywhere, citizens have been reclaiming their say in determining how politics is to relate to political, social, and economic realities. The people are forcing their way in once again. The old mantras of leaving it to the experts, or conjurations of an uncontroversial common European good, today do nothing less than discredit the EU's legitimacy.

Three Structural Tensions

What lessons, then, might we take away from this quick discursive-cultural history of struggles over EU legitimacy? Essentially, it was characterised by three structural tensions that run through all legitimation and delegitimation patterns mentioned so far.

First, they all involved a balancing act between bringing the people in and keeping them out. Ever since the late 1970s, official EU rhetoric turned on "what the people wanted". Yet, the fact that they revolved centrally around the European citizens and their needs and sensitivities did not necessarily mean that these citizens got more of an actual say. Really they remained objects, spectators, and addressees, rather than authors, of EU action. Yes, the will of the people was at the epicentre of these discourses. But it had a double status: it was referred to both as an independent source of legitimacy and, at the same time, an object of manipulation. Culture and the media were, at least partly, instruments of such manipulation as well as justifications in the related discourses. Giving the citizens what they wanted, in many official discourses pre- and post-Maastricht, remained a matter of efficient policy-making – only now this was framed in terms of citizen expectations. It was a matter of greater sophistication in mapping, as well as tweaking, citizens' expectations: in other words, of bringing them closer to the EU, rather than the EU closer to them. Bringing Europeans closer to each other, not least through cultural means, was a key tool in this approximation.

Of course, the tension between bringing the people in and keeping them out was built into the very nature of the European integration project. It arose from its being a top-down enterprise in engineering political reality – at the same time as needing to make plausible that it was somehow in line with "the will of the people" – both in order credibly to claim legitimacy and in order to actually function.

Secondly, the history of contests over EU legitimacy has been a tightrope walk between claiming legitimacy on the grounds of arguments about democracy and about efficient problem solving. My story shows that, rather than being mutually exclusive (as in too many cooks spoiling the broth), the two types of arguments have always, and necessarily, gone together.

Not just any efficient performance output will do to enhance legitimacy – it has to have some credible claim of reflecting the will of the people. In addition, the credibility of such claims relies not on a simple match between citizen preferences and the goals of integration or its policies. Rather, it calls for open processes of contestation over what we want to achieve with it and what standards we want to measure it by.[5] This is why the present disagreements and discontents may end up being a good thing for EU legitimacy on some level. Let me explain what I mean by this, by moving on to the third tension defining the struggle for EU legitimacy as I described it.

Thirdly and finally, the discursive history of EU legitimation can be told as a story of a push and pull between depoliticising forces and counter-forces that actively politicised the stakes of EU politics. It is a story of how it increasingly became undeniable that virtually any solution in integration politics creates winners and losers, of how any discourses glossing over this, and emphasising harmony, effectively became counter-productive. If there is one key lesson, it is that any claims about the EU's legitimacy have to openly acknowledge the essentially controversial nature of EU politics, in order to be plausible. This was a lesson to be drawn already from the constitutional affair, and the current debates around the Euro crisis drive the point home with even greater force. The EU studies literature has been observing politicisation as a phenomenon visible in public opinion data and electoral behaviour. While some have warned against opening Pandora's box and inviting contestation – on the grounds that it could then no longer be contained – other, normative accounts have advocated it, as an end in itself or as instrumental to creating, for example, a European public sphere. I would advocate being upfront about the controversial nature of everything that's at stake in EU politics is absolutely necessary in terms of what has a chance of being plausible, given the preceding discursive history of struggles over EU legitimacy. The good news is that this constant contestation can be a source of, and not only a threat to, EU legitimacy. How so?

Contestation, EU Politics as Play, and Mutual Recognition

One could think of EU politics in terms of the metaphor of a game – and cultural production, exchange and consumption can play a role in probing and promoting this. Resting the political bond that ties us together on such an activity of play is less demanding than basing it on cultural or linguistic commonalities, or even on a "community of project". If we play a game together, we don't have to be alike, we don't have to like each other, or want the same thing – all we need to want to do is play the game against one another, and stick to a certain set of rules. Given the politicisation of EU politics that I sketched above, agreeing to contest or compete with each other might be all that the Europeans are willing to agree on – and it would not be little. While the legitimacy of the EU cannot thrive on contestation alone, it cannot thrive without contestation.

Play, and the "play-element in culture", can have civilising functions. It channels interactions into an activity with distinct rules, codes of behaviour, and clearly marked limits of where the game begins and ends.[6] It teaches us how to lose, to be wrong, and to respect the other.[7] Thinking of politics, and EU politics in particular, as a game, might, like a "well-functioning democracy" built on the "vibrant clash of democratic positions", be a way of trans- forming *antagonism*, or struggle between enemies, into *agonism*, or the struggle between adversaries. It might help to avoid the danger of "[t]oo much emphasis on consensus and the refusal of confrontation", which in turn may lead to citizen apathy, disaffection with political participation, or with European integration and EU politics or, worse still, "the crystallization of collective passions around issues which cannot be managed by the democratic process".[8] Of course, the question remains why we should want to continue playing together. With the threat of parts of the Union breaking apart as tangible as never before, this is a serious question. Simply having locked ourselves into institutions and a whole system designed precisely to intertwine our European fates so much that cooperation has become the only option, seems to be working less well than it used to. More than ever, then, this situation calls for persuasive narratives, arguments, and images for why there should be European integration to begin with. And no such pleads will appear plausible today if they do not acknowledge our essential clashes of interest and identities.

Embracing confrontation and difference points to the centrality of a norm, practice, or aspiration around which the Europeans have built their Union over the past sixty years; that of mutual recognition. Besides being a philosophical concept, and a diplomatic, legal or technical norm, mutual recognition is also a state of mind, a daily practice, or an ethos. Mutual recognition as an ethos involves accepting to live and interact with each other's differences, without either trying to make the other side be like oneself, or simply stopping at the fact of difference and withdrawing into separate spaces.[9] Supporting this aspiration may be one of the most important challenges, and roles, for culture in helping Europe overcome its present discontents, and threats of disintegration.

That the EU, an entirely new kind of political animal, was built around the aspiration of mutual recognition is no small miracle. For, at the same time, the propensity for denying each other this recognition remains imprinted in the Europeans' DNA. A tension between promises and denials of recognition is built into the European project, as it is innate to human nature. The refugee crisis, the Euro crisis, and perhaps even the Brexit debate, have cast a merciless light on this basic tension. Any apparent progress towards mutual recognition that we had witnessed in the last decades has seemed to move into reverse gear. Or at least it is radically tested. Longstanding but dormant clashes of interests and identities are festering back to the surface, touching some raw collective nerves in the process, reviving old tropes of prejudice and othering.

Europe's ongoing crises are manifestations that we are in a moment of renegotiation of who we are, and how we relate to each other. They have forced us to ask why and up to what point we want to stick together in Europe. Once more, we as Europeans, Germans, Greeks, Hungarians, Brits and all the rest, are recalibrating how far and under what conditions we recognise each other, and under what conditions our Union is to last. We are renegotiating the acceptable balance between interference in each other's affairs and deference to each other's ways of doing things and of being: we are engaged in managing the rules of recognition in Europe. One can think of this process as the deeper socio-cultural foundation of managing the political economy of monetary union, and of political union to the extent that it exists. Artists, thinkers, and producers as well as consumers of ideas and culture are called upon in reshaping this socio-cultural foundation in critical ways.

Notes

1.   Kalypso Nicolaïdis, 'Kir Forever? The Journey of a Political Scientist in the Landscape of Mutual Recognition', *The past and future of EU law : the classics of EU law revisited on the 50th anniversary of the Rome Treaty* (2010): pp. 447-455.

2.   Claudia Sternberg, *The Struggle for EU Legitimacy: Public Contestation, 1950-2005* (Basingstoke: Palgrave, 2013); D. Beetham, *The Legitimation of Power*. 2nd Edition. (Basingstoke: Palgrave Macmillan, 2013).

3.   Sternberg, *The Struggle for EU Legitimacy: Public Contestation, 1950-2005* (2013), 46; M. Conway and P. Romijn, 'Introduction to Theme Issue: Political Legitimacy in Mid-Twentieth Century Europe', *Contemporary European History* 13(04) (2004): 377-388; 380; M. Conway and V. Depkat, 'Towards a European History of the Discourse of Democracy: Discussing Democracy in Western Europe 1945-60', in: M. Conway and K. K. Patel, *Europeanization in the Twentieth Century: Historical Approaches* (Basingstoke and New York: Palgrave Macmillan, 2010), 132-156.

4.   Claudia Sternberg, 'Political legitimacy between democracy and effectiveness: trade-offs, interdependencies, and discursive constructions by the EU institutions', *European Political Science Review* 7(4) (2015a): pp. 615-638.

5. Claudia Sternberg, 'What were the French telling us by voting down the "EU constitution"? A case for interpretive research on referendum debates', *Comparative European Politics*: 1-26 (2015b).
6. J. Huizinga, *Homo Ludens. A Study of the Play-Element in Culture* (Abingdon: Routledge, [1949] 2000), p.50.
7. H.G-. Gadamer, *Das Erbe Europas: Beiträge* (Frankfurt am Main: Suhrkamp, 1989), p.30.
8. C. Mouffe, *The Democratic Paradox* (London, New York: Verso, 2000), pp. 102-4.
9. Kalypso Nicolaïdis, 'Trusting the Poles? Constructing Europe through Mutual Recognition', *Journal of European Public Policy* 14(5) (2007): pp. 682-698; Kalypso Nicolaïdis, 'Kir Forever? The Journey of a Political Scientist in the Landscape of Mutual Recognition', *The past and future of EU law : the classics of EU law revisited on the 50th anniversary of the Rome Treaty* (2010): pp. 447-455. K. Gartzou-Katsouyanni, Kalypso Nicolaïdis, and Claudia Sternberg, 'La crise de la zone euro et le déni de l'autre', in *Pour une reconstruction de la reconnaissance mutuelle. Euro, les années critiques*. E. Monnet and Claudia Sternberg (Paris: Presses Universitaires de France, 2015).

Historical texts

Thoughts on the Future

Jean Monnet

Algiers, 5 August 1943

The current circumstances of the war [...] may bring about the imminent defeat of the enemy and the liberation of Europe. We must be prepared for that moment; before it comes, diplomatic arrangements must be made and European nations educated. The main ideas to help restore democratic institutions, the hope that a constructive programme of European reorganisation brings property and peace, and the belief that such solutions will only be found through international cooperation must be planted in people's minds.

By doing so we will have contributed to laying the foundations, which, by believing in democracy and the hope of a better world, will help eliminate the greatest dangers of European reconstruction and peace, namely the belief that by affirming nationalism and national sovereignty in all its political and economic forms, the anxieties of nations can be appeased and future problems can be solved.

[...]

We must therefore act before the enemy collapses. We must act now. That is the duty of the French Committee of National Liberation. It must impose a course of action, sound out the Allies, not necessarily to obtain their approval but to take into account, in the final form of its position, of the essential points that diverge from theirs, as their collaboration – or at least the collaboration by some of them – will be necessary for our undertaking to succeed. The Committee must then speak to France and to the rest of the world.

The goals to achieve are the following: the re-establishment or establishment of a democratic regime in Europe, and economic and political organisation of a 'European entity'. These two conditions are essential for establishing the conditions to make peace in Europe a normal part of life. There will not be peace in Europe if regimes can be established in which the right of opposition is not respected and in which free elections are not held. These two conditions are essential for restoring and maintaining all the essential freedoms of speech, assembly, association and so on, upon which the very foundations of Western civilisation have been built.

There will not be peace in Europe if the States are reconstituted based on national sovereignty, with everything this entails regarding prestige politics and economic protectionism. If European countries again defend themselves against each other, building huge armies will once again be necessary. Under the future peace treaty, some countries will be able to defend themselves, while others will not, as it will be forbidden for them. We have seen this happen in 1919, and we know the consequences. Alliances between European states will be concluded, and we know what they are worth. The weight of military budgets will prevent or delay social reforms and Europe will rebuild itself again based on fear.

European countries are too small to ensure their people the prosperity made possible by modern conditions and consequently necessary. They need larger markets. It is also important that they do not allocate part of their resources to maintaining so-called 'key' industries required by national defence, rendered obligatory by the reflexes of States towards 'national' sovereignty and protectionism, as we saw before 1939.

Unless European States become a federation or a 'European entity' turning them into a common economic unit, prosperity and essential social developments will not be possible.

Obviously it will not be possible to achieve a 'European result' immediately, and that quite a long period will be necessary to allow for important discussions and concluding necessary agreements. However, it is essential that already at the very least measures be taken to ensure that its realisation be made possible.

As mentioned above, if the liberation of Europe occurs, as it seems foreseeable, it will inevitably result in establishing arbitrary authorities in Europe and the reconstitution of sovereign, protectionist States, namely that the previously goals seriously risk not being achieved.

[...]

Consequently, it seems that European reconstitution, and by extension peace, must be planned in two stages, both in terms of the reconstitution of political powers in the different States as well as the point of view of the economy: the first stage will start once the first soldiers of the liberating armies set foot on the continent up until the time when a peace congress is convened. The second stage will start once the peace congress will convene until the conclusion and establishment – if successful – of a European entity.

[...]

For the above-mentioned reasons, the first stage is the most dangerous one. Everything that follows will depend on it.

Politically, it is essential that measures be taken to allow for the immediate creation of provisional governments appointed by democratic consultation in liberated countries.

The various European States must follow the same path, each adopting different constitutional forms to suit their needs. However, nothing could provide more political peace of mind to a troubled Europe than knowing before liberation that the first thing the liberators will do is ensure that a 'provisional government' is established in their countries according to the rules of the Constitution until elections by universal suffrage, held once the prisoners, workers and so on have returned home, have established the final government.

This commitment would suppress forces in the various countries preparing to seize power. In fact, ignoring that a democratically appointed provisional government will be established right after liberation, nations may suspect everything, and consequently coups will be justified or at the very least encouraged. Moreover, if these coups occur, on what grounds will the established de facto authority repress them, other than in the eyes of the people, to maintain its own authority? And if repression were necessary before creating the provisional government, the de facto authority would suppress any coups in order to allow for properly establishing a provisional government. In one case it is civil war, in the other, it is maintaining order within the framework of the institutions.

Once the provisional government is established, it will maintain order on behalf of the nation.

Maintaining order on behalf of a nation can only be done legally. Since the entire European situation is an arbitrary one, rule of law must be restored. Power must be depersonalised, while despotism and personality cults must be eliminated. Before totalitarian regimes existed around 1914 this was the case throughout almost all of Europe.

Vaguely formulated proclamations are not enough. Public opinion must be enlightened. For years, liberalism and democracy, as well as the rule of law and truth were systematically obscured or subjected to violent criticism. They must now be brought back into the light, without hateful controversy or hints of revolt, but with intelligence, diversity and sincerity. Public opinion must also be informed. Young people must be educated by the press, radio and schools, and democracy and respect for the rule of law must be instilled in everyone's mind and conscience.

Some people fear that parties will want to take advantage of the disorder and abandon of nations to impose their will and establish their system. In this case their action would resemble a rebellion against the institutions and would consequently expose them to the same repressive measures, justified by the institutions in which they will be asked to participate in like everyone else.

Economically, it is crucial to prevent economic sovereignties being re-established from the start. Consequently, commitments should already have been asked from all governments in exile or authorities such as the French Committee, such as to not establish custom duties or quotas until a peace treaty has been signed.

Besides the previously mentioned general reasons, it is obvious that Europe, lacking resources, will need everything possible for it to trade, and that people's lives during this period will be made more difficult if hard-to-find essentials were to be weighted down by custom duties. It is also obvious that, if this measure is not adopted, private interests will put pressure on governments to re-establish custom duties and that countries will demand them as a weapon for 'economic negotiations'. In a flash, protectionism among European nations will be the norm and remain in place uncontested for several years. With such protectionism and 'economic nationalism', we will have reverted to the conditions of Europe before 1939:

- Question of import monopolies
- Relief
- Relaunching national industries, at the very least to provide work
- Question of Germany, which could find itself in the position of having the only functioning industry
- Need for a foreign trade monopoly managed by the Allies
- Germany returning machinery, etc., seized in occupied countries
- Financial questions during this interim period
- Lend Lease for overseas procurements, etc.

The plan projected for this interim period will only be successful if it is realistic and takes into account the historical experience of each country. The plan should not artificially divide political and economic factors, as this separation runs contrary to the teachings of history and necessities of government life. This plan can only develop within the framework of legislation, which has been lying dormant for years or more recently abandoned, but will have had the merit having existed, drawn up and implemented in each of the States to be restored. Lastly, the mechanism of elections and more generally of democratic institutions depends on an administrative organisation whose structure would be bad to improvise without referring to the precedents set during the liberal era.

[...]

Under these circumstances, it seems that the first stage should be immediately establishing provisional political authorities with a democratic basis in each State; to maintain the European economy during this transitional period without establishing custom duties and so on; and to not hold the peace congress until duly mandated provisional governments of the various European countries can come together.

[...]

The second stage is essentially the peace congress.

- Plan for the political and economic reconstruction of Europe
- Situation of Europe relative to the US, the UK and the USSR
- Programme for settling the German question, population movements
- Constitution of a European inventory of heavy metallurgy
- European authority for monitoring aircraft manufacturers and airlines
- Association of the US, the UK and the USSR in these systems and verifications
- Political and financial organisation of Europe
- Holding a World Council with European participation

Translated from French by Natasha Cloutier

Extracts from a speech in the Main Auditorium of Cologne University

Konrad Adenauer

Cologne, 24 March 1946

How was it possible that the revival of the true spirit of Germany was of such short duration? How could it be that that German Republic which arose after 1918 endured only 15 years? How could it be that the German Empire founded by Bismarck in 1871, rising swiftly to become the mightiest state in the world, had collapsed again by 1918, after only 47 years – an empire that had seemed the equal, in strength and stability, of well-nigh every other European state of the period? And the National Socialist empire that followed, which was first greeted with jubilation by many unsuspecting Germans, but later, for its abysmal villainy and perfidy, feared indeed, but also despised and execrated, by many, very many more – how was such a thing possible in this our German nation?

How was it possible that this war could be begun by the National Socialist regime – a war that, despite initial dazzling successes, had necessarily to be lost in the end? How was it possible that miracles of bravery and dutifulness could be performed in this war while close by, within the very same nation, crime after crime of the greatest magnitude was being committed? How was it possible that this war was continued, though it was early on clear that it had to be lost, to the point of our own self-destruction?

How was this plunge of the German nation into such abysmal depths possible? And how is this nation now to bear its terrible fate: hunger and cold; hardship and death; a life that offers, for the present, no hope of a better future, led in utter political powerlessness, despised by all the nations of the world!

[...]

I demand no confession of guilt from the German nation as a whole, although many Germans do bear a very heavy burden of guilt, and many others a burden less heavy but a burden of guilt nonetheless. Nor do I believe that people in other countries who have thought reasonably and calmly about this matter demand of us such a public confession of guilt.

But we must proceed to an examination of conscience in our own interest, if we are to find the right way leading out of our present national abyss.

What are the deepest-lying reasons for our having fallen, in the end, into such an abyss? The details do not matter when investigating such a question; many, indeed, are not yet clarified; but the deeper, truly decisive causes of this catastrophe lie in plain sight. They extend back long before 1933. It was National Socialism, it is true, that led us directly into the catastrophe. But National Socialism would not have been able to come to power in Germany if it had not found, in broad strata of the population, a soil well prepared for the poisonous seeds it sowed. I emphasize here: "in broad strata of the population." It is not right to say now that it is the "bigwigs" – the high-ranking officers or the powerful industrialists – who bear the blame alone. Certainly, they bear a full measure of guilt, and their personal guilt – for which they must be called to account by the German people before German courts – is all the greater the more power and influence these people enjoyed. But broad strata within the common people – peasants, petit bourgeois, workers and intellectuals – lacked the proper mental and moral attitude, otherwise the victorious progress of National Socialism through the German people in 1933 and the years after would not be possible. The German nation has, in fact, been suffering for many decades, throughout all its social strata, from a false conception of the state, of power, and of the status of the individual. Our nation has made an idol of the state and raised it onto the altar. The dignity and value of the individual have been sacrificed to this idol. The conviction of the state's omnipotence – that the state and the power assembled in it takes precedence over all other values, including the enduring and eternal values of humanity – rose to dominance in Germany in two historical phases.

First, this idea began to spread outward from Prussia in the period after the "Wars of Liberation". Then, after the victorious war of 1870/71 it gained ascendancy all over Germany.

Thanks to that "spirit of the Volk" that Herder and the Romantics claimed to have discovered, and above all thanks to Hegel's conception of the state as Reason and Morality incarnate, this state became, in the German national consciousness, an almost divine entity. With this exaltation of the state there went, necessarily, hand in hand a diminution in the value assigned to the individual. Power is indivisibly connected with the essence of the state and the institution in which state power is most starkly and imposingly expressed is the army. Thus, militarism became the ruling factor in the thoughts and feelings of extremely large parts of the German population.

After the founding, under Prussian leadership, of the German Empire the state, which had originally been an entity articulated with the life of the people, became more and more a sovereign machine. The great exterior successes which were enjoyed, even if (considered historically) only for a short time, by Bismarck's Empire and its conception of the state and power; the rapidly increasing industrialization; the agglomeration of great masses of people in the cities and sense of "rootlessness" arising from this – all this cleared the path for the disastrous spread of a merely materialistic worldview among the German people. This materialistic worldview, in turn, has necessarily led to a still greater exaggeration and exaltation of the concept of the state and state power and to a further diminution of ethical values and of the idea of the dignity of the individual.

The materialistic understanding of the world propounded by Marxism contributed very largely to this development. Whoever aspires to a centralization of political and economic power in the hands of the state or of one particular class and propounds, in accordance with this, the principle of class struggle is an enemy of the freedom of the individual; he necessarily prepares the way for dictatorship in the thoughts and feelings of those who follow him, even where it is another than himself that actually walks this path to dictatorship that he has prepared. That such a development does indeed occur necessarily is shown by the history of those states in which Karl Marx is the messiah and Marx's doctrine the Gospel.

National Socialism was nothing other than a development to the point of criminality of that worship of power and that disregard, indeed contempt, for the value of the individual that ensues naturally from the materialist worldview. On a nation which had been mentally and spiritually primed for it – first by the exaggerated Prussian conception of the importance of the state, its essence, its power and the unconditional obedience that was owed to it, and then by the materialist worldview – there was able to impose itself relatively quickly, favoured as it was by the grave material situation in which much of the population found themselves, a doctrine which recognized only a total state and a will-lessly guided popular mass; a doctrine which taught that our own race was the master race and our own nation the master nation while dismissing other nations as of lesser worth, in some cases worthy only to be exterminated, but preached as well the extermination, at any price, of all political opponents, even when such opponents emerged within our own race and nation.

Nationalism encountered the strongest spiritual and intellectual opposition in those Catholic and Evangelical Christian regions of Germany which had also best withstood the spell of Karl Marx's doctrine, socialism!

This is a fact beyond dispute!

This conception of the state as the most powerful, indeed as the all-powerful, entity and of the primacy of its rights over the individual's right to dignity and freedom, stands in contradiction with natural law as Christianity understands this. It is our intention to re-establish the principles of Christian natural law.

[...]

The basic proposition contained in the political programme of the CDU – the proposition from which all the demands put forward in our programme proceed – is an idea that lies at the core of Christian ethics: human personhood has a unique dignity and the value of each individual human being is irreplaceable. From this proposition there can be derived a conception of state, economy and culture which is quite new vis-à-vis the conception of these things that has long prevailed in Germany. According to this conception neither the state, nor the economy, nor culture is an end in itself; rather, all have the function of serving, in one way or the other, human personhood. The materialist worldview makes the human being something less than a person: namely, a tiny component in a tremendous machine. This, then, is a worldview which we most decidedly reject.

The meaning and purpose of the state is to awaken the creative forces slumbering in the nation, to draw these forces together, nurture them and protect them. The whole nation must be educated and taught to develop a sense of responsibility and self-reliance. The state should be a community that shares a destiny – but one that is founded on legality and liberty and that is composed of individuals responsible for themselves and others, and that draws together different interests, worldviews and opinions. That is to say, we wish indeed for a state that teaches and educates; but not for one that teaches a willingness to be controlled and led; rather for one that teaches individuals to want, and to be able, to integrate themselves, as free human beings conscious of their own personal responsibility, into the social whole. This education of the nation must be one that is carried out in the spirit of Christianity and democracy; and it must open up above all for all the younger citizens of our country an access to certain convictions and mind-sets that have hitherto been closed to them but that remain, nevertheless, of universal human validity.

In this homeless, jumbled-up, atomised mass which is the spectacle that our nation currently presents to the world every single individual creature must now be addressed and brought, by education, to develop a sense of self-awareness and of responsibility for themselves and others. It is the question of how far we will succeed in achieving this – and not such questions as how many and which of our few remaining firms and companies should be nationalized or how many acres of land should be subject to expropriation – that is the truly fateful question for our nation.

[...]

We want Germany to arise anew. In wanting this, we do not want an empire under Prussian leadership such as was created by Bismarck. We do not want the centralized Germany of National Socialism; but neither do we want a mere confederation of essentially sovereign German states such as the Bavarian Prime Minister, Herr Högner, a member of the Social Democratic Party, called for in his inaugural address to the Bavarian State Advisory Committee. Rather, we want the creation of a genuine federal state – a federal state to whose central authority there are assigned all those powers which are reasonably necessary to maintain and preserve the whole but no powers extending beyond these. We want the individual states that compose this federal state to retain, to a large extent, responsibility for their own affairs in all those spheres in which there exists no necessity, in the sense just outlined, for a central administering authority. The whole of Germany, both the central administrative authorities and those of the individual federal states, should be, as far as possible, decentralized.

People should be counted and addressed at the level of the local municipalities and it is at this level that appeal should be made to them to participate in issues of public concern. For us, the nucleus of all life within a properly-functioning state is the local municipality. It is in the municipality that political forces first learn to exercise themselves and through the municipality that the citizen first concretely acquires a sense of being part of a state.

I am aware of the concerns of Germany's neighbours to the west. I fully understand and appreciate these concerns after the experiences these neighbours have had to undergo in the course of the last hundred years. I feel it is wrong to try to placate these concerns by pointing to the present political balance of power in Europe. Nothing stays as it is and change can come at any time!

A solution must be found to the German question which is of an organic nature and thereby of long duration and which can calm the fears of our western neighbour and give her a sense of enduring safety and security, to which she most certainly has a right. A separation of these regions from Germany is not a solution of this kind.

A separation alone is not a solution to the problem. Whoever undertakes such a separation must also face the question of what will become, afterward, of the rest of Germany. They must ask themselves whether the part of Germany remaining after such a separation will not then become – to adopt a phrase used by a foreign newspaper – a "rotting corpse" in the middle of Europe which will prove as fatal to this latter as a victorious Nazi Germany would have been. I am, and will remain, a German, but I have also always been a European, with the feelings of a European. This is why I have always spoken in favour of coming to an understanding with France, defending this position vis-à-vis the *Reich* government even in the midst of the most serious crises of the 1920s. I never argued for a separating-off of German territory but rather always for coming to some reasonable understanding that would do justice to the interests of both parties. For this reason I argued in the 1920s for an organic integration of the French, Belgian and German economies with one another so as to secure a lasting peace, since economic interests that are coordinated and run parallel with one another are, and always will be, the healthiest and most enduring basis for good political relations between the nations. Today Western Europe, indeed Europe as a whole, enjoys quite different prospects for the future than it did then.

If the moment of international tension which we are just now experiencing passes by without an explosion – and may God grant that it will so pass – then the idea of an international co-operation of all the world's peoples, and of the condemnation of war as a means of dealing with conflicts, shall have withstood its baptism of fire and we shall have moved one great step onward. Then, in my view, the United Nations must set about tackling the problem of a "United States of Europe" inclusive of Germany. Such a "United States of Europe" would be the best, surest and most lasting form of security for Germany's neighbours to the west. But even in the period preceding the establishment of such a "United States of Europe" entirely sufficient assurances can be provided for these neighbours without there being any need for the carving-up of German territory: never again an empire under Prussian leadership, and never again a centralized German empire. Militarism is dead; the bringing of peace and satisfaction to Germany through economic prosperity; support in Germany for the principle of democracy and of mutual understanding between nations; integration with one another of Germany's economic interest and the economic interest of its neighbours to the west, including those of England.

Source: *Konrad Adenauer Stiftung, Düsseldorf. http://www.konrad-adenauer.de/ dokumente/reden/uni-koln. Originally from: Schriftenreihe der Christlich Demo- kratischen Union des Rheinlandes. Heft 8. Köln o. J.*

Translated from the German by Dr. Alexander Reynolds

Extracts from a press conference

Charles de Gaulle

Paris, 5 September 1960

Q. Journalist No. 3
Mister President, could you enlighten us about the projects of European cooperation that you have recently presented to the German, Dutch and Italian leaders, and also tell us, if possible, what are your hopes and perspectives on the subject, taking into account what you know of the discussions that took place between Mister Macmillan and Chancellor Adenauer?

A. Charles de Gaulle
With the Prime Minister, the Minister of Foreign Affairs and others, in accordance with a perfectly defined policy observed by the government, we have as of late inaugurated a series of consultations with the heads of states and governments of Western European countries, more specifically, the ones in Europe we call "The Six". However, this has not stopped us from seeing the British Prime Minister, and we do hope will not stop us from seeing him again occasionally, which will undoubtedly be a good opportunity.

Building Europe and uniting it is obviously something essential, but trivial to say. Why should this hearth of civilisation, of force, of reason and of prosperity choke under its own ashes? In such a case, we must only proceed following realities and not dreams. So what are the realities of Europe? What are the pillars on which we can build it? Honestly, they are the States. States that are indeed very different from one another, each with their own soul, history, language, troubles, glories, and ambitions. States are the only entities to have the right to command and the power to be obeyed. Believing that one can build something efficient to act and be approved by the peoples outside and above States is an illusion. Of course, while waiting to address the problem of Europe in its entirety and head on, it is true that we were able to establish certain agencies that are more or less extranational or supranational. These agencies have their technical value, but they do not have any authority, and therefore are not efficient politically. As long as nothing terrible happens, they can function without too much hassle. However, once dramatic circumstances occur such as a major problem to be solved, we see then that such high authority has nothing on the various national categories, and only States have any authority. This is what we have seen not long ago with the coal crisis. And this is what we have seen with the common market, with agricultural products problems, economic competitions to supply African States or relations between the common market and the free-trade area.

Once more, it is perfectly natural that the States of Europe have at their disposal specialised agencies for their common problems, to prepare, and if need be, to follow up on their decisions. But these decisions belong to them and can only belong to them. They can only be taken through cooperation. Ensuring regular cooperation of the States of Western Europe is what France considers desirable and possible, and as practical in politics, economics, culture and defence. What does this entail? It entails an organised and regular consultation of the governments responsible. And then the work, the specialised agency in each common field, is subject to the government. This requires the periodic deliberation of an assembly formed by the delegates of national parliaments. And in my opinion, it must contain as early as possible a solemn European referendum in order to give this start of Europe a membership quality of popular invention that is essential to it. Actually, among them, the States of Europe have many great means of action as well as very big problems in common, as their past enmities are reduced to very few things. In short, the time is right. Therefore, what France proposes is that this cooperation be organised among them.

Of course, if we go down this road, and hopefully we will, ties will multiply and habits will form. And then, time doing its work, little by little, it is possible that we will arrive at more advanced steps towards European unity. Once more, that is what France proposes. It is all that and nothing else.

Q. Journalist No. 5
Certain criticisms concerning the attitude of France within NATO also play their role in the European discussion. Could you give us a few insights into your idea on the collaboration within NATO of which you have asked to be reformed?

A. Charles de Gaulle
It has been more than 10 years since the Atlantic Alliance was organised as it is today. Back then, I remember that first, the burning and immediate question was only the security of Europe. We had created a limited alliance to Europe in a very narrow zone of action. And at the same time, the United States had its own means of defence and that the States of Western Europe, of continental Europe at least, found themselves in an economic and social position which was uncertain at the very least. These States then postponed the renaissance of their personality in the international order until much later, if they hadn't already given up. And so, we made an alliance based on integration, a system where the defence of each continental European country, of Western Europe, except England, had no national character and where in fact everything was commanded by the Americans who have the main weapons at their disposal, atomic weapons. During the past 10 years much has changed. First, we have seen that the possibilities of conflict and consequently of military operations outside Europe extend throughout the world, particularly the Middle East and Africa, which were danger areas at least as much as Europe was. For them, among the main participants of the Atlantic Alliance there were political differences that, should the occasion arise, might turn into strategic disagreements. Then as well, continental European countries, France in particular, regained its balance and prosperity, and consequently, as it occurred, they regained the awareness of themselves, especially as

concerns their own defence. It is finally one of them – you know which one – who started building an arsenal of atomic weapons. Therefore, in these conditions, France considers what had been done 10 years ago within this narrow zone and on the unique and exclusive basis of integration needed to be revised. And of course I won't say or quote the points that interest France directly. As for the others, if one day there is a general confrontation, well then, they can speak for themselves. As concerns France, there are at least two points of the treaty that must be revised. However, you know that when the North Atlantic Alliance treaty was signed it specified in its text that it could be revised after 10 years. And the 10 years are up. What are the two essential points for France? The first, as I mentioned, is the limitation of the Alliance to the single area of Europe. We believe that, at least among the world powers of the West, something must be organised, as far as the Alliance is concerned, regarding their political and occasionally strategic conduct outside Europe, particularly in the Middle East and Africa, where these three powers are constantly involved. If there is no agreement among the principal members of the Atlantic Alliance on matters other than Europe, how can the Alliance be indefinitely maintained in Europe? In short, this must be remedied. And then, the second point regarding which France would like to see a change is that of the integration of Europe's defence. We feel that the defence of each country, while of course being combined with that of other countries, must have a national character. This does not exclude in the least the principle itself of the Alliance. How, in fact, a government, a parliament or a people in the long run could bring with all their soul and their input to a system, in times of peace, their defence and service, and in times of war their sacrifice, a system where their own defence is not their own responsibility? This is why, a revision, a reanimation of the Alliance from this point of view also seems essential. However, we have taken a few measures to do so, as you know. It is therefore, for example that France now has its fleet at its direct disposal. In fact, what is a fleet? A fleet is a means of remote action. And how can one imagine France leaving its fleet, its means of remote action at the discretion of an exclusively European organisation that has nothing to do with Africa while its own interests and responsibilities are continuously involved in Africa? On the other hand, France believes that if we stockpile atomic weapons on its territory, these weapons must be in their hands. Given the nature of such weaponry and the consequences that their use may have, obviously, France cannot let its own destiny and even its own life be at the discretion of others. That is what France means by the reform of this Atlantic organisation, while repeating that it is indeed absolutely not about separating them from one another. Never has a deep alliance been more necessary among free peoples. Thank you.

Source: *Discours et messages. Avec le renouveau 1958-1962*, par Charles de Gaulle.
© Plon, 1975.

Translated from the French by Natasha Cloutier

The Tragedy of Central Europe

Milan Kundera

1984

1.

In November 1956, the director of the Hungarian News Agency, shortly before his office was flattened by artillery fire, sent a telex to the entire world with a desperate message announcing that the Russian attack against Budapest had begun. The dispatch ended with these words: "We are going to die for Hungary and for Europe."

What did this sentence mean? It certainly meant that the Russian tanks were endangering Hungary and with it Europe itself. But in what sense was Europe in danger? Were the Russian tanks about to push past the Hungarian borders and into the West? No. The director of the Hungarian News Agency meant that the Russians, in attacking Hungary, were attacking Europe itself. He was ready to die so that Hungary might remain Hungary and European.

Even if the sense of the sentence seems clear, it continues to intrigue us. Actually, in France, in America, one is accustomed to thinking that what was at stake during the invasion was neither Hungary nor Europe but a political regime. One would never have said that Hungary as such had been threatened; still less would one ever understand why a Hungarian, faced with his own death, addressed Europe. When Solzhenitsyn denounces communist oppression, does he invoke Europe as a fundamental value worth dying for?

No. "To die for one's country *and* for Europe" – that is a phrase that could not be thought in Moscow or Leningrad; it is precisely the phrase that could be thought in Budapest or Warsaw.

2.

In fact, what does Europe mean to a Hungarian, a Czech, a Pole? For a thousand years their nations have belonged to the part of Europe rooted in Roman Christianity. They have participated in every period of its history. For them, the word "Europe" does not represent a phenomenon of geography but a spiritual notion synonymous with the word "West". The moment Hungary is no longer European – that is, no longer Western – it is driven from its own destiny, beyond its own history: it loses the essence of its identity.

"Geographic Europe" (extending from the Atlantic to the Ural Mountains) was always divided into two halves which evolved separately: one tied to ancient Rome and the Catholic Church, the other anchored in Byzantium and the Orthodox Church. After 1945, the border between the two Europes shifted several hundred kilometers to the west, and several nations that had always considered themselves to be Western woke up to discover that they were now in the East.[1]

As a result, three fundamental situations developed in Europe after the war: that of Western Europe, that of Eastern Europe, and, most complicated, that of the part of Europe situated geographically in the center – culturally in the West and politically in the East.

The contradictions of the Europe I call Central help us to understand why during the last thirty-five years the drama of Europe has been concentrated there: the great Hungarian revolt in 1956 and the bloody massacre that followed; the Prague Spring and the occupation of Czechoslovakia in 1968; the Polish revolts of 1956, 1968, 1970, and of recent years. In dramatic content and historical impact, nothing that has occurred in "geographic Europe", in the West or the East, can be compared with the succession of revolts in Central Europe. Every single one was supported by almost the entire population. And, in every case, each regime could not have defended itself for more than three hours if it had not been backed by Russia. That said, we can no longer consider what took place in Prague or Warsaw in its essence as a drama of Eastern Europe, of the Soviet bloc, of communism; it is a drama of the West – a West that, kidnapped, displaced, and brainwashed, nevertheless insists on defending its identity.

The identity of a people and of a civilization is reflected and concentrated in what has been created by the mind – in what is known as "culture". If this identity is threatened with extinction, cultural life grows correspondingly more intense, more important, until culture itself becomes the living value around which all people rally. That is why, in each of the revolts in Central Europe, the collective cultural memory and the contemporary creative effort assumed roles so great and so decisive – far greater and far more decisive than they have been in any other European mass revolt.[2]

It was Hungarian writers, in a group named after the Romantic poet Sándor Petőfi, who undertook the powerful critique that led the way to the explosion of 1956. It was the theater, the films, the literature and philosophy that, in the years before 1968, led ultimately to the emancipation of the Prague Spring. And it was the banning of a play by Adam Mickiewicz, the greatest Polish Romantic poet, that triggered the famous revolt of Polish students in 1968. This happy marriage of culture and life, of creative achievement and popular participation, has marked the revolts of Central Europe with an inimitable beauty that will always cast a spell over those who lived through those times.

3·

One could say: We'll admit that Central European countries are defending their threatened identity, but their situation is not unique. Russia is in a similar situation. It, too, is about to lose its identity. In fact, it's not Russia but communism that deprives nations of their essence, and which, moreover, made the Russian people its first victim. True, the Russian language is suffocating the languages of the other nations in the Soviet empire, but it's not because the Russians themselves want to "Russianize" the others; it's because the Soviet bureaucracy – deeply a-national, antinational, supranational – needs a tool to unify its state.

I understand the logic. I also understand the predicament of the Russians who fear that their beloved homeland will be confused with detested communism.

But it is also necessary to understand the Pole, whose homeland, except for a brief period between the two world wars, has been subjugated by Russia for two centuries and has been, throughout, subject to a "Russianization" – the pressure to conform to being Russian – as patient as it has been implacable.

In Central Europe, the eastern border of the West, everyone has always been particularly sensitive to the dangers of Russian might. And it's not just the Poles. Frantisek Palacky, the great historian and the figure most representative of Czech politics in the nineteenth century, wrote in 1848 a famous letter to the revolutionary parliament of Frankfurt in which he justified the continued existence of the Hapsburg Empire as the only possible rampart against Russia, against "this power which, having already reached an enormous size today, is now augmenting its force beyond the reach of any Western country". Palacky warned of Russia's imperial ambitions; it aspired to become a "universal monarchy", which means it sought world domination. "A Russian universal monarchy," Palacky wrote, "would be an immense and indescribable disaster, an immeasurable and limitless disaster."

Central Europe, according to Palacky, ought to be a family of equal nations, each of which – treating the others with mutual respect and secure in the protection of a strong, unified state – would also cultivate its own individuality. And this dream, although never fully realized, would remain powerful and influential. Central Europe longed to be a condensed version of Europe itself in all its cultural variety, a small arch-European Europe, a reduced model of Europe made up of nations conceived according to one rule: the greatest variety within the smallest space. How could Central Europe not be horrified facing a Russia founded on the opposite principle: the smallest variety within the greatest space?

Indeed, nothing could be more foreign to Central Europe and its passion for variety than Russia: uniform, standardizing, centralizing, determined to transform every nation of its empire (the Ukrainians, the Belorussians, the Armenians, the Latvians, the Lithuanians, and others) into a single Russian people (or, as is more commonly expressed in this age of generalized verbal mystification, into a "single Soviet people").[3]

And so, again: is communism the negation of Russian history or its fulfillment?

Certainly it is both its negation (the negation, for example, of its religiosity) *and* its fulfillment (the fulfillment of its centralizing tendencies and its imperial dreams).

Seen from within Russia, this first aspect – the aspect of its discontinuity – is the more striking. From the point of view of the enslaved countries, the second aspect – that of its continuity – is felt more powerfully.[4]

4.

But am I being too absolute in contrasting Russia and Western civilization? Isn't Europe, though divided into east and west, still a single entity anchored in ancient Greece and Judeo-Christian thought?

Of course. Moreover, during the entire nineteenth century, Russia, attracted to Europe, drew closer to it. And the fascination was reciprocated. Rilke claimed that Russia was his spiritual homeland, and no one has escaped the impact of the great Russian novels, which remain an integral part of the common European cultural legacy.

Yes, all this is true; the cultural betrothal between the two Europes remains a great and unforgettable memory.[5] But it is no less true that Russian communism vigorously reawakened

Russia's old anti-Western obsessions and turned it brutally against Europe.

But Russia isn't my subject and I don't want to wander into its immense complexities, about which I'm not especially knowledgeable. I want simply to make this point once more: on the eastern border of the West – more than anywhere else – Russia is seen not just as one more European power but as a singular civilization, an *other* civilization.

In his book *Native Realm*, Czeslaw Milosz speaks of the phenomenon: in the sixteenth and seventeenth centuries, the Poles waged war against the Russians "along distant borders. No one was especially interested in the Russians.... It was this experience, when the Poles found only a big void to the east, that engendered the Polish concept of a Russia situated 'out there' – outside the world".[6]

Kazimierz Brandys, in his *Warsaw Diary*, recalls the interesting story of a Polish writer's meeting with the Russian poet Anna Akhmatova. The Pole was complaining: his works – all of them – had been banned.

She interrupted: "Have you been imprisoned?"

"No."

"Have you at least been expelled from the Writers' Union?"

"No."

"Then what exactly are you complaining about?" Akhmatova was genuinely puzzled.

Brandys observes:

Those are typical Russian consolations. Nothing seems horrible to them, compared to the fate of Russia. But these consolations make no sense to us. The fate of Russia is not part of our consciousness; it's foreign to us; we're not responsible for it. It weighs on us, but it's not our heritage. That was also my response to Russian literature. It scared me. Even today I'm still horrified by certain stories by Gogol and by everything Saltykov-Shchedrin wrote. I would have preferred not to have known their world, not to have known it even existed.

Brandys's remarks on Gogol do not, of course, deny the value of his work as art; rather they express the horror of the world his art evokes. It is a world that – provided we are removed from it – fascinates and attracts us; the moment it closes around us, though, it reveals its terrifying foreignness. I don't know if it is worse than ours, but I do know it is different: Russia knows another (greater) dimension of disaster, another image of space (a space so immense entire nations are swallowed up in it), another sense of time (slow and patient), another way of laughing, living, and dying.

This is why the countries in Central Europe feel that the change in their destiny that occurred after 1945 is not merely a political catastrophe: it is also an attack on their civilization. The deep meaning of their resistance is the struggle to preserve their identity – or, to put it another way, to preserve their Westernness.[7]

5.

There are no longer any illusions about the regimes of Russia's satellite countries. But what we forget is their essential tragedy: these countries have vanished from the map of the West.

Why has this disappearance remained invisible? We can locate the cause in Central Europe itself.

The history of the Poles, the Czechs, the Slovaks, the Hungarians has been turbulent and fragmented. Their traditions of statehood have been weaker and less continuous than those of the larger European nations. Boxed in by the Germans on one side and the Russians on the other, the nations of Central Europe have used up their strength in the struggle to survive and to preserve their languages. Since they have never been entirely integrated into the consciousness of Europe, they have remained the least known and the most fragile part of the West – hidden, even further, by the curtain of their strange and scarcely accessible languages.

The Austrian empire had the great opportunity of making Central Europe into a strong, unified state. But the Austrians, alas, were divided between an arrogant Pan-German nationalism and their own Central European mission. They did not succeed in building a federation of equal nations, and their failure has been the misfortune of the whole of Europe. Dissatisfied, the other nations of Central Europe blew apart their empire in 1918, without realizing that, in spite of its inadequacies, it was irreplaceable. After the First World War, Central Europe was therefore transformed into a region of small, weak states, whose vulnerability ensured first Hitler's conquest and ultimately Stalin's triumph. Perhaps for this reason, in the European memory these countries always seem to be the source of dangerous trouble.

And, to be frank, I feel that the error made by Central Europe was owing to what I call the "ideology of the Slavic world". I say "ideology" advisedly, for it is only a piece of political mystification invented in the nineteenth century. The Czechs (in spite of the severe warnings of their most respected leaders) loved to brandish naively their "Slavic ideology" as a defense against German aggressiveness. The Russians, on the other hand, enjoyed making use of it to justify their own imperial ambitions. "The Russians like to label everything Russian as Slavic, so that later they can label everything Slavic as Russian", the great Czech writer Karel Havlicek declared in 1844, trying to warn his compatriots against their silly and ignorant enthusiasm for Russia. It was ignorant because the Czechs, for a thousand years, have never had any direct contact with Russia. In spite of their linguistic kinship, the Czechs and the Russians have never shared a common *world*: neither a common history nor a common culture. The relationship between the Poles and the Russians, though, has never been anything less than a struggle of life and death.

Joseph Conrad was always irritated by the label "Slavic soul" that people loved to slap on him and his books because of his Polish origins, and, about sixty years ago, he wrote that "nothing could be more alien to what is called in the literary world the

'Slavic spirit' than the Polish temperament with its chivalric devotion to moral constraints and its exaggerated respect for individual rights". (How well I understand him! I, too, know of nothing more ridiculous than this cult of obscure depths, this noisy and empty sentimentality of the "Slavic soul" that is attributed to me from time to time!)[8]

Nevertheless, the idea of a Slavic world is a commonplace of world historiography. The division of Europe after 1945 – which united this supposed Slavic world (including the poor Hungarians and Rumanians whose language is not, of course, Slavic – but why bother over trifles?) – has therefore seemed almost like a natural solution.

6.

So is it the fault of Central Europe that the West hasn't even noticed its disappearance?

Not entirely. At the beginning of our century, Central Europe was, despite its political weakness, a great cultural center, perhaps the greatest. And, admittedly, while the importance of Vienna, the city of Freud and Mahler, is readily acknowledged today, its importance and originality make little sense unless they are seen against the background of the other countries and cities that together participated in, and contributed creatively to, the culture of Central Europe. If the school of Schönberg founded the twelve-tone system, the Hungarian Béla Bartók, one of the greatest musicians of the twentieth century, knew how to discover the last original possibility in music based on the tonal principle. With the work of Kafka and Hasek, Prague created the great counterpart in the novel to the work of the Viennese Musil and Broch. The cultural dynamism of the non-German-speaking countries was intensified even more after 1918, when Prague offered the world the innovations of structuralism and the Prague Linguistic Circle.[9] And in Poland the great trinity of Witold Gombrowicz, Bruno Schulz, and Stanislas Witkiewicz anticipated the European modernism of the 1950s, notably the so-called theater of the absurd.

A question arises: was this entire creative explosion just a coincidence of geography? Or was it rooted in a long tradition, a shared past? Or, to put it another way: does Central Europe constitute a true cultural configuration with its own history? And if such a configuration exists, can it be defined geographically? What are its borders?

It would be senseless to try to draw its borders exactly. Central Europe is not a state: it is a culture or a fate. Its borders are imaginary and must be drawn and redrawn with each new historical situation.

For example, by the middle of the fourteenth century, Charles University in Prague had already brought together intellectuals (professors and students) who were Czech, Austrian, Bavarian, Saxon, Polish, Lithuanian, Hungarian, and Rumanian with the germ of the idea of a multinational community in which each nation would have the right of its own language: indeed, it was under the indirect influence of this university (at which the religious reformer Jan Huss was once rector) that the first Hungarian and Rumanian translations of the Bible were undertaken.

Other situations followed: the Hussite revolution; the Hungarian Renaissance during the time of Mathias Korvin with its international influence; the advent of the Hapsburg Empire as the union of three independent states – Bohemia, Hungary, and Austria; the wars against the Turks; the Counter-Reformation of the seventeenth century. At this time the specific nature of Central European culture appeared suddenly in an extraordinary explosion of baroque art, a phenomenon that unified this vast region, from Salzburg to Wilno. On the map of Europe, baroque Central Europe (characterized by the predominance of the irrational and the dominant position of the visual arts and especially of music) became the opposite pole of classical France (characterized by the predominance of the rational and the dominant position of literature and philosophy). It is in the baroque period that one finds the origins of the extraordinary development of Central European music, which, from Haydn to Schönberg, from Liszt to Bartók, condensed within itself the evolution of all European music.

In the nineteenth century, the national struggles (of the Poles, the Hungarians, the Czechs, the Slovaks, the Croats, the Slovenes, the Rumanians, the Jews) brought into opposition nations that – insulated, egotistic, closed-off – had nevertheless lived through the same great existential experience: the experience of a nation that chooses between its existence and its nonexistence; or, to put it another way, between retaining its authentic national life and being assimilated into a larger nation. Not even the Austrians, though belonging to the dominant nation of the empire, avoided the necessity of facing this choice: they had to choose between their Austrian identity and being submerged by the larger German one. Nor could the Jews escape this question. By refusing assimilation, Zionism, also born in Central Europe, chose the same path as the other Central European nations.

The twentieth century has witnessed other situations: the collapse of the Austrian empire, Russian annexation, and the long period of Central European revolts, which are only an immense bet staked on an unknown solution.

Central Europe therefore cannot be defined and determined by political frontiers (which are inauthentic, always imposed by invasions, conquests, and occupations), but by the great common situations that reassemble peoples, regroup them in ever new ways along the imaginary and ever-changing boundaries that mark a realm inhabited by the same memories, the same problems and conflicts, the same common tradition.

7.

Sigmund Freud's parents came from Poland, but young Sigmund spent his childhood in Moravia, in present-day Czechoslovakia. Edmund Husserl and Gustav Mahler also spent their childhoods there. The Viennese novelist Joseph Roth had his roots in Poland.

The great Czech poet Julius Zeyer was born in Prague to a German-speaking family; it was his own choice to become Czech. The mother tongue of Hermann Kafka, on the other hand, was Czech, while his son Franz took up German. The key figure in the Hungarian revolt of 1956, the writer Tibor Déry, came from a German-Hungarian family, and my dear friend Danilo Kiš, the excellent novelist, is Hungario-Yugoslav. What a tangle of national destinies among even the most representative figures of each country!

And all of the names I've just mentioned are those of Jews. Indeed, no other part of the world has been so deeply marked by the influence of Jewish genius. Aliens everywhere and everywhere at home, lifted above national quarrels, the Jews in the twentieth century were the principal cosmopolitan, integrating element in Central Europe: they were its intellectual cement, a condensed version of its spirit, creators of its spiritual unity. That's why I love the Jewish heritage and cling to it with as much passion and nostalgia as though it were my own.

Another thing makes the Jewish people so precious to me: in their destiny the fate of Central Europe seems to be concentrated, reflected, and to have found its symbolic image. What is Central Europe? An uncertain zone of small nations between Russia and Germany. I underscore the words: *small nation.* Indeed, what are the Jews if not a small nation, *the* small nation par excellence? The only one of all the small nations of all time which has survived empires and the devastating march of History.

But what is a small nation? I offer you my definition: the small nation is one whose very existence may be put in question at any moment; a small nation can disappear and it knows it. A French, a Russian, or an English man is not used to asking questions about the very survival of his nation. His anthems speak only of grandeur and eternity. The Polish anthem, however, starts with the verse: "Poland has not yet perished...."

Central Europe as a family of small nations has its own vision of the world, a vision based on a deep distrust of history. History, that goddess of Hegel and Marx, that incarnation of reason that judges us and arbitrates our fate – that is the history of conquerors. The people of Central Europe are not conquerors. They cannot be separated from European history; they cannot exist outside it; but they represent the wrong side of this history; they are its victims and outsiders. It's this disabused view of history that is the source of their culture, of their wisdom, of the "nonserious spirit" that mocks grandeur and glory. "Never forget that only in opposing History as such can we resist the history of our own day." I would love to engrave this sentence by Witold Gombrowicz above the entry gate to Central Europe.

Thus it was in this region of small nations who have "not yet perished" that Europe's vulnerability, all of Europe's vulnerability, was more clearly visible before anywhere else. Actually, in our modern world where power has a tendency to become more and more concentrated in the hands of a few big countries, *all* European nations run the risk of becoming small nations and of sharing their fate. In this sense the destiny of Central Europe anticipates the destiny of Europe in general, and its culture assumes an enormous relevance.[10]

It's enough to read the greatest Central European novels: in Hermann Broch's *The Sleepwalkers*, History appears as a process of gradual degradation of values; Robert Musil's *The Man without Qualities* paints a euphoric society which doesn't realize that tomorrow it will disappear; in Jaroslav Hasek's *The Good Soldier Schweik*, pretending to be an idiot becomes the last possible method for preserving one's freedom; the novelistic visions of Kafka speak to us of a world without memory, of a world that comes after historic time.[11] All of this century's great Central European works of art, even up to our own day, can be understood as long meditations on the possible end of European humanity.

8.

Today, all of Central Europe has been subjugated by Russia with the exception of little Austria, which, more by chance than necessity, has retained its independence, but ripped out of its Central European setting, it has lost most of its individual character and all of its importance. The disappearance of the cultural home of Central Europe was certainly one of the greatest events of the century for all of Western civilization. So, I repeat my question: how could it possibly have gone unnoticed and unnamed? The answer is simple: Europe hasn't noticed the disappearance of its cultural home because Europe no longer perceives its unity as a cultural unity.

In fact, what is European unity based on?

In the Middle Ages, it was based on a shared religion. In the modern era, in which the medieval God has been changed into a *Deus absconditus*, religion bowed out, giving way to culture, which became the expression of the supreme values by which European humanity understood itself, defined itself, identified itself as European.

Now it seems that another change is taking place in our century, as important as the one that divided the Middle Ages from the modern era. Just as God long ago gave way to culture, culture in turn is giving way.

But to what and to whom? What realm of supreme values will be capable of uniting Europe? Technical feats? The marketplace? The mass media? (Will the great poet be replaced by the great journalist?)[12] Or by politics? But by which politics? The right or the left? Is there a discernible shared ideal that still exists above this Manichaeanism of the left and the right that is as stupid as it is insurmountable? Will it be the principle of tolerance, respect for the beliefs and ideas of other people? But won't this tolerance become empty and useless if it no longer protects a rich creativity or a strong set of ideas? Or should we understand the abdication of culture as a sort of deliverance, to which we should ecstatically abandon ourselves? Or will the *Deus absconditus* return to fill the empty space and reveal himself? I don't know, I know nothing about it. I think I know only that culture has bowed out.

9.

Franz Werfel spent the first third of his life in Prague, the second third in Vienna, and the last third as an emigrant, first in France, then in America – there you have a typically Central European biography. In 1937 he was in Paris with his wife, the famous Alma, Mahler's widow; he'd been invited there by the Organization for Intellectual Cooperation within the League of Nations to a conference on "The Future of Literature". During the conference Werfel took a stand not only against Hitlerism but also against the totalitarian threat in general, the ideological and journalistic mindlessness of our times that was on the verge of destroying culture. He ended his speech with a proposal that he thought might arrest this demonic process: to found a World Academy of Poets and Thinkers (*Weltakademie der Dichter und Denker*). In no circumstance should the members be named by their states. The selection of members should be dependent only on the value of their work. The number of members, made up of the greatest writers in the world, should be between twenty-four and forty. The task of this academy, free of politics and propaganda, would be to "confront the politicization and barbarization of the world".

Not only was this proposal rejected, it was openly ridiculed. Of course, it was naive. Terribly naive. In a world absolutely politicized, in which artists and thinkers were already irremediably "committed", already politically *engagé*, how could such an independent academy possibly be created? Wouldn't it have the rather comic aspect of an assembly of noble souls?

However, this naive proposal strikes me as moving, because it reveals the desperate need to find once again a moral authority in a world stripped of values. It reveals the anguished desire to hear the inaudible voice of culture, the voice of the *Dichter und Denker.*[13]

This story is mixed up in my mind with the memory of a morning when the police, after making a mess of the apartment of one of my friends, a famous Czech philosopher, confiscated a thousand pages of his philosophic manuscript. Shortly after we were walking through the streets of Prague. We walked down from the Castle hill, where he lived, toward the peninsula of Kampa; we crossed the Manes Bridge. He was trying to make a joke of it all: how were the police going to decipher his philosophical lingo, which was rather hermetic? But no joke could soothe his anguish, could make up for the loss of ten years' work that this manuscript represented – for he did not have another copy.

We talked about the possibility of sending an open letter abroad in order to turn this confiscation into an international scandal. It was perfectly clear to us that he shouldn't address the letter to an institution or a statesman but only to some figure above politics, someone who stood for an unquestionable moral value, someone universally acknowledged in Europe. In other words, a great cultural figure. But who was this person?

Suddenly we understood that this figure did not exist. To be sure, there were great painters, playwrights, and musicians, but they no longer held a privileged place in society as moral authorities that Europe would acknowledge as its spiritual representatives. Culture no longer existed as a realm in which supreme values were enacted.

We walked toward the square in the old city near which I was then living, and we felt an immense loneliness, a void, the void in the European space from which culture was slowly withdrawing.[14]

10.

The last direct personal experience of the West that Central European countries remember is the period from 1918 to 1938. Their picture of the West, then, is of the West in the past, of a West in which culture had not yet entirely bowed out.

With this in mind, I want to stress a significant circumstance: the Central European revolts were not nourished by the newspapers, radio, or television – that is, by the "media". They were prepared, shaped, realized by novels, poetry, theater, cinema, historiography, literary reviews, popular comedy and cabaret, philosophical discussions – that is, by culture.[15] The mass media – which, for the French and Americans, are indistinguishable from whatever the West today is meant to be – played no part in these revolts (since the press and television were completely under state control).

That's why, when the Russians occupied Czechoslovakia, they did everything possible to destroy Czech culture.[16] This destruction had three meanings: first, it destroyed the center of the opposition; second, it undermined the identity of the nation, enabling it to be more easily swallowed up by Russian civilization; third, it put a violent end to the modern era, the era in which culture still represented the realization of supreme values.

This third consequence seems to me the most important. In effect, totalitarian Russian civilization is the radical negation of the modern West, the West created four centuries ago at the dawn of the modern era: the era founded on the authority of the thinking, doubting individual, and on an artistic creation that expressed his uniqueness. The Russian invasion has thrown Czechoslovakia into a "postcultural" era and left it defenseless and naked before the Russian army and the omnipresent state television.

While still shaken by this triply tragic event which the invasion of Prague represented, I arrived in France and tried to explain to French friends the massacre of culture that had taken place after the invasion: "Try to imagine! All of the literary and cultural reviews were liquidated! Every one, without exception! That never happened before in Czech history, not even under the Nazi occupation during the war."

Then my friends would look at me indulgently with an embarrassment that I understood only later. When all the reviews in Czechoslovakia were liquidated, the entire nation knew it, and was in a state of anguish because of the immense impact of the event.[17] If all the reviews in France or England disappeared, no one would notice it, not even their editors. In Paris, even in a completely cultivated milieu, during dinner parties people discuss television programs, not reviews. For culture has already bowed out. Its disappearance, which we experienced in Prague as a catastrophe, a shock, a tragedy, is perceived in Paris as something banal and insignificant, scarcely visible, a non-event.

11.

After the destruction of the Austrian empire, Central Europe lost its ramparts. Didn't it lose its soul after Auschwitz, which swept the Jewish nation off its map? And after having been torn away from Europe in 1945, does Central Europe still exist?

Yes, its creativity and its revolts suggest that it has "not yet perished". But if to live means to exist in the eyes of those we love, then Central Europe no longer exists. More precisely: in the eyes of its beloved Europe, Central Europe is just a part of the Soviet empire and nothing more, nothing more.

And why should this surprise us? By virtue of its political system, Central Europe is the East; by virtue of its cultural history, it is the West. But since Europe itself is in the process of losing its own cultural identity, it perceives in Central Europe nothing but a political regime; put another way, it sees in Central Europe only Eastern Europe.

Central Europe, therefore, should fight not only against its big oppressive neighbor but also against the subtle, relentless pressure of time, which is leaving the era of culture in its wake. That's why in Central European revolts there is something conservative, nearly anachronistic: they are desperately trying to restore the past, the past of culture, the past of the modern era. It is only in that period, only in a world that maintains a cultural dimension, that Central Europe can still defend its identity, still be seen for what it is.

The real tragedy for Central Europe, then, is not Russia but Europe: this Europe that represented a value so great that the director of the Hungarian News Agency was ready to die for it, and for which he did indeed die. Behind the iron curtain, he did not suspect that the times had changed and that in Europe itself Europe was no longer experienced as a value. He did not suspect that the sentence he was sending by telex beyond the borders of his flat country would seem outmoded and would not be understood.

Translated from the French by Ed White

Notes

1. The responsibility of Central European communists who, after the war, did so much to set up totalitarian regimes in their countries is enormous. But they would never have succeeded without the initiative, the violent pressure, and the international power of Russia. Just after the victory, Central European communists understood that not they but the USSR was the master of their countries; from that point began the slow decomposition of Central European regimes and parties.

2. For the outside observer this paradox is hard to understand; the period after 1945 is at once the most tragic for Central Europe and also one of the greatest in its cultural history. Whether written in exile (Gombrowicz, Milosz), or taking the form of clandestine creative activity (in Czechoslovakia after 1968), or tolerated by the authorities under the pressure of public opinion – no matter under which of these circumstances – the films, the novels, the plays and works of philosophy born in Central Europe during this period often reach the summits of European culture.

3. One of the great European nations (there are nearly forty million Ukrainians) is slowly disappearing. And this enormous, almost unbelievable event is occurring without the world realizing it.

4. Leszek Kolakowski writes (*Zeszyty literacke*, no. 2, Paris, 1983): "Although I believe, as does Solzhenitsyn, that the Soviet system has surpassed Czarism in its oppressive character...I will not go so far as to idealize the system against which my ancestors fought under terrible conditions and under which they died or were tortured or suffered humiliations.... I believe that Solzhenitsyn has a tendency to idealize Czarism, a tendency that neither I nor, I'm sure, any other Pole can accept."

5. The most beautiful union between Russia and the West is the work of Stravinsky, which summarizes the whole thousand-year history of Western music and at the same time remains in its musical imagination deeply Russian. Another excellent marriage was celebrated in Central Europe in two magnificient operas of that great Russophile, Leos Janácek: one of them based on Ostrovski (*Katya Kabanova*, 1921), and the other, which I admire immensely, based on Dostoevsky (*The House of the Dead*, 1928). But it is symptomatic that not only have these operas never been staged in Russia, but their very existence is unknown there. Communist Russia repudiates misalliances with the West.

6. Czeslaw Milosz's books *The Captive Mind* (1953) and *Native Realm* (1959) are basic: the first close analyses that are not Manichaean toward Russian communism and its *Drang nach West*.

7. The word "central" contains a danger: it evokes the idea of a bridge between Russia and the West. T.G. Masaryk, the founding president of Czechoslovakia, had already spoken of this idea by 1895: "It's often said that Czechs have as our mission to serve as a mediator between the West and the East. This idea is meaningless. The Czechs are not next to the East (they are surrounded by Germans and Poles, that is, the West), but also there is no need whatsoever for a mediator. The Russians have always had much closer and more direct contacts with the Germans and the French than with us, and everything the Western nations have learned about the Russians they have learned directly, without mediators."

8. There is an amusing little book named *How to be an Alien* in which the author, in a chapter titled "Soul and Understatement," speaks of the Slavic soul: "The worst kind of soul is the great Slav soul. People who suffer from it are usually very deep thinkers. They may say things like this: 'Sometimes I am so merry and sometimes I am so sad. Can you explain why?' (You

cannot, do not try.) Or they may say: 'I am so mysterious.... I sometimes wish I were somewhere else than where I am.' Or 'When I am alone in a forest at night and jump from one tree to another, I often think that life is so strange.'" Who would dare to make fun of the great Slavic soul? Of course the author is George Mikes, of Hungarian origin. Only in Central Europe does the Slavic soul appear ridiculous.

9. Structuralist thinking started toward the end of the 1920s in the Prague Linguistic Circle. It was made up of Czech, Russian, German, and Polish scholars. During the 1930s, in this very cosmopolitan environment, Mukarovsky worked out his structuralist aesthetics. Prague structuralism was organically rooted in Czech formalism of the nineteenth century. (Formalist tendencies were stronger in Central Europe than elsewhere, in my opinion, thanks to the dominant position of music and, therefore, of musicology, which is "formalist" by its very nature.) Inspired by recent developments in Russian formalism, Mukarovsky went beyond its onesided nature. The structuralists were the allies of Prague avant-garde poets and painters (thereby anticipating a similar alliance that was created in France thirty years later). Through their influence the structuralists protected avant-garde art against the narrowly ideological interpretation that has dogged modern art everywhere.

10. The problem of Central European culture is examined in a very important periodical published by the University of Michigan: *Cross Currents: A Yearbook of Central European Culture.*

11. With this constellation of Central European writers, with Kafka, Hasek, Broch, and Musil, a new post-Proustian, post-Joycean aesthetic of the novel, it seems to me, arises in Europe. Broch is the one I personally care for the most. It's high time this Viennese novelist, one of the greatest of this century, were rediscovered.

12. If journalism at one time seemed to be an appendix to culture, today, by contrast, culture finds itself at the mercy of journalism; it is part of a world dominated by journalism. The mass media decide who will be known and to what degree and according to which interpretation. The writer no longer addresses the public directly; he must communicate with it through the semi-transparent barrier of the mass media.

13. Werfel's speech was not at all naive and it has not lost its relevance. It reminds me of another speech, one that Robert Musil

read in 1935 to the Congress for the Defense of Culture in Paris. Like Werfel, Musil saw a danger not only in fascism but also in communism. The defense of culture for him did not mean the commitment of culture to a political struggle (as everyone else thought at the time) but on the contrary it meant the protection of culture from the mindlessness of politicization. Both writers realized that in the modern world of technology and mass media, the prospects for culture were not bright. Musil's and Werfel's opinions were very coolly received in Paris. However, in all the political and cultural discussions I hear around me, I would have almost nothing to add to what they have said, and I feel, in such moments, very close to them – I feel, in those moments, irreparably Central European.

14. At last, after hesitating, he sent the letter after all – to Jean-Paul Sartre. Yes, he was the last great world cultural figure: on the other hand, he is the very person who, with his theory of "engagement," provided, in my opinion, the theoretical basis for the abdication of culture as an autonomous force, particular and irreducible. Despite what he might have been, he did respond promptly to my friend's letter with a statement published in *Le Monde*. Without this intervention, I doubt whether the police would have finally returned (nearly a year later) the manuscript to the philosopher. On the day Sartre was buried, the memory of my Prague friend came back to my mind: now his letter would no longer find a recipient.

15. By reviews I mean periodicals (monthly, fortnightly, or weekly) run not by journalists but by people of culture (writers, art critics, scholars, philosophers, musicians); they deal with cultural questions and comment on social events from the cultural point of view. In the nineteenth and twentieth centuries in Europe and Russia, all of the important intellectual movements formed around such reviews. The German Romantic musicians clustered around the *Neue Zeitschrift für Musik* founded by Robert Schumann. Russian literature is unthinkable without such reviews as *Sovremennik* or *Viesy*, just as French literature depended on the *Nouvelle Revue Française* or *Les Temps Modernes*. All of Viennese cultural activity was concentrated around *Die Fackel* directed by Karl Kraus. Gombrowicz's entire journal was published in the Polish review *Kultura*. Etc., etc. The disappearance of such reviews from Western public life or the fact that

they have become completely marginal is, in my opinion, a sign that "culture is bowing out".

16. Five hundred thousand people (especially intellectuals) were pushed out of their jobs. One hundred twenty thousand emigrated. About two hundred Czech and Slovak writers have been forbidden to publish. Their books have been banned from every public library and their names have been erased from history textbooks. One hundred and fortyfive Czech historians have been fired. From a single faculty of the university in Prague, fifty teachers were dismissed. (At the darkest moment of the Austro-Hungarian empire, after the revolution of 1848, two Czech professors were driven out of the university – what a scandal at the time!) Every literary and cultural journal has been liquidated. The great Czech cinema; the great Czech theater no longer exist.

17. The weekly publication *Literarni noviny* (*Literary Journal*) which had a circulation of 300,000 copies (in a land of ten million people), was produced by the Czech Writers' Union. It was this publication that over the years led the way to the Prague Spring and was afterward a platform for it. It did not resemble such weeklies as *Time* which have spread throughout Europe and America. No, it was truly literary: in it could be found long art chronicles, analyses of books. The articles devoted to history, sociology, and politics were not written by journalists but by writers, historians, and philosophers. I don't know of a single European weekly in our century that has played as important a historical role or played it as well. The circulation for Czech literary monthlies varied between ten thousand and forty thousand copies, and their level was remarkably high, in spite of censorship. In Poland reviews have a comparable importance; today there are hundreds of underground journals there.

The Bruges Speech[1]

Margaret Thatcher

Bruges, 20 September 1988

Prime Minister, Rector, Your Excellencies, Ladies and Gentlemen,

First, may I thank you for giving me the opportunity to return to Bruges and in very different circumstances from my last visit shortly after the Zeebrugge Ferry disaster, when Belgian courage and the devotion of your doctors and nurses saved so many British lives.

And second, may I say what a pleasure it is to speak at the College of Europe under the distinguished leadership of its Rector [Professor Lukaszewski]. The College plays a vital and increasingly important part in the life of the European Community.

And third, may I also thank you for inviting me to deliver my address in this magnificent hall. What better place to speak of Europe's future than a building which so gloriously recalls the greatness that Europe had already achieved over 600 years ago.

Your city of Bruges has many other historical associations for us in Britain. Geoffrey Chaucer was a frequent visitor here. And the first book to be printed in the English language was produced here in Bruges by William Caxton.

Britain and Europe

Mr. Chairman, you have invited me to speak on the subject of Britain and Europe. Perhaps I should congratulate you on your courage. If you believe some of the things said and written about my views on Europe, it must seem rather like inviting Genghis Khan to speak on the virtues of peaceful coexistence!

I want to start by disposing of some myths about my country, Britain, and its relationship with Europe and to do that, I must say something about the identity of Europe itself.

Europe is not the creation of the Treaty of Rome. Nor is the European idea the property of any group or institution.

We British are as much heirs to the legacy of European culture as any other nation. Our links to the rest of Europe, the continent of Europe, have been the dominant factor in our history.

For three hundred years, we were part of the Roman Empire and our maps still trace the straight lines of the roads the Romans built. Our ancestors – Celts, Saxons, Danes – came from the Continent. Our nation was – in that favourite Community word – "restructured" under the Norman and Angevin rule in the eleventh and twelfth centuries.

This year, we celebrate the three hundredth anniversary of the glorious revolution in which the British crown passed to Prince William of Orange and Queen Mary.

Visit the great churches and cathedrals of Britain, read our literature and listen to our language: all bear witness to the cultural riches which we have drawn from Europe and other Europeans from us.

We in Britain are rightly proud of the way in which, since Magna Carta in the year 1215, we have pioneered and developed representative institutions to stand as bastions of freedom. And proud too of the way in which for centuries Britain was a home for people from the rest of Europe who sought sanctuary from tyranny.

But we know that without the European legacy of political ideas we could not have achieved as much as we did. From classical and mediaeval thought we have borrowed that concept of the rule of law which marks out a civilised society from barbarism.

And on that idea of Christendom, to which the Rector referred – Christendom for long synonymous with Europe – with its recognition of the unique and spiritual nature of the individual, on that idea, we still base our belief in personal liberty and other human rights.

Too often, the history of Europe is described as a series of interminable wars and quarrels. Yet from our perspective today surely what strikes us most is our common experience. For instance, the story of how Europeans explored and colonised – and yes, without apology – civilised much of the world is an extraordinary tale of talent, skill and courage.

But we British have in a very special way contributed to Europe. Over the centuries we have fought to prevent Europe from falling under the dominance of a single power. We have fought and we have died for her freedom. Only miles from here, in Belgium, lie the bodies of 120,000 British soldiers who died in the First World War.

Had it not been for that willingness to fight and to die, Europe would have been united long before now – but not in liberty, not in justice. It was British support to resistance movements throughout the last War that helped to keep alive the flame of liberty in so many countries until the day of liberation.

Tomorrow, King Baudouin will attend a service in Brussels to commemorate the many brave Belgians who gave their lives in service with the Royal Air Force – a sacrifice which we shall never forget.

And it was from our island fortress that the liberation of Europe itself was mounted.

And still, today, we stand together. Nearly 70,000 British servicemen are stationed on the mainland of Europe. All these things alone are proof of our commitment to Europe's future.

The European Community is one manifestation of that European identity, but it is not the only one.

We must never forget that east of the Iron Curtain, people who once enjoyed a full share of European culture, freedom and identity have been cut off from their roots. We shall always look on Warsaw, Prague and Budapest as great European cities.

Nor should we forget that European values have helped to make the United States of America into the valiant defender of freedom which she has become.

Europe's future

This is no arid chronicle of obscure facts from the dust-filled libraries of history. It is the record of nearly two thousand years of British involvement in Europe, cooperation with Europe and contribution to Europe, contribution which today is as valid and as strong as ever [sic].

Yes, we have looked also to wider horizons – as have others – and thank goodness for that, because Europe never would have prospered and never will prosper as a narrow-minded, inward-looking club.

The European Community belongs to all its members. It must reflect the traditions and aspirations of all its members.

And let me be quite clear. Britain does not dream of some cosy, isolated existence on the fringes of the European Community. Our destiny is in Europe, as part of the Community.

That is not to say that our future lies only in Europe, but nor does that of France or Spain or, indeed, of any other member. The Community is not an end in itself.

Nor is it an institutional device to be constantly modified according to the dictates of some abstract intellectual concept. Nor must it be ossified by endless regulation.

The European Community is a practical means by which Europe can ensure the future prosperity and security of its people in a world in which there are many other powerful nations and groups of nations.

We Europeans cannot afford to waste our energies on internal disputes or arcane institutional debates. They are no substitute for effective action.

Europe has to be ready both to contribute in full measure to its own security and to compete commercially and industrially in a world in which success goes to the countries which encourage individual initiative and enterprise, rather than those which attempt to diminish them.

This evening I want to set out some guiding principles for the future which I believe will ensure that Europe does succeed, not just in economic and defence terms but also in the quality of life and the influence of its peoples.

Willing co-operation between sovereign states

My first guiding principle is this: willing and active co-operation between independent sovereign states is the best way to build a successful European Community.

To try to suppress nationhood and concentrate power at the centre of a European conglomerate would be highly damaging and would jeopardise the objectives we seek to achieve.

Europe will be stronger precisely because it has France as France, Spain as Spain, Britain as Britain, each with its own customs, traditions and identity. It would be folly to try to fit them into some sort of identikit European personality.

Some of the founding fathers of the Community thought that the United States of America might be its model.

But the whole history of America is quite different from Europe. People went there to get away from the intolerance and constraints of life in Europe. They sought liberty and opportunity; and their strong sense of purpose has, over two centuries, helped to create a new unity and pride in being American, just as our pride lies in being British or Belgian or Dutch or German.

I am the first to say that on many great issues the countries of Europe should try to speak with a single voice. I want to see us work more closely on the things we can do better together than alone. Europe is stronger when we do so, whether it be in trade, in defence or in our relations with the rest of the world.

But working more closely together does not require power to be centralised in Brussels or decisions to be taken by an appointed bureaucracy. Indeed, it is ironic that just when those countries such as the Soviet Union, which have tried to run everything from the centre, are learning that success depends on dispersing power and decisions away from the centre, there are some in the Community who seem to want to move in the opposite direction.

We have not successfully rolled back the frontiers of the state in Britain, only to see them re-imposed at a European level with a European super-state exercising a new dominance from Brussels.

Certainly we want to see Europe more united and with a greater sense of common purpose. But it must be in a way which preserves the different traditions, parliamentary powers and sense of national pride in one's own country; for these have been the source of Europe's vitality through the centuries.

Encouraging change

My second guiding principle is this: Community policies must tackle present problems in a practical way, however difficult that may be.

If we cannot reform those Community policies which are patently wrong or ineffective and which are rightly causing public disquiet, then we shall not get the public support for the Community's future development. And that is why the achievements of the European Council in Brussels last February are so important.

It was not right that half the total Community budget was being spent on storing and disposing of surplus food. Now those stocks are being sharply reduced.

It was absolutely right to decide that agriculture's share of the budget should be cut in order to free resources for other policies, such as helping the less well-off regions and helping training for jobs. It was right too to introduce tighter budgetary discipline to enforce these decisions and to bring the Community spending under better control.

And those who complained that the Community was spending so much time on financial detail missed the point. You cannot build on unsound foundations, financial or otherwise, and it was the fundamental reforms agreed last winter which paved the way for the remarkable progress which we have made since on the Single Market.

But we cannot rest on what we have achieved to date. For example, the task of reforming the Common Agricultural Policy is far from complete.

Certainly, Europe needs a stable and efficient farming industry. But the CAP has become unwieldy, inefficient and grossly expensive. Production of unwanted surpluses safeguards neither the income nor the future of farmers themselves. We must continue to pursue policies which relate supply more closely to market requirements, and which will reduce over-production and limit costs. Of course, we must protect the villages and rural areas which are such an important part of our national life, but not by the instrument of agricultural prices.

Tackling these problems requires political courage. The Community will only damage itself in the eyes of its own people and the outside world if that courage is lacking.

Europe open to enterprise

My third guiding principle is the need for Community policies which encourage enterprise.

If Europe is to flourish and create the jobs of the future, enterprise is the key. The basic framework is there: the Treaty of Rome itself was intended as a Charter for Economic Liberty.

But that it is not how it has always been read, still less applied. The lesson of the economic history of Europe in the 70's and 80's is that central planning and detailed control do not work and that personal endeavour and initiative do. That a State-controlled economy is a recipe for low growth and that free enterprise within a framework of law brings better results.

The aim of a Europe open to enterprise is the moving force behind the creation of the Single European Market in 1992. By getting rid of barriers, by making it possible for companies to operate on a European scale, we can best compete with the United States, Japan and other new economic powers emerging in Asia and elsewhere.

And that means action to free markets, action to widen choice, action to reduce government intervention.

Our aim should not be more and more detailed regulation from the centre: it should be to deregulate and to remove the constraints on trade.

Britain has been in the lead in opening its markets to others. The City of London has long welcomed financial institutions from all over the world, which is why it is the biggest and most successful financial centre in Europe. We have opened our market for telecommunications equipment, introduced competition into the market services and even into the network itself – steps which others in Europe are only now beginning to face. In air transport, we have taken the lead in liberalisation and seen the benefits in cheaper fares and wider choice. Our coastal shipping trade is open to the merchant navies of Europe. We wish we could say the same of many other Community members.

Regarding monetary matters, let me say this. The key issue is not whether there should be a European Central Bank. The immediate and practical requirements are: to implement the Community's commitment to free movement of capital – in Britain, we have it; and to the abolition through the Community of exchange controls – in Britain, we abolished them in 1979; to establish a genuinely free market in financial services in banking, insurance, investment; and to make greater use of the ecu.

This autumn, Britain is issuing ecu-denominated Treasury bills and hopes to see other Community governments increasingly do the same.

These are the real requirements because they are what the Community business and industry need if they are to compete effectively in the wider world.

And they are what the European consumer wants, for they will widen his choice and lower his costs.

It is to such basic practical steps that the Community's attention should be devoted. When those have been achieved and sustained over a period of time, we shall be in a better position to judge the next move.

It is the same with frontiers between our countries. Of course, we want to make it easier for goods to pass through frontiers. Of course, we must make it easier for people to travel throughout the Community.

But it is a matter of plain common sense that we cannot totally abolish frontier controls if we are also to protect our citizens from crime and stop the movement of drugs, of terrorists and of illegal immigrants.

That was underlined graphically only three weeks ago when one brave German customs officer, doing his duty on the frontier between Holland and Germany, struck a major blow against the terrorists of the IRA.

And before I leave the subject of a single market, may I say that we certainly do not need new regulations which raise the cost of employment and make Europe's labour market less flexible and less competitive with overseas suppliers.

If we are to have a European Company Statute, it should contain the minimum regulations. And certainly we in Britain would fight attempts to introduce collectivism and corporatism at the European level – although what people wish to do in their own countries is a matter for them.

Europe open to the world

My fourth guiding principle is that Europe should not be protectionist.

The expansion of the world economy requires us to continue the process of removing barriers to trade, and to do so in the multilateral negotiations in the GATT. It would be a betrayal if, while breaking down constraints on trade within Europe, the Community were to erect greater external protection.

We must ensure that our approach to world trade is consistent with the liberalisation we preach at home. We have a responsibility to give a lead on this, a responsibility which is particularly directed towards the less developed countries.

They need not only aid; more than anything, they need improved trading opportunities if they are to gain the dignity of growing economic strength and independence.

Europe and defence

My last guiding principle concerns the most fundamental issue – the European countries' role in defence.

Europe must continue to maintain a sure defence through NATO. There can be no question of relaxing our efforts, even though it means taking difficult decisions and meeting heavy costs. It is to NATO that we owe the peace that has been maintained over 40 years.

The fact is things are going our way: the democratic model of a free enterprise society has proved itself superior; freedom is on the offensive, a peaceful offensive the world over, for the first time in my life-time.

We must strive to maintain the United States' commitment to Europe's defence. And that means recognising the burden on their resources of the world role they undertake and their point that their allies should bear the full part of the defence of freedom, particularly as Europe grows wealthier. Increasingly, they will look to Europe to play a part in out-of-area defence, as we have recently done in the Gulf.

NATO and the Western European Union have long recognised where the problems of Europe's defence lie, and have pointed out the solutions. And the time has come when we must give substance to our declarations about a strong defence effort with better value for money.

It is not an institutional problem. It is not a problem of drafting. It is something at once simpler and more profound: it is a question of political will and political courage, of convincing people in all our countries that we cannot rely for ever on others for our defence, but that each member of the Alliance must shoulder a fair share of the burden.

We must keep up public support for nuclear deterrence, remembering that obsolete weapons do not deter, hence the need for modernisation. We must meet the requirements for effective conventional defence in Europe against Soviet forces which are constantly being modernised.

We should develop the WEU, not as an alternative to NATO, but as a means of strengthening Europe's contribution to the common defence of the West.

Above all, at a time of change and uncertainly in the Soviet Union and Eastern Europe, we must preserve Europe's unity and resolve so that whatever may happen, our defence is sure.

At the same time, we must negotiate on arms control and keep the door wide open to cooperation on all the other issues covered by the Helsinki Accords.

But let us never forget that our way of life, our vision and all we hope to achieve, is secured not by the rightness of our cause but by the strength of our defence. On this, we must never falter, never fail.

The British approach

Mr. Chairman, I believe it is not enough just to talk in general terms about a European vision or ideal. If we believe in it, we must chart the way ahead and identify the next steps. And that is what I have tried to do this evening.

This approach does not require new documents: they are all there, the North Atlantic Treaty, the Revised Brussels Treaty and the Treaty of Rome, texts written by far-sighted men, a remarkable Belgian – Paul Henri Spaak – among them.

However far we may want to go, the truth is that we can only get there one step at a time. And what we need now is to take decisions on the next steps forward, rather than let ourselves be distracted by Utopian goals. Utopia never comes, because we know we should not like it if it did.

Let Europe be a family of nations, understanding each other better, appreciating each other more, doing more together but relishing our national identity no less than our common European endeavour.

Let us have a Europe which plays its full part in the wider world, which looks outward not inward, and which preserves that Atlantic community – that Europe on both sides of the Atlantic – which is our noblest inheritance and our greatest strength.

May I thank you for the privilege of delivering this lecture in this great hall to this great college.

Source: *Margaret Thatcher Foundation: COI transcript*
http://www.margaretthatcher.org/document/107332

Note

1. Speech given to the College of Europe.

Extracts from a speech in the European Parliament

Václav Havel

Strasbourg, 8 March 1994

Mr. Chairman,
Members of Parliament,

I am most grateful to you for the honour of addressing the European Parliament, and I can scarcely think of a better way of using this opportunity than to try to answer three questions. First, why is the Czech Republic, which I represent here, requesting membership in the European Union? Secondly, why is it in the interest of all of Europe to expand the European Union? And thirdly, what, in my opinion, are the more general tasks confronting the European Union today?

Europe is a continent of extraordinary variety and diversity geographically, ethnically, nationally, culturally, economically and politically. Yet at the same time all its parts are and always have been so deeply linked by their destiny that this continent can accurately be described as a single albeit complex political entity. Anything crucial in any area of human endeavour occurring anywhere in Europe always has had both direct and indirect consequences for our continent as a whole. The history of Europe is, in fact, the history of a constant searching and reshaping of its internal structures and the relationship of its parts. Today, if we talk about a single European civilization or about common European values, history, traditions, and destiny, what we are referring to is more the fruit of this tendency toward integration than its cause.

From time immemorial, Europe has had something that can be called an inner order, consisting of a specific system of political relations that circumscribed it and tried in one way or another to institutionalize its natural interconnectedness. This European order, however, usually was established by violence. The more powerful simply imposed it upon those less powerful. In this sense, the endless series of wars in Europe can be understood as an expression of the constant effort to alter the status quo and replace one order with another. From the ancient Roman Empire, through the Holy Roman Empire, and down to the power systems created by the Congress of Vienna, the Treaty of Versailles and finally by Yalta all these were merely historical attempts to give European coexistence a certain set of game rules. A thousand times in its history Europe has been unified or divided in various ways; a thousand times one group has subjected another, forced its version of civilization on another and established self-serving political relations; a thousand times Europe's internal balance has been dramatically sought, found, transformed, and torn down. And a thousand times the French, the Swedes, the Germans or the Czechs have dealt with apparently internal matters, only to have their actions affect the rest of Europe.

I do not believe, therefore, that the idea of a European Union simply fell out of the sky, or was born in the laboratory of political theoreticians or on the drawing boards of political engineers. It grew quite naturally out of an understanding that European integrity was a fact of life, and from the efforts of many generations of Europeans to project the idea of unity into a specific "supranational" European structure.

We may all be different, but we are all in the same boat. We can fight for our places and means of coexistence on this boat, but we also can agree on them peacefully. I understand European unity as a magnanimous attempt to choose the second of these possibilities, and to give Europe for the first time in its history the kind of order that would grow out of the free will of everyone, and be based on mutual agreement and a common longing for peace and cooperation. It would be a stable and solid order, one based not merely on military and political treaties, which anyone can break or ignore at will, but on such a close cooperation between European nations and citizens that it would limit, if not exclude, the possibility of new conflicts. This is not a mere dream. Soon half a century will separate us from the end of the Second World War. During that time all of Western Europe has successfully averted the threat of many potential conflicts, precisely by building, step by step, such an integrating system.

This alone is enough to demonstrate that this newest type of European order is not, or need not be, a mere utopia, but that it can work in real terms.

I do not perceive the European Union as a monstrous super-state in which the autonomy of all the various nations, states, ethnic groups, cultures, and regions of Europe would gradually be dissolved. On the contrary, I see it as the systematic creation of a space that allows the autonomous components of Europe to develop freely and in their own way in an environment of lasting security and mutually beneficial cooperation based on principles of democracy, respect for human rights, civil society, and an open market economy.

The Czech Lands lie at the very centre of Europe and some-times even think of themselves as its very heart. For this reason, they have always been a particularly exposed place, unavoid-ably involved in any European conflict. In fact, many European conflicts began or ended there. Like a number of other Central European countries, we have always been a dramatic crossroads of all kinds of European intellectual and spiritual currents and geopolitical interests. This makes us particularly sensitive to the fact that everything that happens in Europe intrinsically concerns us, and that everything that happens to us intrinsically concerns all of Europe. We are among the expert witnesses to the political reality of Europe's interconnectedness. That is why our sense of co-responsibility for what happens in Europe is especially strong, and also why we are intensely aware that the prospect of European integration presents an enormous historic opportunity to Europe as a whole, and to us.

I think I have essentially answered my first question that is, why the Czech Republic wants to become a member of the European Union. Yes, we are able and happy to surrender a portion of our sovereignty in favour of the commonly administered sovereignty of the European Union, because we know it will repay us many times over, as it will all Europeans. The part of the world we live in can hope for a gradual transformation from an arena of eternally warring rulers, powers, nations, social classes and religious doctrines, competing for territories of influence or hegemony, into a forum of down-to-earth dialogue and effective cooperation between all its inhabitants in a commonly shared, commonly administered and commonly cultivated space dedicated to coexistence and solidarity.

I believe my thoughts about the interconnectedness of Europe have, to a considerable degree, answered the second question as well: why the European Union should gradually expand. Europe was divided artificially, by force, and for that very reason its division had to collapse sooner or later. History has thrown down a gauntlet we can, if we wish, pick up. If we do not do so, a great opportunity to create a continent of free and peaceful cooperation may be lost. Only a fool who has learned nothing from the millennia of European history can believe that tranquillity, peace and prosperity can flourish forever in one part of Europe without regard for what is happening in the other. The era of the Cold War, when the enforced cohesion of the Soviet Bloc contributed to the cohesion of the West, is definitively over.

We must all accept that the world is radically different today than it was five years ago. The vision of Europe as a stabilizing factor in the contemporary international environment, one that does not export war to the rest of the world but rather radiates the idea of peaceful coexistence, cannot become reality if Europe as a whole is not transformed. The gauntlet simply must be taken up. What is going on in the former Yugoslavia should be a grave reminder to any of us who think that in Europe we can ignore with impunity what is going on next door. Unrest, chaos and violence are infectious and expansionary. We Central Europeans have directly felt the truth of this countless times, and I think it is our responsibility repeatedly to draw others' attention to this experience, especially those fortunate enough not to have undergone it as often as we have.

Western Europe has been moving toward its present degree of integration for nearly fifty years. It is clear that new members, particularly those attempting to shed the consequences of Communist rule, cannot be accepted overnight into the European Union without seriously threatening to tear the delicate threads from which it is woven. Nevertheless, the prospect of its expansion, and of the expansion of its influence and spirit, is in its intrinsic interest and in the intrinsic interest of Europe as a whole. There is simply no meaningful alternative to this trend. Anything else would be a return to the times when European order was not a work of consensus but of violence. And the evil demons are lying in wait. A vacuum, the decay of values, the fear of freedom, suffering and poverty, chaos these are the environments in which they flourish. They must not be given that opportunity.

For if the future European order does not emerge from a broadening European Union, based on the best European values and willing to defend and transmit them, it could well happen that the organization of this future will fall into the hands of a cast of fools, fanatics, populists and demagogues waiting for their chance and determined to promote the worst European traditions. And there are, unfortunately, more than enough of those.

Members of Parliament,

Allow me now to turn to the third question I have posed. That is, the question of the tasks with which, in my opinion, the European Union is now confronted. There are certainly many of them, and all of them are difficult. One, however, appears to me especially important, and it is this I would like to talk about.

I confess that when I studied the Maastricht Treaty and the other documents on which the European Union is based, I had a somewhat ambiguous response. On the one hand, it is undoubtedly a respectable piece of work. It is scarcely possible to believe that a common framework could be given to such a complex and diverse legal and economic order, involving so many different European countries. It is amazing that common rules of the game have been created, that all the legislative, administrative and institutional mechanisms that enable the smooth running of this great body have been invented and that, in so colourful a political environment, agreement on an enormous number of concrete matters was reached and many different interests harmonized in a way that will benefit everyone. It is, I repeat, a remarkable labour of the human spirit and its rational capacities.

However, into my admiration, which initially verged on enthusiasm, there began to intrude a disturbing, less exuberant feeling. I felt I was looking into the inner workings of an absolutely perfect and immensely ingenious modern machine. To study such a machine must be a great joy to an admirer of technical inventions, but for me, whose interest in the world is not satisfied by admiration for well-oiled machines, something was seriously missing, something that could be called, in a rather simplified way, a spiritual or moral or emotional dimension. The treaty addressed my reason, but not my heart.

Naturally, I am not claiming that an affirmation of the European Union can be found in a reading of its documents and norms alone. They are only a formal framework to define the living realities that are its primary concern. And the positive aspects of those realities far outweigh whatever dry official texts can offer. Still, I cannot help feeling that my sensation of being confronted with nothing more than a perfect machine is somehow significant; that this feeling indicates something or challenges us in some way.

The large empires, complex supranational entities or confederations of states that we know from history, those which, in their time, contributed something of value to humanity, were remarkable not only because of how they were administered or organized, but also because they were always buoyed by a spirit, an idea, an ethos I would even say by a charismatic quality out of which their structure ultimately grew. For such entities to work and be vital, they always had to offer, and indeed did offer, some key to emotional identification, an ideal that would speak to people or inspire them, a set of generally understandable values that everyone could share. These values made it worthwhile for people to make sacrifices for the entity that embodied them, even, in extreme circumstances, the sacrifice of their very lives.

The European Union is based on a large set of values, with roots in antiquity and in Christianity, which over 2,000 years evolved into what we recognize today as the foundations of modern democracy, the rule of law and civil society. This set of values has its own clear moral foundation and its obvious metaphysical roots, whether modern man admits it or not. Thus it cannot be said that the European Union lacks a spirit from which all the concrete principles on which it is founded grow. It appears, though, that this spirit is rather difficult to see. It seems too hidden behind the mountains of systemic, technical, administrative, economic, monetary and other measures that contain it. And thus, in the end, many people might be left with the understandable impression that the European Union to put it a bit crudely is no more than endless arguments over how many carrots can be exported from somewhere, who sets the amount, who checks it and who will eventually punish delinquents who contravene the regulations.

That is why it seems to me that perhaps the most important task facing the European Union today is coming up with a new and genuinely clear reflection on what might be called European identity, a new and genuinely clear articulation of European responsibility, an intensified interest in the very meaning of European integration in all its wider implications for the contemporary world, and the re-creation of its ethos or, if you like, its charisma.

Reading the Maastricht Treaty, for all its historical importance, will hardly win enthusiastic supporters for the European

Union. Nor will it win over patriots, people who will genuinely experience this complex organism as their native land or their home, or as one aspect of their home. If this great administrative work, which should obviously simplify life for all Europeans, is to hold together and stand the tests of time, then it must be visibly bonded by more than a set of rules and regulations. It must embody, far more clearly than it has so far, a particular relationship to the world, to human life and ultimately to the world order. Far more clearly than before, it must impress upon millions of European souls an idea, a historical mission and a momentum. It must clearly articulate the values upon which it is founded and which it intends to defend and cultivate. It also must take care to create emblems and symbols, visible bearers of its significance.

It should be perfectly clear to everyone that this is not just a conglomerate of states created for purely utilitarian reasons, but an entity that in an original way fulfils the longings of many generations of enlightened Europeans who knew that European universalism can when projected into political reality become the framework for a more responsible human existence on our continent. More than that, it is the way to achieve the genuine inclusion of our continent as a partner in the multicultural environment of contemporary global civilization.

Naturally, my intention is not to advise the European Union on what it should do. I can only say what I, as a European, would welcome.

I would welcome it, for instance, if the European Union were to establish a charter of its own that would clearly define the ideas on which it is founded, its meaning and the values it intends to embody. Clearly, the basis of such a charter could be nothing other than a definitive moral code for European citizens. All those hundreds of pages of agreements on which the European Union is founded would thus be brought under the umbrella of a single, crystal-clear and universally understandable political document that would make it obvious at once what the European Union really is. At the same time, it also would be to its advantage if it were made even more obvious who represents it and embodies and guarantees its values. If the citizens of Europe understand that this is not just an anonymous bureaucratic monster to limit or even deny their autonomy, but simply a new type of human community that actually broadens their freedom significantly, then the European Union need not fear for its future.

You will certainly understand that at this moment my concern is not so much any particular suggestion but something deeper: how to make the spirit of the European Union more vivid and compelling, more accessible to all. For it seems to me that this is a project of such historical importance that it would be an unforgivable sin were it to languish and ultimately disappoint the hopes invested in it only because its very meaning were drowned in disputes over technical details.

Ladies and gentlemen,

I have come from a land that did not enjoy freedom and democracy for almost sixty years. You will perhaps believe me when I say that it is this historical experience that has allowed me to respond at the deepest level to the revolutionary meaning of European integration today. And perhaps you will believe me when I say that the very depth of that experience compels me to express concern for the proper outcome of this process and to consider ways to strengthen it and make it irreversible.

Allow me, in conclusion, to thank you for approving the Europe Agreement on the association of the Czech Republic with the European Union two weeks after it was signed. In doing so, you have shown that you are not indifferent to the fate of my country.

Source: *Historical Archives European Parliament, 1994. No. 3-445/60.*

Extracts from a speech in the European Parliament

François Mitterrand

Strasbourg, 17 January 1995

Mr President, ladies and gentlemen, as you are aware, of course, since 1 January this year, France has held the presidency of the European Union.

[...]

I represent France, a country which is conscious of the threats surrounding it in this context, and which is well acquainted with the rivalry of languages. When I think of other peoples, however, which are equally deserving of respect, but whose languages are not as geographically widespread as French, which in turn is not as geographically widespread as some other languages, I wonder what will become of the soul, the means of expression of, for instance, Gaelic, Flemish or Dutch?

And, since I do not wish to appear to be referring only to the nations which are the smallest or weakest, because they are the least populous – and this is not a question of demography – I would say that in fact, if we really think about it, Italy, Germany and France are also under threat. Today, possibly only Anglo-American culture and Spanish culture are in a position to face up to these challenges. And, not withstanding my friendship for these countries, I would rather speak my own language than theirs.

Firstly, let us consider the audio-visual sector. Perhaps you think that I am being excessively partisan? I hope not. We are all conscious of the fact that in the audio-visual sector, awareness, imagination and knowledge are increasingly being shaped by images, and that there will be no Europe without European images. At a time when we are celebrating the centenary of the cinema, the most popular art form of the century has never been under greater threat in all our countries. In some of these countries, moreover, there is no longer a threat, because the film industry has already disappeared. Community assistance was unable to halt the decline. It was not able to encourage the creation of a genuine European audio-visual area or to provide our countries' industries in this sector with an international dimension.

It is a matter of urgency to increase the appeal and promote the circulation of works produced within the European Union. I am not calling for protective measures. I do not wish to deny the considerable and frequently remarkable contribution of culture from outside the Union, but the European public have the right to see the works of their own creative artists. They cannot be deprived of this right because of arbitrary decisions taken elsewhere, or because of the logic of a blind market – or the blind logic of the market. I have no wish to offend anyone. Achieving this goal requires ambitious reforms, which are made inevitable by the new technological and economic environment. We must put an end to the dispersal of our efforts. We must focus our assistance on certain priorities – in particular, distribution. We must adept the nature and volume of the resources to the scale of the task. Is the House aware that the ECU 200 million allocated to the MEDIA programme represents only one day's worth of Community spending?

The French presidency will endeavor to achieve some of these goals. But six months – what can be done in just six months? Perhaps this should lead us to review the length of the mandate given to the various presidencies – although I am not asking for any extension of my own.

[...]

The French presidency will give its backing to an overhaul of the legal framework for audio-visual broadcasting. It will promote the development of new technologies and their application in the areas of culture and education. It will apply itself to reorganizing in depth the system of aid for the broadcasting industries. I must stress that this a subject which is close to my heart. We cannot be satisfied with the existing level of resources. Even less can we move backwards in relation to what was achieved in 1989, with the "Television without Frontiers" directive, and in 1993, with the GATT agreements. I hear some people say that we should give up everything in the name of some sort of freedom of trade. I hear some people say that we should abandon broadcasting quotas, change nothing in the media sector – in short, "laisser faire". Well that is not the opinion of France.

However, moving images are not the only area in which the Europe of cultures is being built. There is a need for Europe to be better known – I would go so far as to say better loved – by its people. I am returning here to an earlier part of my speech. The people of Europe must love Europe. Why, in the past, have their defended their native land – and they must continue to do so if necessary? Because they love it. And why do they love their native land? Because it represents their home, their scenery, their landscape, their friends, their identity. If Europe lacks all this, there will be no Europe. But we know that it is within our reach, if we prove capable of taking Europe forward with sufficient courage and, if necessary, sufficient caution.

I would repeat that moving images are not, of course, the only area in which the Europe of cultures is being built. To strengthen our approach, let us rediscover those places and objects which represent our common past. I should like to see the devising and implementation of a vast project to develop the sites of our European heritage. At the same time, let us teach about Europe. Let us educate our children on the subject. Let our schools prepare them for citizenship. Let them develop the teaching of history, geography and culture. Let us encourage the twinning of schools and universities, exchanges of schoolchildren and students. Let us stress the importance of multilingualism. To this end, France will be submitting a draft intergovernmental convention on the teaching of at least two foreign languages. At the same time, let us step up our efforts to promote the translation of written works. I have long observed that the French, my fellow country-men, frequently complain that their great authors are seldom translated in, for example, some of the countries of Central and Eastern Europe. And I have also observed that in fact, we, the French, do not translate their works either: we complain of a fault of which we ourselves are guilty – because the Europe of cultures is the whole of Europe.

If there is any area in which the distinction between the European union and Central and Eastern Europe makes no sense, it is this. I would therefore like to submit the following two proposals to the House. The first, which is a modest one, but practical and specific, can be implemented immediately. Let us extend to all the countries of Europe those cultural measures which are symbolic of the Europe of fifteen: literary prizes, translation prizes, youth orchestras, the European capital of culture, to mention but a few. The second is more ambitious. I believe that the European Union should adopt a large-scale initiative designed to help our neighbours in Central and Eastern Europe to make good – especially in the area of culture – the effects of the isolation in which they lived for half a century. A European cultural foundation or agency could draw up an original programme of cooperation with these countries, backed with considerable resources, designed to foster the preservation of their heritage, the renovation of their libraries and museums, the rebuilding of their audio-visual production and broadcasting capacities, and the promotion of creative works and live performances. These countries are rich in creative artists. Their efforts were long frustrated, through no fault of their own, but simply because they were dominated by more powerful people, who had no interest in such things. It is our duty to come to their assistance when they need it. Then we must have confidence in them: they will make their way perfectly well on their own. We must not attempt to lecture them, but instead to learn from them. In this way, we shall show that, far from being eroded, the cultural identity of nations that is reinforced by the process of European integration. The Europe of cultures, ladies and gentlemen, is a Europe of nations as opposed to a Europe of nationalism.

[...]

I thank you for your patience and attention with which you have been kind enough to listen to me, and I should like to finish with a few remarks of a more personal nature. Fate would have it that I was born during the First World War and fought in the Second. I therefore spent my childhood in the surroundings of families torn apart, all of them mourning loved ones and feeling great bitterness, if not hatred towards the recent enemy, the traditional enemy. However, ladies and gentlemen, such enemies have changed from century to century, as traditions have always changed. I have had occasion to say to this House before that France has engaged in wars with every European country, with the exception, I believe, of Denmark. We have to wonder why...

But my generation has almost completed its work; it is carrying out its last public acts, and this will be one of my last. It is therefore vital to us to pass on our experience. Many of you will remember the teaching of your parents, will have felt the suffering of your countries, will have experienced the grief, the pain of separation, the presence of death – all as a result of the mutual enmity of the peoples of Europe. It is vital to pass on not this hatred, but, on the contrary, the opportunity for reconciliation which we have, thanks – it must be said – to those who, after 1944-45, themselves blood-stained and with their personal lives destroyed, had the courage to envisage a more radiant future which would be based on peace and reconciliation. That is what we have done.

However, I did not acquire my own convictions in this way, by chance. I did not acquire them in the German prisoner-of-war camps in which I was a captive, or in a country which itself was occupied – a situation which many of you will have experienced. I remember that even families which practiced the virtues of humanity, of kindness, spoke with animosity when they talked about the Germans. When I was an escaped prisoner of war – or rather, when I was in the process of escaping – I met some Germans, then I spent some time in a prison in Baden-Württemberg, and I used to talk to the people, Germans, there and I came to realize that the Germans liked the French more than the French liked the Germans.

I say this without wishing to denigrate my country, which is no more nationalistic than any other, far from it. I say this to make it clear that, at that time, everyone saw the world from his or her own viewpoint, and that those viewpoints were generally distorting. We must overcome such prejudices. What I am asking you to do is almost impossible, because it means overcoming our past. And yet, if we fail to overcome our past, let there be no mistake about what will follow: ladies and gentlemen, nationalism means war!

War is not only our past, it could also be our future! And it is us, it is you, ladies and gentlemen, the Members of the European Parliament, who will henceforth be the guardians of our peace, our security and our future!

Source: *Historical Archives European Parliament, 1995. No. 4-456/45.*

The Special Quality of Europe is Culture

György Konrád

2001

What is the role of culture in European Integration? Permanent and determining. Coherent European culture existed before European economic and political association, since the former depends on relationships between individuals, while the latter depends upon relationships between states, and individuals come together easier than states.

Europe's innovation – cultural pluralism – is victorious world-wide. It is a tendency parallel to the spread of philosophy of human rights, whose basis is a requirement to respect the human individual.

Europe's special quality is no plan, but rather something which already exists: a sensitive attraction to diversity, kept coherent by European humanism. This pluralist sensitivity penetrates to the details, all the way to the core of personality and to all of its momentary states. At the same time, it does not break with those fundamental principles, outgrowths of Judeo-Christian and antique-humanist traditions, which have been rationalized by European worldly thought since the Enlightenment. Europe's special quality lies in the balance between the universal and the particular, the general and the specific, the shared and the individual.

What unites Europe? Is it only the community of economic interest? Ideologies were unable to unite the continent. Neither the nationalist-socialist nor the communist-socialist vision provided an appropriate basis for unification. Both were destructive fantasies, and both meant submission of the European people to the power centers of those two experiments. The crazy

20th century is now closed and, with it, the history of the two world wars and the shadow of a third. We are through with two ideological utopias, the nationalist and the communist. Both killed many and eventually succumbed. And what is there now? Is ideology absent?

Europe owes its success to respect for pluralism which recognized the mutual dependency of mankind and is able to bow before a child. European pluralism learns to accept and love people in their uniqueness.

This humanism takes into account our mortality and respects the dignity of the personal, single lifetime. The European faces death individually, with relatively little hedging, little hedging, little consolation of after-life, reincarnation, or being lifted to a place where we will partake of all manner of corporeal and spiritual joy. The personality no longer escapes to a collective next world, it does not transcend itself in nations, empires, corporations – but imparts increasing weight to our presence here, to our individual earthly life, and feels no obligation to regard life in the here and now as a vale of tears.

Europe is really a community of values. Our greatest treasure, our "wonder weapon" is European humanism, which reckons with the variety and sovereignty of human realities and personalities. European pluralism is a tendency of societal development which has wintered centuries and remains irrepressibly valid. It signifies the separation of intellectual and physical power, the separation of religion and state, the concord for protection of individuals' legal rights against public authority and it signifies the venturing independence of citizens.

Europe's special quality is the emancipation of the individual, liberation from the compelling authority of religious-ideological modes of thought which were deemed obligatory. Rule that is ideological, nationalist, communist, fundamentalist, theocratic – in a word, rule governed by ideas discriminates on the basis of loyalty to the ideas themselves, and does not ensure equal rights for citizens. A society that is enlightened, realistic, worldly, pluralist, and willing to negotiate is the result of a long process:

it is a slow-growing plant. The reliability of the civilized citizen denotes an inner value system for whose survival fear of punishment is insufficient.

Europe was united by the community of reflection. The classics are one family. There were no national boundaries in the arts; rules need borders. Works of art do not cry out for borders, on the contrary, their diffusion is promoted when borders are less and less significant, and more and more virtual. In general, material-physical obstacles to contact between people are weakening, while media which link, convey and interpret are gaining in strength. Cultural values, words and signs cannot be kept within borders. Cultural traffic, too, has become global.

Europeans think with their entire individual and collective past, and this experience is present in their instinctive sympathies or antipathies. The work of thought is influenced by values and their hierarchy. What are our ideals, and which are our highest values, which standpoints are subordinate to other considerations?

We are not functioning machines. No person really knows only one language, a banker is not only about money, and engineer not only about technology, a musician not only about music, a chef not only about cooking and a mother not only about child rearing. Every person is a complete universe, every leaf is a unique whole; the real challenge of the spirit to use a gentle touch in discovering the secrets of the personality.

The era of reductionism is past. The more daring intellectual achievement is to comprehend another person, or another person's work in its own complexity, and not the malicious enjoyment of recognizing that it can be taken apart or deconstructed.

Post-modern value relativity must not cast doubt on the universal requirement to respect the human individual, nor on the universal validity of acknowledging human rights.

On the basis of post-modern value relativity, all types of crime may be sanctioned as the needs of a special character. Naturally, passions and arguments stand behind all acts. We may regard them with understanding, even with empathy, until they conflict with the universal and absolute requirement of protection of human life, which may be disregarded only as the result of exceptional inner blindness.

If those in developed nations say: "For me, democracy and electrical power are necessary; tyranny and candlelight are good enough for the less advanced", they speak as lords spoke of serfs, saying leftovers were good enough for them.

Value relativity renders uncertain not only European integration, but the entire complex of international agreements. The productive position is dialogue, tension and drama between universal values and empathy which flexibly understands relativities. We must not concede either pole of the opposition. The essence of Europe is *brains over brawn*. After going through the barbarian accumulation of quantity, we are on an expedition of discovery toward the unencumbered, the immaterial, the virtual; we are on our way from the world of quantity to the world of quality, which requires more complex intelligence, more ingenious associations, and a higher civilizational level, along with a philosophy which fathoms the material environment.

According to one thesis, in the 21st century quality will be emphasized more and quantity correspondingly less. Well-turned reflection as opposed to crude mass. This process will be accompanied by the strengthening of the sovereignty of culture.

We will experience the revolt of personal thought against passive consumption of information. The eclipsing of the propensity toward quantity in consumption by the demand for quality in consumption is already perceptible. Personality wishes to leave its mark on every object. It wants to, because this is its role, and is its immortality.

Acting on a guilty conscience, the intelligentsia cast doubt on the value of knowledge as opposed to ignorance. It is not true that freedom must denote comfortable vulgarity. Freedom is understanding ourselves and others, and self-restraint above all. It is not selfish, exclusively passive, chattering randomness. An active, initiating role for the intelligentsia is proper in a democracy; the intelligentsia is even allowed to be strict in democracy.

Restraint on the part of mankind is the end goal for survival of the species. The objective of European integration is European self-restraint: that we should not kill each other, that we should make war against each other. If we do not make war, we will be compelled to understand each other.

Cities are emblems of European pluralism. It is truly miraculous that so many nations live together, that cohabitation of so many kinds of human will not create a madhouse. In cities, the widest variety of forces and intentions are able to live together instead of killing each other. No party has exclusive rule and the secret is compromise borne of dialogue. Our exceptional inheritance is worldly urbanity, along with recognition of our diversity and the theatrical nature of the soul.

We live together with our ambivalence and our mysteries, regarding them not as unfortunate, or as criminal, but rather as fortunate gifts. Our societies are increasingly diverse, yet they do not lose their coherence. From the outside, coherent pluralism, or the comprehension of inner contradictions may seem like cynism, but this is a reflection of a distorted mirror, the opposite of reality.

Cultural-artistic activity has accompanied European history throughout, art always was and doubtless always will be. Artists from one society. We know of each other. The existing media already connect European culture and intimate familiarity of the societal-cultural network. Cultural integration progresses without any special outside help.

But why shouldn't we help? In the interests of Europe becoming one broader homeland, culture can do the most, and has done the most up to now. Moreover, cultural union is the least expensive and progresses most organically.

The feeling of being related, a kind of European interweaving, develops almost automatically, taking possession of that which it has seen in other countries as well. Identities are becoming differentiated in both directions. Affinities are formulated both above and below the level of nation-states. The European community has its own conscience, but a small village does too.

One sign of European differentiation is the mushrooming of local newspapers and television stations, creating numerous lively forums in small communities. Rather than contradicting each other, the European tradition and the tradition of small cities reinforce each other.

Every small city has its own artist subculture, society, circle of friends, forum, publication, meeting place, workshop, bar, habits. Artists come in swarms and societies of artists have their own unmistakable intimate style. I don't think we need fear that special characters will be dissolved into the European mass.

Following the warrier, the ideal has become the venturer, who may be characterized by talent, ideas and original insights rather than great material wealth. The talented venture will have as much money as he or she needs. The venture fills up a lifetime. And that lifetime is the greatest value, it is our granted, inherited asset.

If the manufacturers of toothpaste seduce, we shall seduce as well. The objectives of the intelligentsia are compatible with capitalist market economies and political democracy, and with the viewpoint of human rights, since we are only able to work in democracy, and only in a democracy do we have access to information and networks. This framework is suitable for us.

If there is to be competition, let it be so, let us compete, let us measure our values, our tastes, our norms, our ability to comprehend, our tests. The intellectual who sulks and whines in the corner belongs to yesterday.

Wealth exists for the sake of culture and not the other way around. Culture is imperious, it demands we improve our lives, puts us through trials, and spurs us to higher goals.

I'm willing to risk making the supposition that in the age of quality, industrial society will be supplanted by artistic society, in which pragmatic thought too, must apply artistic modes of association in order to operate successfully.

The utopia of everyday life is contained within European worldly humanism. Utopia is life itself, without any qualification: survival, continuity, ordinary days. Utopia was here and we participated in it. Some of its constituents were conflict, sadness, and natural death which generally came too early.

Source: *Epilogue in Wolfgang Beck, Laurent J.G. van der Maesen, Fleur Thomése, and Alan Walker (eds.), Social Quality: A Vision for Europe (The Hague, London, Boston: Kluwer Law International, 2001), pp. 369-374.*

The Europe of Melancholy

Tomasso Padoa-Schioppa

2006

When I began to think about what I wanted to say to you here today,[1] my thoughts went back forty years to the time when I was at the Bocconi University in Milan. To tell the truth, it is hard to believe that it is so long since I was a student. Today, my thoughts are with the young people currently attending university, and above all with those, perhaps a considerable number, who are still unsure as to what to do after university, as to how they might combine necessity with freedom, the need to earn a living with their desire to serve a cause they believe in, and to be public-spirited in both the private and public spheres of their working lives.

I was drawn to the Bocconi as a result of my decision – influenced in part by my reading of Luigi Einaudi's *Il buongoverno*[2] – to study economics, a discipline that could accommodate my disparate and vague interests and motivations: a scientific but at the same time a humanistic field, knowledge and action, polis and home.

I subsequently chose public service, and not research, business or politics. I say "chose" because my generation, as it entered the working world in the 1970s, really did have the possibility to choose; in this, we were exceptionally fortunate, perhaps the most fortunate generation of the past century. Italy, in its transition from a poor country of peasants and subsistence farmers, consumers of their own products, into a modern transformation economy, highly competitive in the nascent European market, created a wealth of jobs and opportunities for graduates and non graduates alike. The fears and resistance, strong in the industrial and academic worlds, of those who had warned that we were not strong enough to rise to the European challenge were belied.

The politicians were more farsighted than the ruling class which often regarded them with arrogance, as it also does today.

I would like to talk to students about today's and tomorrow's Europe and suggest that they take Europe as a point of reference both in their working lives, whatever profession or line of work they may enter, and in their lives as Italian citizens, irrespective of their political leanings: in short, as a professional, cultural, political and civil point of reference. This is the subject of my discourse.

I am well aware that proposing Europe, to say nothing of European political union, as a point of reference in the current historical phase amounts to swimming against the tide: Europe is not a fashionable idea, and it is indeed perceived by many as a hopeless one. However, I am also aware that the very prospect of swimming against the tide can appeal to, or at least intrigue, some young people. Yet, I am not seeking to appeal to a vein of dissension here, but rather to the critical spirit, to the desire to view the world with passion while also, dispassionately, looking at it with far-sighted judiciousness.

The Black Bile

Spheres such as politics, economics, the institutions, and associationism are the ones in which Europe seems to live and grow. Europe talks about trade, competition, technical regulations, subsidies, currency, and unemployment; on a more specifically political and institutional level, it talks about Parliament, the Commission, voting procedures, enlargement and majorities. So why am I proposing, as the central thread of my reflections here, the idea of melancholy, which seems to belong not to these areas, but rather to the life of the individual? A malaise so private that the melancholy themselves strive to hide it from the world?

I have chosen it because this state of mind, ancient, mysterious and ambivalent, perhaps characterises better than any other the phase that Europe, in all its greatness and all its dejection, is currently living through. In short, I do not believe that Europe is melancholy because it is in a state of crisis; on the contrary, I believe that Europe is in a state of crisis because our society is melancholic. This is true of economics, and also of politics.

In fact, for over twenty-five centuries, the black bile has preoccupied Europe's physicians, philosophers, artists, theologians and psychologists, and they have probed the question with a depth and constancy not matched in other cultures. Perhaps melancholy is a peculiarly European trait: if we can manage to understand it, perhaps this understanding might help us to find a way out of the present difficulties.

Society, like the individual, can be affected by diseases that weaken the body and the spirit; it, too, is overcome by states of mind that influence its course and its choices. By probing the gloomy depths where these states of mind live and identifying the nature of the current disease we are better able to understand the phenomena that manifest themselves on the surface, in the political and economic spheres, too. We can talk of the mood of society and of the mood of an individual. We talk of euphoria on the markets, and we can talk of Europe's melancholy. "Depression" is a technical term used both in economics and in psychology, two disciplines whose relationship has been recognised by the Nobel Prize.

What is more, the earliest reflections on melancholy and on the influence of Saturn sought a common basis for the microcosm and the macrocosm. And in Robert Burton's famous treatise on melancholy (*The Anatomy of Melancholy*), we read that kingdoms, provinces, political bodies are equally sensitive and subject to this disease, as widely demonstrated by Botero in his politics. He says: "as in the human body, there are various alterations determined by different humours, thus there are many diseases in the community" as is easily intuited from the specific symptoms.[3]

So, Europe today seems sick above all with melancholy. I cite, first of all, its main symptoms: loss of faith, inaction, loss of interest in the outside world, a withdrawing into itself, and low self-esteem. There is also the introverted nature of the condition: Freud, distinguishing between mourning and melancholy, remarked that in mourning, the world is impoverished and void, in melancholy it is the Ego itself that is impoverished and void.[4] Finally, I think of melancholy as a characteristic trait of extraordinary natures, those drawn to the absolute, the disease of heroes (Gellio), of spiritual exaltation (Plato), and of excellence (Aristotle). Certainly, it is a loss of faith, but of a faith that has solid foundations. As Kierkegaard writes "Never, ever has the thought occurred to me that, among all my contemporaries, there was one more alone than me [...] and deep down inside, I was, in my eyes, the most miserable of all".[5]

Interestingly, the unique and ambivalent nature of melancholy is confirmed by the fact that, in the section on synonyms and opposites, the Devoto-Oli (dictionary of the Italian language) contains no entry for "melancholy".

The Chronicles of Crisis

If, conducting a search of the daily Italian and international press for the past six months, we were to combine the words "Europe" and "crisis", Google would come up with an almost endless list of references. Perhaps "Europe" would show the highest correlation with the word "crisis", ahead of words such as "oil", "Iraq", "employment", "soccer" and "Alitalia".

We hear the sound of funeral bells ringing for Europe on a daily basis, every time we open a newspaper or turn on the television. On the rare occasions that the bells instead ring joyfully, the celebratory tone that accompanies them is so irritating as to leave one almost favourably disposed towards the anti-European rhetoric of those commentators who, in their editorials, delight in the devaluation or revaluation of the euro, the disharmony over Iraq, the violation of the stability pact, the low turnout at the European polling stations, France's rejection of the Constitutional Treaty, and the endless squabbles between the governments.

In recent years I have made a mental note of a great many instances in which illustrious papers like *The Financial Times*, after devoting four front-page columns to announcements of imminent European disasters, have, a few days later, devoted just a few sober lines, tucked away at the bottom of page 4, to the averting of that same disaster: I refer to issues such as the switch to the euro, the European Convention, and the enlargement of the European Union. Similarly, I recall the insistent way in which – a few days after the entry into circulation of the first euro banknotes – TV journalists, interviewing people in the streets, encouraged them to complain about the difficulties they were encountering, yet the people questioned, whether in Paris, Dublin, Milan or Hamburg, responded with smiles and expressed enthusiasm over the historic event that was the arrival of the single currency.

Bad news makes us depressed. Yet, in its turn, bad news – indeed, the fact that bad news makes a good news story – is the fruit of the black bile that is currently pervading European society, making it, as it were, lacking in appetite, bored with consuming, with investing, with generating offspring, with conceiving ambitious plans, and with seeking to look far ahead. When I use the expression "European society" I am clearly referring to a *geographical* and *social* space, but today it is easy to confuse this space with the fragile political construction that we call the "European Union", and to direct all our bile at it, and at the promise of "ever closer union" that it contains.

Thus we enter the spiral of melancholy. Employment levels fail to increase and it is all the fault of the rules decided in Brussels (the same rules that, for over thirty years, have favoured growth levels far superior to those recorded in the United States). We face the threat of terrorism, and pin the blame on the Schengen Agreement (the same agreement that has allowed Italy to reorganise and strengthen its border controls). Globalisation is transforming the world and getting rid of barriers; yet we say that it is Europe that is eliminating barriers and suppressing languages, traditions and local production. Bureaucracy gets on the nerves of citizens and businesses and we complain about "Brussels red tape", forgetting that the Italian region of Lombardy, or the city of Munich for example, each have more employees than the European Commission in Brussels does. Perhaps because it is a rainy city, even the rain is blamed on Brussels, not only by the political class, which has the excuse of wanting to avoid courting unpopularity, but also by the intelligentsia, from which we might legitimately expect a more dispassionate analysis.

The Literature of Success

This, however, is only part of the picture. Because while, on the one hand, the daily news relentlessly rehashes the sad story of the European crisis, on the other there is emerging a growing body of political writings – in the form of essays and books rather than newspaper articles and TV reports – that tells an entirely different tale, and that we might call the literature of success. It analyses all that Europe has done in the fields of economics, the institutions, international relations, state and market building, peacekeeping, development aid, and relations with neighbouring countries and territories, and it judges the European Union a resounding success, a new political model that should inspire international relations in the future: the blueprint for the world order in the age of global economic integration and the most important development of the past half century.[6]

A common feature of this recent literature is the fact that it does not examine European integration through the prism of an existing model, be it the nation-state, the confederation, or the federation. It seems to leave out of consideration twentieth-century Europeanism's two main historical references and sources of inspiration: the birth of the United States of America at the end of the eighteenth century and the nation-states in the course of the nineteenth. In addition, it does not seem to be pervaded by the ideological, enterprising, and sometimes even prophetic spirit that runs through many writings in support of or against European unity. The literature of success considers not so much ideas as facts; it observes Europe as it really is, with a pragmatic eye, without asking itself whether, and into what new form, it should evolve further. It is no coincidence that its authors are British and American; they practise the method of British empiricism suggested by Hume: never confusing *is* with *ought* to be.

Robert Cooper,[7] a Brussels-based British diplomat close to Prime Minister Blair, maintains that 1989 marked a far more profound change in the course of European (and possibly world) history than other key years, such as 1789, 1815 or 1919. This is because 1989 brought to an end not only the Cold War, but also the system instituted by the Peace of Westphalia in 1648.

In that system, peace – illusory in that it was merely a state of non-war – rested on the equilibrium between the forces and on the non-interference among states. In the twentieth century, the conditions for this kind of peace, already precarious, were totally lost as a result of the rise of a Continental power of exorbitant strength (united Germany), and of the advent of technology that disproportionately increased the costs of war, and of a mass society that turned war into a clash not of armies but of peoples. Now, the world, and not only Europe, is looking for a new formula for peace, just as it did after the devastation of the Thirty Years War, when it found it, or rather believed it had found it, in the treaty of 1648.

According to Cooper, the new formula – the generator of a new order of peace that he terms post-modern – is the one that Europe worked out after the end of the Second World War, and is successfully applying in vital areas such as economic relations and security.

"The post-modern system," Cooper writes, "does not rely on balance, nor does it emphasize sovereignty or the separation of domestic and foreign affairs."[8] The rules, he says, are self-imposed. In the European Union, everyone is concerned to keep European law alive. "The European Union is a highly developed system for mutual interference in each other's domestic affairs."[9]

According to Cooper, the Treaty of Rome, which established the European Economic Community (EEC, 1957), constitutes the first example of a post-modern community; but there are others, such as the Treaty on Conventional Armed Forces in Europe (CFE, 1990), under whose terms participating countries undertake to keep each other informed of the location of their heavy armaments and agree to be inspected. Cooper maintains that it is important to realise that this is a genuine revolution. The normal, logical behaviour of an army is to conceal its strengths and its military capacity from its potential enemies. In the logic of war, treaties that regulate these areas are absurd: first of all, one should never enter into agreements with the enemy given that, if it really is an enemy, it is not to be trusted; second, one should never allow the enemy to come and peruse one's military bases or count the arms in one's possession. And yet the CFE Treaty makes provision for just this. "Security, which once depended on walls, is today based on openness, transparency and mutual vulnerability."[10]

Certainly, the European application of the post-modern formula is restricted to internal relations and to relations with the surrounding geographical area, with Russia for example. But the formula can, and in Cooper's view should, govern all international relations in the post-modern, or we might say, post-Westphalian world.

I will shortly take a look at what is, in my opinion, the flaw in Cooper's thesis. The thing I am seeking to underline here, however, is the vision of European construction as a new, original and successful endeavour – the true, and positive, new development that has emerged in international relations since the Second World War.

Comparing the American dream with the European dream, Jeremy Rifkin examines these two protagonists of globalisation and international politics. As he analyses their economic systems and social models, he argues that it is the United States that is in fact the Old World, and Europe the New World. According to Rifkin, the American dream embodies the thought of a particular historical moment, which history made concrete and transported by sheer force to American shores in the XVIII century, where it has since determined the American experience right through to present day. He goes on to say that successive generations of Americans chose to live out the Protestant Reformation and the Enlightenment "in their purest forms, making us the most devoutly Protestant people on Earth and the most committed to scientific pursuits, private property, capitalism, and the nation-state".[11]

But this model, he observes, is reaching the end of its historical cycle. It is ill suited to a world in which not only the economy, but also the function of government, is structured as a network and not bound to a defined territory; in which the quality of life and of social relations is seen to be more important than the individual accumulation of material goods, where the natural world is more threatened than threatening. The reality suited to this new world is not the heavy and monolithic America, but rather, Europe, which is, to use some of Rifkin's adjectives, discursive, networked, transnational and orchestral: this Europe that is not a state, that does not have a territory, because its territory continues to belong to its member states, that is neither centralised nor hierarchical, and that has no clearly defined borders. "Europe is busy preparing for a new era, while America is desperately trying to hold on to the old one."[12]

Let us take the economy, today considered Europe's weak point. As Rifkin reminds us, the European Union is the world's largest integrated market; it is the leading exporter of goods and services in the world economy; it is creating integrated networks in the fields of transport, energy, telecommunications and finance; and it is running important educational programmes (such as Socrates, Leonardo, and Erasmus). Unlike America, Europe does not rely on credit in order to maintain its high standard of living. Its total product is almost the equivalent of America's, but of superior quality, given that a smaller share of it goes on military expenditure and crime fighting, and is wasted on energy. Fourteen of the world's leading banks are European, as are eight of the ten leading insurance companies, the top five life insurance companies, six of the top eleven telecommunications companies, and six of the top twelve car manufacturers. In the line-up of the world's best fifty companies, compiled by Global Finance, forty-nine are European.

But it does not end with the economy. In Europe, there is a better quality of life, greater protection of privacy, more stringent environmental protection, a keener sense of social solidarity, and a more cautious attitude to scientific experimentation and technological innovation, and Europe also has a greater capacity to propose and to transmit to other countries and world regions its own model of social, political and international relations. The book contains analyses, facts and references relating to each of these fields.

Rifkin writes in support of a thesis, and his work might almost be described as a pamphlet; he is addressing, above all, the American reader, seeking to put him on his guard against the illusion of omnipotence that currently seems to be influencing a section of America's politicians and intellectuals. But his "pamphlet" is, in reality, a hefty, 400-page work, full of facts and figures, which here, for simplicity's sake, I do not cite. His analysis is detailed, and his arguments strong, numerous and convergent.

Similar considerations can be found in Mark Leonard's brief and highly effective book. Europe, he observes, has founded a new system of government and a new way of operating in the field of international relations. Both are based not on secrecy but on transparency, not on exclusion but on inclusion, and not on threat but on persuasion. Europe's method is law, and European law is also the instrument of its foreign policy. Leonard talks of "passive aggression": "rather than relying on the threat of intervention to secure its interests, Europe relies on the threat of not intervening – of withdrawing the hand of friendship, and the prospect of membership."[13]

Through this method, the European Community (subsequently Union) has transformed not only the economy, but also the rule of law, institutions and politics of countries aspiring to join it, including the ten countries that joined the European Union in 2004; today "for countries such as Turkey, Serbia, or Bosnia, the only thing worse than having the bureaucracy of Brussels descend on your political system, insisting on changes, implementing regulations, instigating state privatisations and generally seeping into every crack of everyday political life, is to have its doors closed to you".

America and Europe face similar threats on their doorsteps, "drug trafficking, large flows of migrants across leaky borders, networks of international crime", but their responses could not be more different. "The US has sent troops into neighbouring countries more than 15 times over the last 50 years but many of the countries around it have barely changed [...] The European response, on the other hand, has been to hold out the possibility of integration to neighbouring countries."

Europe Is Not a Finished Thing

Thus, what we can say is that while the newspapers paint a picture of a Europe in crisis, books present Europe as a triumphant success story. Certainly, it is difficult to find even one detailed and intellectually rigorous analysis of the crisis that has the breadth and depth of a book or an essay, rather than the superficiality of the umpteenth account of breakdowns in negotiations, or of the latest tirade against bureaucracy, politics, and modernity generally.

All this is true; and yet I do not feel that the question ends here. Yes, the anti-European rhetoric is short on arguments and, as a result of the literature of success, the onus is now firmly on it to produce some proof. And yet at the same time, no one who sees the profound reasons for European unification can simply dismiss as false the depiction of a weary Europe, lacking the capacity to influence world history that, for centuries, it possessed.

The signs that prove the truth of this depiction are right under our noses: the inability to find a common stance on the major questions of foreign and security policy and on agricultural policy reform, the huge wastage of resources due to the refusal to join forces in pursuit of common objectives, the ridiculous show of meanness over the reduction of the Community budget, the undignified quarrels over how to spend the meagre funds that are available and the diatribes on the stability pact, the Lisbon promises and the blocking of the Bolkestein directive, the revolt of the French electorate and the desertion of Europe's polling stations.

These disparate and contradictory signs need to be understood singly before we can consider them as a whole. In them, we find, in fact, the contradictions and hypocrisies typical of any normal political process, but we can also see the arduousness and tortuousness of the path to what Machiavelli called "gli ordini nuovi" (the new orders); we find the miserable failings of Europe's ruling classes and a discontent among Europe's citizens and voters, which can largely be attributed to these very failings.

Whereas for *the press* these signs all seem to shout out only one word, "crisis", for *the books* they amount to little more than distant background noise, hardly worthy of note.

The coryphaei of success seem to say: "it is fine as it is, you have finished Europe and it is perfect. Stop here, there's no need to take things any further." Indeed, Robert Cooper, in an illuminating passage in his book, points out that although some still dream of a European state, they are a minority, a very small minority. He calls it a dream left over from a previous age and says that if the nation-state is a problem then the superstate is certainly not a solution.[14]

And it is here that we find the hidden flaw, the ambiguous element that prevents the literature of success from being able to reassure us. The flaw is the fact that Europe is regarded as a finished thing, whereas, in fact, it is not finished at all. Of course, if we consider the centuries of history in which it is rooted, then we can say that Europe, in the space of just fifty years, has made enormous progress. But if we consider the speed at which the world is changing and its desperate and urgent need for what Europe has conceived of, but what, gripped by sloth, it is still hesitant to realise, then we can see that it still has not come nearly far enough. To use Michael Howard's wonderful expression, Europe has "invented peace" but has failed to turn its invention into reality.

The Method Is New, Not the Formula

Let us ask ourselves a question: does all that Europe has progressively achieved since 1950 constitute a new and now perfect formula for political aggregation, or is it an unfinished work that seems new precisely because it is unfinished? In my view there can be no doubt: the second answer is the correct one, the first is just a misleading illusion.

In politics (which is about power) there is no such thing as a new formula for union, just as in mechanics (which is about motion) there are no formulas that can free us from the force of gravity or give us perpetual motion. The basic rules of politics, just like the foundations of peace and of law, cannot be separated from the availability of means of coercion. The history of relations among states amounts to a succession of truces and fiercely fought battles: the peace described by Dante in *Monarchia* and by Kant in *Perpetual Peace* is possible only if it is built on a superior power. Certainly, truces can be enduring and wonderful, particularly if they come in the wake of terrible wars that have imparted harsh lessons in wisdom and moderation. But they are still truces.

Thus, the European Union, the EU, is not yet a union; it is a truce, not peace. The entity that, in Maastricht, was given this name lacks the essential requisite of a political union: a founding pact on the strength of which staying together, deciding together, and acting together are guaranteed *not only in moments of accord, but also in moments of discord*. If, and only if, this solid pact exists can a union truly be said to have been created, because it is only at this point that its members recognise that being together is a higher and stronger motivation than all the differences in outlook and preferences that will always emerge (within ourselves first, and only subsequently in our dealings with others) over the concrete questions that reality forces us to confront. In this essential sense, the European Union is still not complete. And the results achieved so far, remarkable as they are, are thus fragile, partial, reversible or, to use an economic term, unsustainable.

Seduced by this young Europe, rather in the way one might be by the charm of an adolescent, many forget that this same person, in order to become an adult, will have to lose much of his or her appeal. The charm will be lost, but strength and maturity will take its place.

Cooper and Leonard thus give us the truth, but not the *whole* truth, nor, in my opinion, its crux. They fail to acknowledge that the Europe that has been created so far is *not* ready for today's or for tomorrow's world, that it does *not* possess the means to prevent its civilisation from coming to an end or its economy from declining, that it is *not* strong enough to stop – and perhaps only Europe could do this – the world from plunging into self-destruction, as it did in the last century. Europe has not completed the transition from truce to peace and therefore is not properly equipped to help the world itself build peace.

The formula for union, as I said earlier, is not new, even though the variation on it that Europe is working out can probably be said to be original. It makes provision for the distribution of the power of government on a number of levels, according to the dimensions and the nature of the questions of common interest, of the *res publicae* (plural, note, not singular). Applying the formula means overcoming the idea that a state can be called a state only if it recognises no power over itself; it means recognising that a supranational power restores rather than suppresses sovereignty. In the technical language of political science, this formula is termed the federal model, even though nowadays simply to utter this term is to expose oneself to outbursts of irritation of the kind once (but no longer) prompted by crude and vulgar language.

As for the method, this is certainly new. Europe is trying to build a union of states not, as it did for centuries, through recourse to arms or marriages of convenience between reigning dynasties, but through democracy and law, through the gentle force of persuasion and consensus: it is an amazing feat, especially if one considers that the states that are part of it are among the world's oldest and proudest, the very ones that, for so long, proclaimed and applied the doctrine of their own unlimited sovereignty. Even though it has not been finished, it is nevertheless a new and a majestic endeavour.

But let us not foolishly confuse very two different ideas of unfinished here. We all know very well that history is never finished, or complete. But Europe is not only unfinished in this general sense: it is also unfinished in the more specific and worrying sense that it has not yet realised its own design for union. Europe today is already enjoying more benefits from having set about this project and from having realised a part of it than rightly it should be doing: it is already reaping the rewards of a future that can by no means be taken for granted. Even before it has been completed, Europe is already cashing in on its reputation.

And it is precisely from this, in my view, that Europe's spiral of melancholy derives. "The only thing we have to fear is fear itself, said Roosevelt, in an attempt to shake up the America of the Great Depression. The depression, the black bile, of Europeans is at once the cause and the effect of the failure to do enough, of the failure to seize opportunities, of the time that has been wasted, of the fear to carry the task through to completion. It is the guilty conscience that results from our saturnine procrastination, from the undeserved advantages we enjoy, from the task we have left undone and from which we avert our gaze. This guilty conscience is feeding our gloom and paralysing Europe.

It is not that the meagreness of what we have accomplished explains this depression, since the work done is anything but meagre, and the fact that it is unfinished should spur us into action rather than deter us from it. Instead, it is that our own melancholy prevents us from carrying it through; it is fear, our own oppressive heaviness that stops us from forging ahead. And we feel responsible for this heaviness, guilty in some cases, and we respond to this not by rolling up our sleeves and, with humility, setting to work, but by indulging in the displays of melancholy that have been known for over twenty-five centuries: we procrastinate, we decry ourselves, we pour scorn on what has been done, we are sluggish.

Can We Hope for an External Power?

"Noi ci allegrammo, e tosto tornò in pianto": I have lost count of the number of times that, when thinking of today's unfinished Europe, these words of Dante have sprung to mind.

After the end of the Cold War, and with the failure of the experiment in real socialism, huge spaces for democracy and for the market opened up the world over. And while Fukuyama, today a well-known follower of the old nationalist ideology that inspires the American government, was announcing the end of history, a pattern all too familiar to Europe (characterised by successions of equilibrium, hegemony, opposing alliances, threats, wars and truces) was preparing its return.

There are almost two hundred countries that declare themselves sovereign in the Westphalian sense of the word, replicas or would-be replicas of the nation-state that is resistant to the placement of any restriction on its power. The United States, despite supporting – in the last century – efforts to give the world a post-Westphalian order (first through the League of Nations, and subsequently through the UN), heads this list. But the aspirations and the influence of other giant nation-states, such as China, Russia, India, Brazil, Mexico, Iran and Nigeria, are growing rapidly. No European state will ever be able, by itself, to enter this select circle. And in the meantime, there abound challenges that are beyond the capacity for government even of the largest of these countries: guaranteeing security against terrorism, the rise of the Asian continent, the lack of renewable sources of energy, the instability of the international market, and the problems related to climate change.

History seems to be moving rapidly towards application of the logic of Westphalia on a global scale. When it was only Europe that was governed by this logic, tensions and ultimately wars, resulted from the upsetting of a regional equilibrium. They were resolved, in the end, through the intervention of an external power. This external power was the United States, Europe's own offspring. Reproduced on a global scale, the logic of Westphalia is far, far more destructive than it was during the century and a half of European domination, because the world does not have an external power to look to, to say nothing of a benevolent, democratic and enlightened external power, which is what America was for us Europeans.

But doesn't it? Could it not be that Europe itself might be that "external power" that the world needs; external not in a spatial sense, of course, but in the sense that, because it heralds an order other than the Westphalian, post-modern order, it is already projected forwards in time? There are many factors that combine to put us, in Europe, in a unique position. We are equipped with *knowledge* – we have experienced the system of unlimited sovereignties right through to its catastrophic conclusion, and we thus know that it is precarious and unsustainable. We have a *responsibility*, a moral and political debt to honour, for having made the world pay for our internal struggles and our colonial domination and for having generated the evil model that harbours the seeds of destructive conflict. We have *resources*, the means to play an influential role in world affairs; we are already the leading providers of development aid and we do not live on credit. We have *principles*, because we accept solidarity and multilateralism as constituent parts of the world order. We have *credibility* because we have already planted in our territory and begun to tend, with promising results, the seeds of a different pattern of inter-state relations.

The literature that I have called the literature of success describes very effectively this privileged position and special role enjoyed by Europe, and it is truly remarkable just how many results Europe, despite being almost defenceless and politically unfinished, has already recorded in the sphere of world politics.

Today, the threat to security is global, because the framework of the states is global, as is the non-territorial violence of terrorism, the hatred of the poor for the rich, the loss of control of the relationship between man and nature, and the fanaticism and hatred practised in the name of religion. The fact that Europe is unfinished now constitutes a grave danger not only to Europe, but to the world, because only Europe holds the key to solve these global threats. The two conflicts that we call the World Wars were, in truth, European Wars. In the same way, the only possible world peace, by which I mean true peace and not an illusory truce, is perhaps a *pax europea*.

The Way out of Melancholy

It is now almost sixty years since Churchill delivered, in Zurich, one of the most memorable speeches of the last century. In September 1946, much of Europe was in ruins, hungry, and weighed down by resentment, shame and desperation. It was destroyed, but it had saved its civilisation.

Six years earlier, having been called upon by his party to lead the government (more as a way of getting rid of him than really to put him at the helm), Churchill had, in the space of just five days (his first five days at number 10 Downing Street) completely altered the course of the war. How he managed to do this, almost single-handedly, is recorded in John Lukacs' masterly reconstruction of the events of that time.[15] Lukacs recounts, almost by the hour, how from May 24th to May 28th, 1940 – as his foreign secretary schemed with Germany, the generals declared military resistance impossible, France capitulated, the Soviet Union was with Hitler, practically all of Europe was occupied by the Nazis or governed by their dummies, and America watched but did not intervene – Churchill managed to transmit to his countrymen his own furious determination that Britain would fight, and would continue to fight whatever the cost. These were not the days in which Hitler lost the war, but they were certainly the ones in which he lost the possibility of winning it.

How can one fail to spot, here, those signs of passion, of folly, of heroism and of spiritual exaltation that, according to Plato, are typical of the *humor melancholicus*? How can one fail to see, also, embodied in Churchill, a heavy drinker, the analogy between the range of manifestations associated with the black bile and the range of effects associated with alcohol, an analogy that Aristotle broadly developed precisely in order to explain "why it is that all those who have achieved eminence in philosophy or politics, or poetry or the arts are clearly melancholic?"

Of melancholy, Churchill was well acquainted not only with the passion, the exaltation and the heroism, but also with the dark desperation, the sense of void, and the desolate loneliness that he, employing and making famous an image already used by James Boswell, Walter Scott, and R.L. Stevenson, called "the black dog" on his back. Reflecting from an ethical and religious perspective, Romano Guardini remarks that melancholy is "nostalgia for that which is simply perfect [...] the price to be paid for the birth of eternity in man [...] the unease of the man who perceives the closeness of infinity".[16]

There is a remedy for the "tragedy of Europe", Churchill declared in Zurich, and "it is to re-create the European Family [...] We must build a sort of United States of Europe [...], a sense of enlarged patriotism and common citizenship [...]. The first step in the re-creation of the European Family must be a partnership between France and Germany. In this way only can France recover the moral and cultural leadership of Europe." He went on to say "But I must give you a warning. Time may be short. At present there is a breathing-space."

Guardini considers the remedy to melancholic tension to lie in ethics and in faith. Even the secular Churchill, in Zurich, repeated the expression "act of faith": "If Europe is to be saved from infinite misery, and indeed from final doom, there must be this act of faith in the European Family and this act of oblivion against all the crimes and follies of the past."

Today we can say that this task is still unfinished, but that the "breathing-space" remains.

At the start of this piece, I mentioned my wish to urge students today to take united Europe as a professional, civil and political point of reference. I will now explain the connection between this wish and the considerations that I have set forth here.

During my years in Frankfurt, I held regular monthly meetings, each lasting an hour, exclusively for the European Central Bank's youngest functionaries – young people who rarely entered my office and, when they did so, rarely ventured to speak up – for an absolutely free discussion on any topic of their choice.

These extremely well-read thirty-year-olds, graduates of leading universities, had been adolescents when the Maastricht Treaty was signed, just as I had been when a history and philosophy teacher at my high school in Trieste spoke to us over the school's internal radio of the newly-signed Treaty of Rome. But that teacher's speech helped to direct my life, providing it with a political point of reference long before I had decided the course my studies would take, or indeed chosen my profession. As an adolescent, my earliest recollections were of the bombing of Genoa and of the bridges along the Riviera, of the round-ups by the German troops and the passage of the American ones, of my reunion with my father, almost a stranger to me, on his return from the front and from imprisonment. War did not figure in the childhood recollections of those thirty-year-olds in Frankfurt, and their memories of their adolescence were full of inter-railing and Erasmus projects.

Those young people were crossing the boundary between university and the working world. They were fascinated by economics and proud to be at the summit of Europe, and yet they viewed their daily work as a narrowing of their horizons, a descent into detail, a sort of shelving of and failure fully to exploit all the knowledge they had acquired, a sinking into repetitive routine. Exaltation and mortification, the full spectrum of melancholy.

The topics of our discussions rose above the routine of our daily work, but they were still connected with it: Where is the enlarged Europe heading? What will become of the Constitution? How can we boost growth? What can be done to turn the ECB into what we want it to be? I often noted an attitude in these young people that was more contemplative than active, a certain refusal to believe that they really could "make a difference". It was not easy to convince them that the answers to their questions would come by themselves, that the future of the euro, the future of the ECB, the future of Europe itself, and of the project for union designed by their grandfathers or great-grandfathers was now in their hands. The Europe this generation knows is peaceful and prosperous, but it is also melancholic and even apathetic. It is a Europe that looks finished, but is not; a Europe that lives under the shadow not of destruction but of decline.

And yet there is a task that is waiting to be completed, one that demands and deserves effort and sacrifice. Adopting a point of reference means taking as one's guide something that, while connected to the times and the place in which we live, lies on a higher and more distant plane and, as such, is able to give meaning and direction to our advance. This something is not a prediction, and neither is it a wager: it is an objective and a purpose. It requires us to lift our gaze and see beyond our own particular moment in time.

And so my advice to students is this: do not become discouraged, do not lose the determination that has seen you through your studies, do not withdraw into the private sphere, do not worship the idol of career or of financial gain, and do not turn to psychologists. Give yourselves, choose yourselves, points of reference. The way out of melancholy is to look inside ourselves and to set our sights high.[17]

Source: *Tomasso Padoa-Schioppa, 'The Europe of Melancholy', The Federalist, Year XLVIII, 2006, Number 1, page 9. http://www.thefederalist.eu.*

Notes

1. This is a version of the lecture delivered by the author on October 28th, 2005, to inaugurate the Academic Year 2005-2006 of the Luigi Bocconi University in Milan. The text is published in Italian in the journal *Il Mulino*, LV (2006), n. 1.

2. L. Einaudi, *Il buongoverno: saggi di economia e politica (1897-1954)* (1954), edited by E. Rossi, Rome-Bari, Laterza, 2004. This text is still recommended reading, also for students of economics.

3. R. Burton, *The Anatomy of Melancholy* (1621).

4. S. Freud, 'Lutto e malinconia' (1915-1917), in *Opere*, vol. VIII, Turin, Bollati Boringhieri (1976), p. 128.

5. S.A. Kierkegaard, *Vom Sinn der Schwermut*, in R. Guardini, *Ritratto della malinconia* (Brescia, Morcelliana, nuova ed. 1993), p. 15.

6. I cite several authors from this body of political writing: R. Cooper, *The Breaking of Nations: Order and Chaos in the Twenty-First Century* (London: Atlantic Books, 2003); J. Rifkin, *The European Dream: How Europe's Vision of the Future is Quietly Eclipsing the American Dream* (New York: Penguin, 2004); T.R. Reid, *The United States of Europe: The New Superpower and the End of American Supremacy* (London: Penguin, 2004); M. Leonard, *Why Europe Will Run the 21st Century* (London: Fourth Estate, 2005); G. Morgan, *The Idea of a European Superstate: Public Justification and European Integration* (Princeton, N.J.: Princeton University Press, 2005). As the reader will see, some of the subtitles are even more revealing than the titles.

7. Cooper, *The Breaking of Nations*.

8. Cooper, *The Breaking of Nations*.

9. Cooper, *The Breaking of Nations*.

10. Cooper, *The Breaking of Nations*.

11. Rifkin, *The European Dream*, p. 85.

12. Rifkin, *The European Dream*, p. 83.

13. Leonard, *Why Europe Will Run the 21st Century*, cit., p. 51.

14. Cooper, *The Breaking of Nations*, cit., p. 37.

15. J. Lukacs, *Five Days in London. May 1940* (New Haven, Conn., London, 1999).

16. Guardini, *Ritratto della malinconia*, cit., pp. 63, 67-69.

17. Translation not reviewed by the author.

New Alliances and Recomposition Logic

For a Western Union between Europe and the United States

Édouard Balladur

2008

For centuries the West has dominated the world. By removing barriers, developing trade and getting continents to communicate, Western Europe, followed by the United States, as rivals or associates, have extended their hold and acted as examples, as authors of international rule and masters of its sanction.

Today, the West is both divided and threatened. History is being written without it, and one day history may turn against it. To be sure to avoid this Westerners need to be aware of the risk of convincing themselves that affirming a greater solidarity among themselves is the only way. They are united in their traditions, cultures and ideals, and economically, morally, politically and strategically close as well. They are most threatened by the disorder of the world and the emergence of new powers that do not share the same values, whose notions of life, humans and society are different. A real union between Europe and the United States would see them reinforcing each other.

Europe and the United States do not have good relations. When problems arise, Europe and the United States still do not understand that the dangers threatening them are largely same ones, and that they must show a united front: conflicts in Africa between insecure states with contested borders, instability in Latin America, upheavals in the balance of power in Asia-Pacific and the Middle East, UN weakness, constant violations of the actual foundations of international law, economic instability, monetary disorder, and today a financial crisis of an unprecedented seriousness, energy shortage fears, massive movements of populations fleeing poverty, an increase in ethnic and religious conflicts, the arms race, temptation of withdrawal, fear of the future, and so on. The military Alliance that is supposed to unite them is unbalanced, as Americans stay sedentary and Europeans, resigned.

Without the West, will the world build balance on new foundations?

The West faces competition, an unprecedented situation for many centuries, which gradually diminishes its place and influence. Today, not only the marginalisation of the West is taking place, but also its rejection. How many nations contest not only its material, economic and military domination, were it declining, but also its entire moral values and principles of collective life?

Challenged in its power and values, afraid of being marginalised, even rejected, dreading the threat of violent actions instigated by terrorist States or international criminal organisations, affected in its economic prosperity and influence, the West must face all of this. What new message must it send to the world? How must it organise itself? Is it ready to show a united front faced with common threats?

The war led by the United States in Iraq has exacerbated the differences. It is about more than material or political interests; there is a real ideological and moral divide between America and numerous European countries. Even if political change must one day appease tensions in Europe like in the United States, awareness has been raised: on an issue vital for their future, Europe and America have difficulty coordinating their efforts, a dreadful perspective for both of them!

However, the West still exists, even if it struggles to define and organise itself. The transatlantic community constitutes its best definition, as it is material reality, written in facts. The economic integration between the two sides of the Atlantic continues to progress. The European Union is the privileged land for American investments, itself the first investor in the United States. For 10 years American businesses have invested 10 times more in The Netherlands than in China, and Europe has invested more in Texas than the United States has in Japan. Trading goods increases at a rate of 10% a year, to the point where it is referred to as a 'transatlantic economy'. Together the European Union and the United States still produce more than 55% of the world's goods.

The security of Europe and the United States is closely linked, nowadays less faced with the risks of the Cold War to those caused by terrorism, nuclear proliferation and uncontrolled globalisation. Today they are the first victims of the international financial crisis: who would argue that in a time of turmoil their interests are not linked?

Europe and America feed the same collective ideals: their history is largely common, their principles as well, they are linked to the respect of fundamental human rights and individual liberty, they believe in a market economy, in competition, in progress born from individual drive, and above all, they are proud of having invented human rights.

Europe must avoid American isolationism and withdrawal

Let us not forget, United States imperialism is a less ancient and maybe less natural tradition than isolationism. It is time for Europeans to realise that the errors and failures of America, far from reinforcing Europe, also weaken it. Conversely, when Europe and the United States act as partners confident in serving a just cause, they are successful: we've seen it with the end of the Cold War; let us hope that we will also see it if we can overcome the financial crisis due a complacency that has perverted liberalism, which must be accompanied by respecting the rules of good governance.

A weak America is not in Europe's interest – quite the contrary. A strong and confident America, without claiming to impose its views on everyone else, is the best guarantee of stability and general security.

This does not mean that Europe must renounce its views to submit to the ones of its natural partner, but it must also make an effort to broaden its views. The systematic hostility toward American policy does not serve Europe. Europe and America must define an ambitious partnership for all the problems they both face and create solidarity to remedy the disarray that threatens Western nations.

Europe must be more efficient in order to create a Western Union

Europe must be more than just a respected ally. The Union must be created in order to recommend and act on its own, as well as convince the United States every time it needs to warn it or carry out a joint action with it. The Union must also have the means to avoid being caught up in trifles like regulating the size of rear-view mirrors of trucks.

If we want to progress in good faith, the status quo is not an option. Until Europe is reformed, reforming the Atlantic Alliance will be not possible. It would be useless to talk of sharing different responsibilities in the chains of command between participating nations, to bemoan that too many Europeans States would rather buy military equipment from American companies than regret Americans acting on their own when they feel the need. This unequal situation perpetuates a feeling of irresponsibility in too many European countries and will not be remedied as long as the United States refuses to discuss with the Union as equals. For this to be acceptable, the Union needs to actually exist and be better organised.

The idea of a 'three circles policy' in Europe was born from the refusal of a political revolution that would have seen all nations agree to submit to the power of a real European State capable of making major decisions. Since this is not the case, we must go off the beaten track to avoid preconceived notions. Europe would never have been able to progress consistently. In the politics of the 'circles' we can see a breakdown of the Union in several categories of States, but it is the only way forward. Three circles could be created:

- The first circle, common law, a great market where everyone would be included, corresponding to the European Union in its entirety.
- Within this common law circle, there would be a second circle of specialised cooperation comprising the more ambitious States that are determined to go faster and further together. In fact, this already exists in the area of currency and security, but gives rise to mistrust and jealousy.
- The third circle would be separate from the Union; it would comprise neighbouring States with which it could sign close partnership contracts.

These partnerships would concern southern countries and those East of the Mediterranean. Then, the goal could be achieved: the United States would become a partner of equal importance with equal cohesion, solid, reliable and heard without the agreement of which no common effort could be conceivable. Otherwise, the Western Union will not see the light of day. Once reorganised, the European Union could establish closer cooperation with the United States, guaranteeing both better security and greater influence.

- A few years ago I had already made proposals to nominate a European coordinator for transatlantic relations working with the president of the Union; the creation by the European Union and the United States of a permanent joint secretariat whose mission would be to prepare the meetings that take place between ministers or heads of states, the meetings of multilateral financial institutions in which they participate, seeing how much this is needed today, as well as negotiations carried out within the World Trade Organization. The objective would be to avoid presenting divergent positions within international bodies as well as studying measures to increase economic integration on both sides of the Atlantic.

–   We must become more ambitious and imagine the progressive creation of a great common commercial market between Europe and the United States by establishing a customs union and adopting similar rules in matters of fiscal, legal, competition law or business law. Who does not see the discussions within the International Monetary Fund, World Trade Organization or G8 taking place under better conditions for interests that would gradually become, if not joint ones, at least infinitely closer, even if differences persisted?

The current crisis should convince us all of the necessity of this coordination. It is still necessary to avoid sticking to general ideas and convincing ourselves that the time has come for a thorough reform not only of the international monetary system, but also of the regulations concerning issuing and distributing credit to companies and individuals. Economic globalisation is an inevitable fact, a given that we cannot escape. However, it still needs be well organised in order to avoid the disorder that endangers prosperity like it does today.

–   The time has come to seriously commit to ending the disorganised fluctuation of currencies that threaten the prosperity of the world and its progress, which will eventually destroy the very idea of liberalism. In 1987 I was able to get our partners to sign the Louvre Accord in which Europe, the United States and Japan agreed to maintain monetary stability by coordinating their economic policies and the interventions of central banks on currency markets. For a few years these agreements had satisfactory results, then we forgot about them and monetary speculation started up again.

Later, on several occasions, I tried to convince France's partners to build a new and more stable international monetary system; I did not succeed. They all refused the minimum of discipline required, despite liberalism not being synonymous with complacency but, on the contrary, assuming that common principles be defined and respected. Today we see where this self-deception had led us: the anarchic circulation of capital, monetary instability, uncontrolled distribution of credit with no link to the real needs of the economy, worry, crisis, and no common authority able to impose a few essential rules and proper sanctions.

We must not get discouraged and continue the task at hand. Today, this regards the ties between the euro and the US dollar. A relation close to the one established between European currencies by the European monetary system could be created between the US dollar and the euro, the fluctuation margins oriented and controlled by the two central banks, the Federal Reserve and the European Central Bank, the coordinated economic and budgetary policies, and the harmonised monetary policies. The fluctuation of currency was justified by the belief that only a freely functioning market could generate stable and lasting prosperity, but the time has come to discard this preconceived notion. I believe that liberalism only has advantages when it is accompanied by order or rules that everyone must respect.

It should also be possible to harmonise the rules concerning credit, obligations respected by banks and financial institutions, the transparency of transactions, the objectivity of agencies charged with evaluating and indexing companies.

– As for foreign policy, this new Union between Europe and the United States would anticipate that any important initiative cannot be taken without partners consulting each other, which would avoid, for example, the controversies and misunderstandings which gave rise to the intention of the Americans of installing an anti-missile shield East of Europe. As well, the two partners would set new objectives in their relations with the rest of the world, such as better respect of human rights, a strong willingness to protect the environment and credible actions to help developing nations.

- As for military issues, the emergence of a Western Union between Europe and the United States would help rebalance the functioning of the North Atlantic Treaty Organization (NATO) in order to better share responsibilities. One will also need to clarify and adapt the strategic idea inspiring the Alliance by specifying the conditions of its intervention outside its growing traditional geographical field, the rules of which allow its members to intervene in some regions of the world without the agreement of their allies, but by using the means of the Alliance.

To face such serious questions and try to provide answers, the organised and improved consultation between Europeans and Americans will not be enough, nor will the strengthening of the military Alliance.

An Executive Board of the Western Union would bring together the leaders every three months. For the United States, it is simple: the president aided by ministers of their choice. For the Union, it is less clear: the president of the Union, hoping that the ratification of the Treaty of Lisbon will allow it for several years, aided by people they designate. Upon discussing questions that do not concern all members of the Union, such as currency or defence, one can imagine that it be represented by the president of the Union aided by the president of the group of States linked to a specialised cooperation, the president of the Eurogroup, for example, when monetary problems are discussed. It would be best not to commit to rigid notions in order to be able to adapt according to the experience.

Would this Executive Board have as its single mission to organise the confrontation of points of view, harmonise their positions, and as a new development, do so at regular intervals? Would we have to give it, like we did with the European Council, real decision-making powers, and in what form, with what majority and what sanctions? It is too early to answer such questions without running the risk of being unrealistic. Creating a limited organisation that meets frequently, where neither the Europeans, nor the Americans can decide anything about common interest problems without having discussed it together previously, would already be great progress. If the attempt was successful, then the Western Union could go further. But to be honest, I don't see the possibility of this today.

Can the West really choose another policy?

Many reject the actual principle of a closer association between Europe and the United States in the name of safeguarding an increasingly fragile independence, without seeing that refusing this association would obscure each other's future. A revolution in people's mind is therefore needed in Europe as well as in the United States.

The United States must convince itself that it will be more successful in maintaining the balance of the world if it is more closely associated with a Europe that can finally get organised. The United States will have to overcome their tendency of making decisions on their own. European nations, without giving up who they are, must open their eyes and collaborate more closely with each other, as it is the only way to discuss with the United States on an equal footing.

I am well aware that in the world, Europe and the United States do not have the same interests, the same ambitions, the same views or the same policies with regards to all nations. We must not restrict them to an exclusive dialogue, which would affect their will to act together. Both partners have ties they intend to maintain and will be part of several organisations, so it is not about denying them the right. Each party would need to prioritise their choices and make them compatible with one another.

Close collaboration between Europe and the United States would not always lead to identical policies in all the regions of the world, but at the very least they will have discussed it beforehand in order to better understand each other and perhaps get along. The fact that Europe is not only turned towards the Atlantic, but also towards Africa and Eastern Europe, particularly Russia, while the United States is not only concerned with what is going on in Europe, but also in Latin America or the Pacific Rim that hold an increasingly important place in their preoccupations and apprehensions, should not impede closer ties between Europeans and Americans. Quite the contrary, thanks to one another, everyone could have a more precise view of the state of the world, of the most relevant actions to carry out, while much ambiguity would dissipate, misunderstandings clarified and rivalry avoided.

The West will then find a role suited to the one it played for four centuries when, due to intellectual reform and economic revolution, it propagated a material civilisation unequalled today around the world. Today it must demonstrate that its messianism was not just hypocrisy. It is a spiritual message the world needs, going beyond differences and confrontations. The West, if it can show tolerance, disinterest, idealism and intelligence, can find a mission suitable to its history without losing any of its material influence, provided that it can convince us of its sincerity, as it will need to act. Also provided that it urgently demonstrates the ability to overcome its difficulties and contradictions, its ability to imagine liberalism that is not synonymous with anarchy, but with rules everyone must follow and its ability to finally ensure that economic progress benefits everyone.

Source: *Édouard Balladur, 2008, 'Pour une Union Occidentale', Revue internationale et stratégique, 4, 72.* © Librairie Artheme Fayard 2007

Translated from the French by Natasha Cloutier

Remarks to the Turkish Parliament

Barack Obama

Ankara, 6 April 2009

Mr. Speaker, Madam Deputy Speaker, distinguished members, I am honored to speak in this chamber, and I am committed to renewing the alliance between our nations and the friendship between our people.

This is my first trip overseas as President of the United States. I've been to the G20 summit in London, and the NATO summit in Strasbourg, and the European Union summit in Prague. Some people have asked me if I chose to continue my travels to Ankara and Istanbul to send a message to the world. And my answer is simple: *Evet* yes. Turkey is a critical ally. Turkey is an important part of Europe. And Turkey and the United States must stand together – and work together – to overcome the challenges of our time.

This morning I had the great privilege of visiting the tomb of your extraordinary founder of your republic. And I was deeply impressed by this beautiful memorial to a man who did so much to shape the course of history. But it is also clear that the greatest monument to Ataturk's life is not something that can be cast in stone and marble. His greatest legacy is Turkey's strong, vibrant, secular democracy, and that is the work that this assembly carries on today.

This future was not easily assured, it was not guaranteed. At the end of World War I, Turkey could have succumbed to the foreign powers that were trying to claim its territory, or sought to restore an ancient empire. But Turkey chose a different future. You freed yourself from foreign control, and you founded a republic that commands the respect of the United States and the wider world.

And there is a simple truth to this story: Turkey's democracy is your own achievement. It was not forced upon you by any outside power, nor did it come without struggle and sacrifice. Turkey draws strength from both the successes of the past, and from the efforts of each generation of Turks that makes new progress for your people.

Now, my country's democracy has its own story. The general who led America in revolution and governed as our first President was, as many of you know, George Washington. And like you, we built a grand monument to honor our founding father – a towering obelisk that stands in the heart of the capital city that bears Washington's name. I can see the Washington Monument from the window of the White House every day.

It took decades to build. There were frequent delays. Over time, more and more people contributed to help make this monument the inspiring structure that still stands tall today. Among those who came to our aid were friends from all across the world who offered their own tributes to Washington and the country he helped to found.

And one of those tributes came from Istanbul. Ottoman Sultan Abdulmecid sent a marble plaque that helped to build the Washington Monument. Inscribed in the plaque was a poem that began with a few simple words: "So as to strengthen the friendship between the two countries." Over 150 years have passed since those words were carved into marble. Our nations have changed in many ways. But our friendship is strong, and our alliance endures.

It is a friendship that flourished in the years after World War II, when President Truman committed our nation to the defense of Turkey's freedom and sovereignty, and Turkey committed itself into the NATO Alliance. Turkish troops have served by our side from Korea to Kosovo to Kabul. Together, we withstood the great test of the Cold War. Trade between our nations has steadily advanced. So has cooperation in science and research.

The ties among our people have deepened, as well, and more and more Americans of Turkish origin live and work and succeed within our borders. And as a basketball fan, I've even noticed that Hedo Türkoğlu and Mehmet Okur have got some pretty good basketball games.

The United States and Turkey have not always agreed on every issue, and that's to be expected – no two nations do. But we have stood together through many challenges over the last 60 years. And because of the strength of our alliance and the endurance of our friendship, both America and Turkey are stronger and the world is more secure.

Now, our two democracies are confronted by an unprecedented set of challenges: An economic crisis that recognizes no borders; extremism that leads to the killing of innocent men and women and children; strains on our energy supply and a changing climate; the proliferation of the world's deadliest weapons; and the persistence of tragic conflict.

These are the great tests of our young century. And the choices that we make in the coming years will determine whether the future will be shaped by fear or by freedom; by poverty or by prosperity; by strife or by a just, secure and lasting peace.

This much is certain: No one nation can confront these challenges alone, and all nations have a stake in overcoming them. That is why we must listen to one another, and seek common ground. That is why we must build on our mutual interests, and rise above our differences. We are stronger when we act together. That is the message that I've carried with me throughout this trip to Europe. That is the message that I delivered when I had the privilege of meeting with your President and with your Prime Minister. That will be the approach of the United States of America going forward.

Already, America and Turkey are working with the G20 on an unprecedented response to an unprecedented economic crisis. Now, this past week, we came together to ensure that the world's largest economies take strong and coordinated action to stimulate growth and restore the flow of credit; to reject the pressures of protectionism, and to extend a hand to developing countries and the people hit hardest by this downturn; and to dramatically reform our regulatory system so that the world never faces a crisis like this again.

As we go forward, the United States and Turkey can pursue many opportunities to serve prosperity for our people. The President and I this morning talked about expanding the ties of commerce and trade. There's enormous opportunity when it comes to energy to create jobs. And we can increase new sources to not only free ourselves from dependence of other energies – other countries' energy sources, but also to combat climate change. We should build on our Clean Technology Fund to leverage efficiency and renewable energy investments in Turkey. And to power markets in Turkey and Europe, the United States will continue to support your central role as an East-West corridor for oil and natural gas.

This economic cooperation only reinforces the common security that Europe and the United States share with Turkey as a NATO ally, and the common values that we share as democracies. So in meeting the challenges of the 21st century, we must seek the strength of a Europe that is truly united, peaceful and free.

So let me be clear: The United States strongly supports Turkey's bid to become a member of the European Union. We speak not as members of the EU, but as close friends of both Turkey and Europe. Turkey has been a resolute ally and a responsible partner in transatlantic and European institutions. Turkey is bound to Europe by more than the bridges over the Bosphorous. Centuries of shared history, culture, and commerce bring you together. Europe gains by the diversity of ethnicity, tradition and faith – it is not diminished by it. And Turkish membership would broaden and strengthen Europe's foundation once more.

Now, of course, Turkey has its own responsibilities. And you've made important progress towards membership. But I also know that Turkey has pursued difficult political reforms not simply because it's good for EU membership, but because it's right for Turkey.

In the last several years, you've abolished state security courts, you've expanded the right to counsel. You've reformed the penal code and strengthened laws that govern the freedom of the press and assembly. You've lifted bans on teaching and broadcasting Kurdish, and the world noted with respect the important signal sent through a new state Kurdish television station.

These achievements have created new laws that must be implemented, and a momentum that should be sustained. For democracies cannot be static – they must move forward. Freedom of religion and expression lead to a strong and vibrant civil society that only strengthens the state, which is why steps like reopening Halki Seminary will send such an important signal inside Turkey and beyond. An enduring commitment to the rule of law is the only way to achieve the security that comes from justice for all people. Robust minority rights let societies benefit from the full measure of contributions from all citizens.

I say this as the President of a country that not very long ago made it hard for somebody who looks like me to vote, much less be President of the United States. But it is precisely that capacity to change that enriches our countries. Every challenge that we face is more easily met if we tend to our own democratic foundation. This work is never over. That's why, in the United States, we recently ordered the prison at Guantanamo Bay closed. That's why we prohibited – without exception or equivocation – the use of torture. All of us have to change. And sometimes change is hard.

Another issue that confronts all democracies as they move to the future is how we deal with the past. The United States is still working through some of our own darker periods in our history. Facing the Washington Monument that I spoke of is a memorial of Abraham Lincoln, the man who freed those who were enslaved even after Washington led our Revolution. Our country still struggles with the legacies of slavery and segregation, the past treatment of Native Americans.

Human endeavor is by its nature imperfect. History is often tragic, but unresolved, it can be a heavy weight. Each country must work through its past. And reckoning with the past can help us seize a better future. I know there's strong views in this chamber about the terrible events of 1915. And while there's been a good deal of commentary about my views, it's really about how the Turkish and Armenian people deal with the past. And the best way forward for the Turkish and Armenian people is a process that works through the past in a way that is honest, open and constructive.

We've already seen historic and courageous steps taken by Turkish and Armenian leaders. These contacts hold out the promise of a new day. An open border would return the Turkish and Armenian people to a peaceful and prosperous coexistence that would serve both of your nations. So I want you to know that the United States strongly supports the full normalization of relations between Turkey and Armenia. It is a cause worth working towards.

It speaks to Turkey's leadership that you are poised to be the only country in the region to have normal and peaceful relations with all the South Caucasus nations. And to advance that peace, you can play a constructive role in helping to resolve the Nagorno-Karabakh conflict, which has continued for far too long.

Advancing peace also includes the disputes that persist in the Eastern Mediterranean. And here there's a cause for hope. The two Cypriot leaders have an opportunity through their commitment to negotiations under the United Nations Good Offices Mission. The United States is willing to offer all the help sought by the parties as they work towards a just and lasting settlement that reunifies Cyprus into a bizonal and bicommunal federation.

These efforts speak to one part of the critical region that surrounds Turkey. And when we consider the challenges before us, on issue after issue, we share common goals.

In the Middle East, we share the goal of a lasting peace between Israel and its neighbors. Let me be clear: The United States strongly supports the goal of two states, Israel and Palestine, living side by side in peace and security. That is a goal shared by Palestinians, Israelis, and people of goodwill around the world.

That is a goal that the parties agreed to in the road map and at Annapolis. That is a goal that I will actively pursue as President of the United States.

We know the road ahead will be difficult. Both Israelis and Palestinians must take steps that are necessary to build confidence and trust. Both Israelis and Palestinians, both must live up to the commitments they have made. Both must overcome longstanding passions and the politics of the moment to make progress towards a secure and lasting peace.

The United States and Turkey can help the Palestinians and Israelis make this journey. Like the United States, Turkey has been a friend and partner in Israel's quest for security. And like the United States, you seek a future of opportunity and statehood for the Palestinians. So now, working together, we must not give into pessimism and mistrust. We must pursue every opportunity for progress, as you've done by supporting negotiations between Syria and Israel. We must extend a hand to those Palestinians who are in need, while helping them strengthen their own institutions. We must reject the use of terror, and recognize that Israel's security concerns are legitimate.

The peace of the region will also be advanced if Iran forgoes any nuclear weapons ambitions. Now, as I made clear in Prague yesterday, no one is served by the spread of nuclear weapons, least of all Turkey. You live in a difficult region and a nuclear arm race would not serve the security of this nation well. This part of the world has known enough violence. It has known enough hatred. It does not need a race for an ever-more powerful tool of destruction.

Now, I have made it clear to the people and leaders of the Islamic Republic of Iran that the United States seeks engagement based on mutual interest and mutual respect. We want Iran to play its rightful role in the community of nations. Iran is a great civilization. We want them to engage in the economic and political integration that brings prosperity and security. But Iran's leaders must choose whether they will try to build a weapon or build a better future for their people.

So both Turkey and the United States support a secure and united Iraq that does not serve as a safe haven for terrorists. I know there were differences about whether to go to war. There were differences within my own country, as well. But now we must come together as we end this war responsibly, because the future of Iraq is inseparable from the future of the broader region. As I've already announced, and many of you are aware, the United States will remove our combat brigades by the end of next August, while working with the Iraqi government as they take responsibility for security. And we will work with Iraq, Turkey, and all Iraq's neighbors, to forge a new dialogue that reconciles differences and advances our common security.

Make no mistake, though: Iraq, Turkey, and the United States face a common threat from terrorism. That includes the al-Qaeda terrorists who have sought to drive Iraqis apart and destroy their country. That includes the PKK. There is no excuse for terror against any nation. As President, and as a NATO ally, I pledge that you will have our support against the terrorist activities of the PKK or anyone else. These efforts will be strengthened by the continued work to build ties of cooperation between Turkey, the Iraqi government, and Iraq's Kurdish leaders, and by your continued efforts to promote education and opportunity and democracy for the Kurdish population here inside Turkey.

Finally, we share the common goal of denying al-Qaeda a safe haven in Pakistan or Afghanistan. The world has come too far to let this region backslide, and to let al-Qaeda terrorists plot further attacks. That's why we are committed to a more focused effort to disrupt, dismantle, and defeat al-Qaeda. That is why we are increasing our efforts to train Afghans to sustain their own security, and to reconcile former adversaries. That's why we are increasing our support for the people of Afghanistan and Pakistan, so that we stand on the side not only of security, but also of opportunity and the promise of a better life.

Turkey has been a true partner. Your troops were among the first in the International Security Assistance Force. You have sacrificed much in this endeavor. Now we must achieve our goals together. I appreciate that you've offered to help us train and support Afghan security forces, and expand opportunity across the region. Together, we can rise to meet this challenge like we have so many before.

I know there have been difficulties these last few years. I know that the trust that binds the United States and Turkey has been strained, and I know that strain is shared in many places where the Muslim faith is practiced. So let me say this as clearly as I can: The United States is not, and will never be, at war with Islam. In fact, our partnership with the Muslim world is critical not just in rolling back the violent ideologies that people of all faiths reject, but also to strengthen opportunity for all its people.

I also want to be clear that America's relationship with the Muslim community, the Muslim world, cannot, and will not, just be based upon opposition to terrorism. We seek broader engagement based on mutual interest and mutual respect. We will listen carefully, we will bridge misunderstandings, and we will seek common ground. We will be respectful, even when we do not agree. We will convey our deep appreciation for the Islamic faith, which has done so much over the centuries to shape the world – including in my own country. The United States has been enriched by Muslim Americans. Many other Americans have Muslims in their families or have lived in a Muslim-majority country – I know, because I am one of them.

Above all, above all we will demonstrate through actions our commitment to a better future. I want to help more children get the education that they need to succeed. We want to promote health care in places where people are vulnerable. We want to expand the trade and investment that can bring prosperity for all people. In the months ahead, I will present specific programs to advance these goals. Our focus will be on what we can do, in partnership with people across the Muslim world, to advance our common hopes and our common dreams. And when people look back on this time, let it be said of America that we extended the hand of friendship to all people.

There's an old Turkish proverb: "You cannot put out fire with flames." America knows this. Turkey knows this. There's some who must be met by force, they will not compromise. But force alone cannot solve our problems, and it is no alternative to extremism. The future must belong to those who create, not those who destroy. That is the future we must work for, and we must work for it together.

I know there are those who like to debate Turkey's future. They see your country at the crossroads of continents, and touched by the currents of history. They know that this has been a place where civilizations meet, and different peoples come together. They wonder whether you will be pulled in one direction or another.

But I believe here is what they don't understand: Turkey's greatness lies in your ability to be at the center of things. This is not where East and West divide – this is where they come together. In the beauty of your culture. In the richness of your history. In the strength of your democracy. In your hopes for tomorrow.

I am honored to stand here with you – to look forward to the future that we must reach for together – and to reaffirm America's commitment to our strong and enduring friendship. Thank you very much. Thank you. Thank you.

Source: *Barack Obama, President Obama's Remarks in Turkey, 6 April 2009. https://www.whitehouse.gov/the-press-office/remarks-president-obama-turkish-parliament*

Germany in and with and for Europe[1]

Helmut Schmidt

Berlin, 4 December 2011

Friends, Ladies and Gentlemen,
Let me begin on a personal note. When Sigmar Gabriel, Frank-Walter Steinmeier and my party asked me once again for a contribution, I recalled with pleasure that, 65 years ago today, I was kneeling on the floor with my wife, Loki, painting invitation posters for the SPD in the Neugraben district of Hamburg. But I must admit that at my age I am beyond good and evil in respect of any party politics. For a long time now my two major interests have been the tasks facing this country and the role it should play in the crucial arena of European integration.

I am pleased to share this lectern with Jens Stoltenberg from Norway who, in the midst of the profound misfortune his country has suffered, has provided us and all Europeans with a shining example of unwavering, constitutional, liberal and democratic leadership.

When you're as old as I am, you have a natural tendency to take a long-term perspective – both backwards into history and forwards into the future, in which you place your hopes and your aspirations. That said, I nonetheless found it impossible to give a straightforward answer to a very simple question put to me just a few days ago by Wolfgang Thierse, who asked me when I thought Germany would finally become a normal country. I answered by saying that Germany would not be a "normal" country in the foreseeable future. Standing in the path to normality is the enormous and unique burden of our history. A further stumbling block is the economically and demographically dominant central position Germany occupies in the middle of our very small continent with its multitude of different nation states.

Which brings me to the heart of the complex subject matter I wish to address: Germany in, with and for Europe.

I   Motives and origins of European integration

Although a few of the 40-odd nation states in Europe – Italy, Greece and Germany, for example – were late in developing the national identity they have today, bloody wars have been fought time and again all over the continent. Seen from central Europe, the history of the continent might well be regarded as a never-ending succession of struggles between the periphery and the centre and, vice versa, between the centre and the periphery. The decisive battlefield has always been the centre, however.

Whenever the rulers, states or peoples at the heart of Europe were weak, their neighbours from the periphery would penetrate into the enfeebled centre. The greatest destruction and the largest losses of human life in relative terms were suffered during the first Thirty Years War 1618-48, which was played out for the most part on German soil. At that time, Germany was no more than a geographical concept, vaguely defined as the area in which German was spoken. The French came at a later date under Louis XIV and again under Napoleon. The Swedes did not come a second time. The British and the Russians, however, came several times, the latter most recently under Stalin.

Whenever the dynasties or the states in the centre of Europe were strong – or felt they were strong – they, in turn, ventured into the periphery. That was the case with the Crusades, which were also campaigns of conquest directed not just at Asia Minor and Jerusalem, but also at eastern Prussia and all three present-day Baltic states. In modern times it applied to the war against Napoleon and the three wars waged by Bismarck in 1864, 1866 and 1870/71.

It was true, above all, of the second Thirty Years War from 1914 to 1945. And it was especially true of Hitler's advances as far as the North Cape, the Caucasus, the Greek island of Crete, southern France and even Tobruk close to the border between Egypt and Libya. The catastrophe unleashed by Germany on Europe encompassed the disaster which befell the European Jews and the devastation of the German nation state.

Before that, however, the Poles, the Baltic nations, the Czechs, the Slovaks, the Austrians, the Hungarians, the Slovenians and the Croats had shared the fate of the Germans in that they had all suffered for centuries because of their geopolitical location at the heart of this small continent of Europe. To put it differently, we Germans have frequently made others suffer because of our position of power at the centre.

Nowadays, the conflicting territorial claims and the conflicts over languages and borders, which were still crucial aspects of national identity in the first half of the 20th century, have *de facto* largely lost their significance, for us Germans at least.

Whereas knowledge and recollection of the wars waged in the Middle Ages have largely faded in the public mind and in the published opinion in the countries of Europe, memories of the two world wars in the 20th century and of German occupation continue to play a dominant role beneath the surface.

For us Germans it seems to me critical that almost all Germany's neighbours – and virtually all Jews the world over – remember the Holocaust and the abominable deeds that took place during German occupation of the countries at the periphery. We are not sufficiently aware of the fact that in almost all our neighbouring countries there is a latent suspicion of Germans that will probably persist for many generations to come.

Future generations of Germans will have to live with this historical burden, too. And the present generations should not forget that it was suspicion of Germany and its future development that paved the way for the start of European integration in 1950.

Churchill had two objectives in mind when, in the great speech he gave in Zurich in 1946, he urged the French to live on good terms with the Germans and to join with them in setting up the United States of Europe. His first objective was to build a common defence against the perceived threat posed by the Soviet Union; the second was to integrate Germany into a broad Western alliance. Churchill was far-sighted enough to anticipate that Germany would grow strong again.

When Robert Schuman and Jean Monnet put forward the Schuman Plan for a European Coal and Steel Community in 1950, four years after Churchill's speech, they did so for the same reason: to re-integrate Germany. Ten years later, the same motive inspired Charles de Gaulle to extend the hand of reconciliation to Konrad Adenauer.

All these endeavours were based on a realistic awareness of the dreaded possibility that Germany would regain its strength in the future. It was not the idealism of Victor Hugo, who called for the unification of Europe in 1849, nor any other form of idealism that characterised the early phase of European integration between 1950 and 1952, which was limited to Western Europe. The leading statesmen in Europe and America at the time (George Marshall, Eisenhower and Kennedy, but above all Churchill, Jean Monnet, Adenauer and de Gaulle along with de Gasperi and Henri Spaak) were motivated not by any form of European idealism but by their knowledge of European history. Their actions were inspired by a realistic awareness of the need to prevent a continuation of the struggle between the states at the periphery and Germany at the centre. An appreciation of this original motivation for European integration – and it remains a key element to this day – is crucial to the resolution of the current, extremely dangerous European crisis.

The more the Federal Republic of Germany grew in economic, military and political stature in the course of the 1960s, 70s and 80s, the more the Western European leaders came to regard European integration as a safeguard against the conceivable prospect of a renewed German susceptibility to the lure of power. The initial resistance to the unification of the two German post-war states mounted by Margaret Thatcher, Mitterand and

Andreotti in 1989/90 was clearly prompted by concern about a strong Germany at the heart of this small continent of Europe.

Permit me to make a personal digression at this point. I listened to Jean Monnet when I was involved in the work of his committee Pour les États-Unis d'Europe (For the United States of Europe). That was in 1955. Jean Monnet remains one of the most far-sighted Frenchmen I have ever met – not least because of his plan for a gradual approach to European integration.

Ever since then I have been a supporter both of European integration and of Germany's inclusion into Europe not on any idealistic grounds but out of an awareness of the strategic interests of the German nation. (That led to a dispute between me and the party chairman, Kurt Schumacher, a man I held in great esteem. It might have been a trivial matter for him, but for me – a 30-year-old former soldier returned home from the war – it was a deadly serious issue). In the 1950s my position prompted me to back the plans of the Polish Foreign Minister at the time, Rapacki. In the early 1960s I wrote a book criticising the official Western strategy of nuclear retaliation that NATO used to threaten the powerful Soviet Union – a strategy to which we remain committed to this very day.

II   The European Union is necessary

In the 1960s and early 1970s, de Gaulle and Pompidou continued the process of European integration – not because they wanted to draw their own country in, for better or worse, but in order to bind Germany in. Subsequently, the good relationship I enjoyed with Giscard d'Estaing resulted in a period of Franco-German cooperation and the continuation of European integration – a period that was successfully resumed by Mitterand and Kohl after the spring of 1990. Between 1950/52 and 1991 the European Community grew little by little from six to twelve Member States.

Thanks to the extensive preparatory work carried out by Jacques Delors (then President of the European Commission),

Mitterand and Kohl were able to launch the common currency – the euro – in Maastricht in 1991, which was introduced ten years later in 2001. Here again, the underlying cause was the French concern about an over-powerful Germany or, to be more precise, an over-powerful deutschmark.

In the meantime the euro has become the second most important currency in the global economy. Both internally and externally this European currency has so far proved more stable than the U.S. dollar – and more stable than the deutschmark in the last ten years of its existence. All that has been written and said about an alleged "crisis of the euro" is irresponsible nonsense uttered by the media, journalists and politicians.

The world has changed dramatically since Maastricht in 1991/92, however. We have witnessed the liberation of the countries of Eastern Europe and the implosion of the Soviet Union. We have experienced the phenomenal rise of China, India, Brazil and other "emerging economies", which used to be sweepingly referred to as the "Third World". In addition, the real economies in most parts of the world have been "globalised". In other words, almost all the countries in the world are dependent on each other. Players in the globalised financial markets, in particular, have acquired a power that, for the time being, remains completely uncontrolled.

At the same time the world's population has soared almost unnoticed to seven billion. When I was born, there were just two billion people in the world. All these enormous changes are having a tremendous impact on the peoples of Europe, their countries and their prosperity.

On the other hand, all the European countries are ageing and their populations are shrinking. By the middle of the 21st century there will probably be as many as nine billion people on the planet. The European nations together will then account for just seven per cent of the world's population. Seven percent of nine billion! For more than two centuries – up to the year 1950 – Europeans made up over twenty per cent of the global population. But for the past fifty years we Europeans have been shrinking in numbers, not just in absolute figures but also, and above all, compared to Asia, Africa and Latin America. Similarly, the Europeans' share of the global national product, i.e. the value added of the world's population, is shrinking. By 2050 it will drop to around ten per cent; in 1950 it was still at around thirty per cent.

In 2050, each of the European nations will constitute just a fraction of one per cent of the world's population. In other words, if we cherish the notion that we Europeans are important for the world, we have to act in unison. As individual states – France, Italy, Germany, Poland, Holland, Denmark or Greece – we will ultimately be measured not in percentages, but in parts per thousand.

That is why the European nation states have a long-term strategic interest in their mutual integration. This strategic interest in European integration will become increasingly significant. As yet, the countries are mostly unaware of the fact. Their governments have failed to make it clear to them.

Should the European Union fail to ensure its capacity to take common action in the decades ahead, however limited that might be, a self-inflicted marginalisation of the European countries and of European civilisation cannot be ruled out. If this happens, a revival of competition between the countries of Europe and of battles for prestige cannot be excluded either. If that were the case, the integration of Germany could hardly continue. The old game between the centre and the periphery might well be resumed.

The process of global enlightenment, the spread of human rights and human dignity as well as of constitutional and democratic government would no longer receive any effective impetus from Europe. Taking these aspects into consideration, the European Community emerges as a vital necessity for the nation states of our old continent. This necessity goes beyond the motives that inspired Churchill and de Gaulle. It goes beyond the motives demonstrated by Monnet and Adenauer as well. Today, it also overarches the motives of Ernst Reuter, Fritz Erler, Willy Brandt and Helmut Kohl.

I would add that one of the issues at stake here is still undoubtedly to bind Germany in. For that reason we Germans must be quite clear in our minds about the tasks we have to address and our own role in the context of European integration.

III Germany needs continuity and reliability

If, at the end of 2011, we look at Germany from the outside through the eyes of our close and more distant neighbours, it becomes clear that for the last years this country has been a cause of uneasiness and, more recently, of political concern. In the immediate past, considerable doubts have emerged about the continuity of German policy. The trust placed in the reliability of German policy has been damaged.

On the one hand, these doubts and concerns are the result of foreign policy mistakes made by German politicians and governments. On the other hand, they have to do with the economic strength of our country following its reunification, which took the world by surprise. Beginning in the 1970s, at a time when Germany was still divided, our economy has developed into the biggest in Europe. In technological, financial and social terms it is one of the most productive economies in the world. The economic strength and the social peace we have enjoyed for decades now, which in comparative terms is very stable, have provoked envy, particularly since our unemployment rate and our debt to equity ratio are well within the international norm.

However, it has not really dawned on us that our economy is not only closely integrated into the common European market but is also highly globalised, which means it is dependent on global market conditions. Next year, therefore, German exports will not grow very much.

In addition, there has been a very undesirable development in the form of persistently high surpluses in our balance of trade and balance of payments. For years now, the surpluses have constituted around five per cent of our national product. They are more or less the size of China's surpluses. We are not conscious of the fact, because the surpluses are no longer expressed in deutschmarks but in euros. Our politicians need to bear this in mind, however, as in reality all our surpluses are the deficits of other countries. The claims we have on others are their debts. This is an annoying violation of the "external balance" we once elevated to the status of a legal ideal. It is a violation that must worry our partners. Recently, voices have been raised abroad – mostly in America, although in the meantime they have come from all quarters – urging Germany to play a leading role in Europe. All these factors taken together have aroused further suspicion among our neighbours. And they have revived unpleasant memories, too.

These economic developments and the simultaneous crisis in the ability of the European Union institutions to take action have pressured Germany into playing a key role again. The Chancellor has willingly accepted this role alongside the French president. In many European capitals and in the media of many of our neighbouring countries, however, there is once more a growing concern about German dominance. This time the issue at stake is not a central power that is exceedingly strong in military and political terms, but a centre that is exceedingly powerful in economic terms.

At this point it is time to issue a serious, carefully considered warning to German politicians, the media and the general public.

If we Germans were to be tempted by our economic strength into claiming a leading political role in Europe or at least playing the role of first among equals, an increasing majority of our neighbours would mount effective resistance. The concern among the states on the periphery about the centre of Europe becoming too strong would return very quickly. The likely consequences of such a development would cripple the EU and Germany would lapse into isolation.

The Federal Republic of Germany is a very large country with a very competitive economy that needs to be integrated into Europe – to protect it from itself, amongst other things. Ever since 1992 therefore – since the times of Helmut Kohl – Article 23 of the Basic Law has obliged us to cooperate "... in the development of the European Union". Article 23 also obliges us, as an element of this cooperation, to heed "the principle of subsidiarity". The present crisis affecting the ability of the EU institutions to take action does not change these principles in any way.

In view of our central geopolitical location, the unfortunate role we played in European history up to the middle of the twentieth century and the strong economy we have today, every German government is called upon to show the utmost sensitivity towards the interests of our partners in the European Union. And our willingness to help is indispensable.

The great work of reconstruction we Germans have carried out over the past sixty years has not been exclusively the result of our own efforts. It would have been impossible without the help of the victorious Western powers, without our integration into the European Community and the Atlantic Alliance, without the assistance of our neighbours, without the political awakening in eastern central Europe and without the end of communist dictatorship. We Germans have every reason to be grateful. At the same time we have the duty to prove ourselves worthy of the solidarity we have received by exercising solidarity ourselves with our neighbours.

By contrast, it would be pointless – and probably even harmful – for us to strive for global political prestige and a role of our own in the international political arena. At all events, it is crucial that we maintain our close cooperation with France and Poland and with all our neighbours and partners in Europe.

I strongly believe that it is of cardinal importance for our long-term strategic interests that Germany should not isolate itself nor allow itself to be isolated. Isolation within the West would be dangerous. Isolation within the European Union or the euro area would be extremely dangerous. For me, this particular German interest enjoys a much higher priority than any tactical interest pursued by political parties of whatever hue.

German politicians and the German media damn well have the duty to consistently convey this message to the general public.

Now it might be the case, as has happened recently, that someone claims that from now on Europe will speak German; that a German foreign minister considers telegenic appearances in Tripoli, Cairo or Kabul to be more important than political contacts with Lisbon, Madrid and Warsaw or with Prague, Dublin, The Hague, Copenhagen and Helsinki; that someone else feels called upon to prevent a European "transfer union". That is nothing more and nothing less than arrogant pretentiousness and it is harmful to boot.

It is a fact that, for decades now, Germany has been a net contributor. We could afford to play that role in Adenauer's time and have continued to do so ever since. And of course Greece, Portugal and Ireland have always been net recipients.

It may be that the political class in Germany today is not sufficiently aware of this solidarity. Hitherto, however, it was a matter of course. The same is true of the principle of subsidiarity: what a country cannot regulate or manage on its own must be dealt with by the European Union. That principle has been written into the Treaty of Lisbon as an obligation.

Following the Schuman Plan, Konrad Adenauer – led by his correct political instinct and in the face of opposition from both Kurt Schumacher and, later on, Ludwig Erhard – took up the offers made by the French. Although Germany was still divided at the time, Adenauer was correct in his assessment of Germany's long-term strategic interests. All Adenauer's successors – Brandt, Schmidt, Kohl and Schröder – continued his policy of integration.

Short-term, domestic policy and foreign policy tactics have never called the long-term strategic interests of the Germans into question. For decades now, all our neighbours and partners have therefore been able to rely on the continuity of Germany's European policy, irrespective of any changes in government. It is essential that this continuity be maintained in the future.

IV   The present situation of the EU calls for vigorous action

German conceptual contributions have always been a matter of course. Things should remain that way in the future. However, we should not try to anticipate the distant future. The facts, omissions and errors of Maastricht twenty years ago could only be partially remedied by changes to the treaty. The present proposals for an amendment to the current Treaty of Lisbon do not strike me as very helpful for the immediate future, bearing in mind the difficulties we have experienced so far with ratification by all the treaty states and the negative outcomes of referenda.

I would, therefore, concur with what the Italian President, Napolitano, had to say in a remarkable speech in late October, in which he urged us to concentrate on what needs to be done now. And that we must exploit the opportunities offered by the present EU Treaty, particularly as regards the tightening of budget rules and the strengthening of economic policy in the euro currency area.

The current crisis affecting the capacity to act of the European Union institutions that were set up in Lisbon must not be allowed to go on for years. With the exception of the European Central Bank, the institutions – the European Parliament, the European Council, the Commission in Brussels and the Councils of Ministers – have provided precious little effective assistance following the resolution of the severe banking crisis of 2008 and especially since the subsequent sovereign debt crisis.

There is no panacea for overcoming the present EU leadership crisis. Several steps will need to be taken, some simultaneous, others consecutive. This will require not only a capacity to make judgments and take action, but also patience. In this situation German conceptual contributions should not be confined to slogans. They should not be bandied about on television but discussed confidentially in committees set up by the EU institutions. In this discussion we Germans should refrain from holding up our economic and social system, our federal system or our financial and budgetary system as models or standards for our European partners to emulate. Instead, we should present them as just one option among many.

We all bear a common responsibility for what Germany does or does not do now and the future consequences that will have for Europe. We therefore need European common sense. In addition to common sense, however, we must have a compassionate heart for our neighbours and partners.

On one important point I agree with Jürgen Habermas, who recently said that "... for the first time in the history of the EU we are experiencing a real weakening of democracy". Indeed, not only the European Council including its president, but also the European Commission including its president as well as the various Councils of Ministers and the entire bureaucracy in Brussels have together pushed democracy aside. At the time we introduced general elections to the European Parliament I succumbed to the illusion that the parliament would wield its own political clout. In actual fact, however, it has so far failed to exert any perceptible influence on the management of the crisis, since its consultations and decisions have had no public impact.

Let me, therefore, make the following appeal to Martin Schulz. It is high time that you and your fellow parliamentarians – Christian Democrats, Socialists, Liberals and Greens – acted in unison to make your voices heard in public, and in no uncertain tones. The best area for the European Parliament to flex its muscles is probably the supervision of banks, stock exchanges and their financial instruments, which has been totally inadequate since the G20 meeting in 2008.

Umpteen thousands of financial traders in the USA and Europe, plus a number of rating agencies, have succeeded in turning the politically responsible governments in Europe into hostages. It is highly unlikely that Barack Obama will do much about it. The same is true of the British government. In 2008/2009, governments the world over managed to rescue the banks with the help of guarantees and the taxpayers' money. Since 2010, however, this herd of highly intelligent, psychosis-prone financial managers has gone back to its old game of profits and bonuses. Theirs is a game of chance to the detriment of all the non-players, which Marion Dönhoff and I criticised as extremely dangerous back in the 1990s.

If no one else is prepared to act, then the members of the euro area must do so. They could make use of Article 20 of the EU Treaty of Lisbon, in which there is express provision for individual or several EU Member States to ... "establish enhanced cooperation among themselves". At all events, the members of the euro currency union should work together to introduce radical regulations for the common financial market in the euro currency area. These regulations should cover the separation of normal commercial banks from investment and shadow banks; a ban on the short selling of securities at a future date; a ban on trading in derivatives, unless they have been approved by the official stock exchange supervisory body; and the effective limitation of transactions affecting the euro area carried out by the currently unsupervised rating agencies. I will not bore you with any further details.

Naturally, the globalised banking lobby would again move heaven and earth to prevent this. After all, it has thwarted all the far-reaching regulations that have been introduced so far. It has deliberately engineered a situation in which its herd of dealers has put European governments in the predicament of having to constantly invent new "rescue mechanisms" – and to extend them by means of "leverage". It is high time something was done about this. If the Europeans have the courage and the strength to introduce radical financial market regulation, we have the prospect of becoming an area of stability in the medium term. But if we fail in this respect, Europe's influence will continue to decline – and the world will move towards a duumvirate consisting of Washington and Peking.

All the steps envisaged and announced so far will undoubtedly be needed in the euro area in the immediate future. They include the rescue fund, the leverage ratios and the requisite monitoring mechanisms, a common economic and fiscal policy as well as a series of tax, spending, social and labour market reforms in the different countries. A common debt will be inevitable too. We Germans should not refuse to accept this for selfish national reasons.

We should also avoid advocating an extreme deflationary policy for the whole of Europe. On the contrary, Jacques Delors is quite right to insist that a balancing of the budgets should be accompanied by the introduction and financing of growth-enhancing projects. No country can consolidate its budget without growth and without new jobs. Those who believe that Europe can recover solely by making budgetary savings should take a close look at the fateful effect of Heinrich Brüning's deflationary policy in 1930/32. It triggered a depression and intolerable levels of unemployment, thus paving the way for the demise of the first German democracy.

V   To my friends

In conclusion, my friends, let me say that there is really no need to preach international solidarity to Social Democrats. For a century and a half, German Social Democrats have been internationalists to a far greater extent than generations of Liberals, Conservatives or German Nationalists. We Social Democrats have upheld the cause of freedom and human dignity. We have held fast to representative parliamentary democracy. These fundamental values make it our duty to exercise European solidarity today.

In the 21st century, Europe will undoubtedly continue to consist of nation states, each with its own language and history.

For that reason Europe will definitely not become a federal state. However, the European Union cannot afford to degenerate into a mere confederation. The European Union must remain a dynamically developing alliance, for which there is no parallel in the whole of human history. We Social Democrats must contribute to the gradual evolution of this alliance.

The older you get, the more you tend to take a long-term perspective. As an old man I still hold fast to the three fundamental values of the Godesberg Programme: freedom, justice and solidarity. My feeling is that nowadays justice requires, in particular, equal opportunities for children, school pupils and young people in general.

Looking back to the year 1945 or to 1933 – I had just turned fourteen at the time – the progress that has been achieved in the meantime strikes me as almost incredible: the progress Europeans have made since the Marshall Plan of 1948 and the Schuman Plan of 1950; the progress we owe to Lech Walesa and Solidarnosz, to Václav Havel and Charter 77 and to the Germans in Leipzig and East Berlin since the major political changes in 1989/91.

Today, most of Europe enjoys human rights and peace. That is something we could never have imagined in 1918, 1933 or 1945. Let us, therefore, strive to ensure that the historically unique European Union emerges unshaken and with self-confidence from its current period of weakness.

Source: *Friedrich-Ebert-Stiftung, http://library.fes.de/pdf-files/id/ipa/08888.pdf*

Note

1.   Speech given at the SPD conference in Berlin.

Biographies

Yoeri Albrecht (the Netherlands) is director of De Balie, a national cultural debating centre in Amsterdam. He is also non-executive director of the board of media house Vereniging Veronica (owner of ANP and NRC Handelsblad) and a member of the European Council on Foreign Relations. He is a long-standing journalist, opinion leader, television/radio maker and media advisor. Over the years he has been active in several cultural, political and media institutions. Albrecht holds a master's degree in history and a postgraduate degree in international law from Leiden University and he studied European Politics in Oxford.

Mathieu Segers (the Netherlands) is Professor of Contemporary European History and European Integration at Maastricht University and Dean of the University College Maastricht. He was a Fulbright-Schuman fellow at the Center for European Studies of Harvard University and Senior Research Fellow at the Department of Politics and IR at the University of Oxford. His current research focuses on the history and prehistory of European integration and trans-Atlantic relations, on which he published in international scholarly journals of different disciplines. His book on The Netherlands and European integration won the Dutch prize for best political book in 2013. He is a columnist for the Dutch daily *Het Financieele Dagblad* and a staff member of the Netherlands Scientific Council for Government Policy.

Tom Holland (United Kingdom) is a British writer and historian, who has published several popular works on classical and medieval history. He is the author of award-winning books such as Rubicon: The Triumph and Tragedy of the Roman Republic (2003), Persian Fire (2005), Millennium: The End of the World and the Forging of Christendom (2008), In the Shadow of the Sword (2012) and Dynasty (2015). He has translated Herodotus for Penguin Classics and is the presenter of BBC Radio 4's Making

History. Holland has written and presented a number of television documentaries on subjects ranging from Islam to dinosaurs.

Larry Siedentop (United Kingdom) is a US-born British political philosopher. He studied at Harvard University and has a DPhil from the University of Oxford. Siedentop is the acclaimed author of *Democracy in Europe* (2001) and *Inventing the Individual* (2014) in which he presents radical and challenging new insights on the origins of our ideas on notions of individuality, liberty, moral responsibility and equality. He frequently contributes to major newspapers such as the *Financial Times* and *The Times*. In 2004, Siedentop was made CBE (Commander of the Order of the British Empire) for his contributions to political thought and higher education.

Stella Ghervas is a Swiss author, essayist and historian with roots in Eastern Europe. Her research focuses on the political and cultural foundations of European unification. She has lectured on four continents and is currently Assistant Professor of History at the University of Alabama at Birmingham and Associate of the Department of History at Harvard University. Among her many publications are *Réinventer la tradition: Alexandre Stourdza et l'Europe de la Sainte-Alliance*, which was awarded the Guizot Prize of the Académie Française in 2009, and *Conquering Peace: From the Enlightenment to the European Union*, which is forthcoming from Harvard University Press. For more information see: http://www.ghervas.net.

Benno Barnard (the Netherlands) is a Dutch poet, novelist, playwright and translator. Since his literary debut in 1981 he has published a number of poems, essays and novels, often reflecting on post-war European identity. Barnard has received increasing media attention after his lecture *Leve God, weg met Allah* at the University of Antwerp was interrupted by Sharia4Belgium. As a result, he since then regularly takes part in public debates on the re-evaluation of Christianity and Western values in general.

Barnard's work has been translated into several languages and he has received a number of important literary awards.

Ivan Krastev (Bulgaria) is a political scientist and commentator. He is currently chairman of the Centre for Liberal Strategies in Sofia and permanent fellow at the Institute for Human Sciences in Vienna (IWM). Krastev teaches, speaks and writes regularly about the crisis of democracy in Europe. His recent work includes provocative books such as *In Mistrust We Trust: Can Democracy Survive When We Don't Trust Our Leaders?* (2013) and *Democracy Disrupted: The Politics of Global Protest* (2014). *Krastev is a founding board member of the European Council on Foreign Relations.*

Philipp Blom (Germany) is a German historian, novelist, journalist and translator. After obtaining his PhD in Modern History at Oxford University, he has worked as a journalist, editor and writer, contributing to newspapers, magazines and radio programmes throughout Europe and the US. Blom's historical books on European history, such as *The Vertigo Years* (2008) and *A Wicked Company* (2010), have been awarded several international prizes. For his current project, 'At Breaking Point', Blom is working on a historical overview of culture and life during the interwar period in Europe and the United States.

Kalypso Nicolaïdis (Greece) is a Greek-French Professor of International Relations at the University of Oxford where she is also director of the Centre for International Studies. Nicolaïdis has published widely on various aspects of European integration, international relations and global governance. Her latest book publications include: *Echoes of Empire: Memory, Identity and Colonial Legacies*, edited with Gabi Maas and Berny Sebe (2015); *Normative Power Europe Revisited*, edited with Richard Whitman (2013); *European Stories: Intellectual Debates on Europe in National Contexts*, edited with Justine Lacroix, (2010); and *Mediterranean Frontiers: Borders, Memory and Conflict in a Transnational Era*, edited with Dimitar Bechev (2009). Nicolaïdis has advised several European governments and European institutions on European affairs, is on the Council of ECFR and was recently part of the Gonzales Reflection group on the future of Europe 2030 at the European Council.

Claudia Sternberg (Germany) is a German scholar working in the United Kingdom. Her research explores the relationship between citizens and political power, and the roles that ideas, ideologies and narratives can play in shaping it. Her book *The Struggle for EU Legitimacy: Public Contestation, 1950-2005* (2013) asks what it would mean for the EU to be a legitimate body, and where our ideas on this question come from. The book traces the history of constructions, and contestations, of the EU's legitimacy in discourses of the European institutions and in public debate. The book was awarded the UACES Prize for Best Book in Contemporary European Studies. Sternberg's current research investigates how the Eurozone crisis has led Europeans to deny each other recognition, and how to recover the promise of mutual recognition, on which the European integration project was built.

Isaiah Berlin (1909-97, Latvia) was a British-Latvian social and political theorist, philosopher, historian of ideas, educator and essayist. For much of his life he was renowned for his conversational brilliance, his defence of liberalism, his attacks on political extremism and intellectual fanaticism, and his accessible, coruscating writings on the history of ideas. Berlin was knighted in 1957, and was awarded the 'Order of Merit' in 1971. He is popularly known for his essay *Two Concepts of Liberty* (1958), which he delivered as his inaugural speech at Oxford University and remains one of the most influential and widely discussed texts in the field of political theory.

Jean Monnet (1888-1979, France) was a French political economist and diplomat. He is regarded by many as the chief architect of

European unity and the founding father of the European Union. While he was never elected to public office, Monnet worked behind the scenes of American and European governments as a well-connected, pragmatic internationalist. In 1955, Monnet founded the Action Committee for the United States of Europe in order to revive European construction. It brought political parties and European trade unions together to become a thriving force behind the initiatives that laid the foundation for the European Union as it eventually emerged.

Konrad Adenauer (1876-1967, Germany) was a German statesman who served as the first Chancellor of (West) Germany, from 1949 to 1963. Adenauer was a lawyer until he became a member of the Cologne City Counsel and eventually was appointed Lord Mayor of the city. During the Second World War he was shortly imprisoned, and although he was reappointed mayor by the Americans, he left the position in 1945. Adenauer was the founder and first leader of the Christian Democratic Union (CDU), a political party that still is the most influential party in Germany. During his years in power, West Germany achieved democracy, stability, international respect and economic prosperity. As a Christian Democrat and firm anti-communist, Adenauer supported the NATO and established ties with Germany's former enemies, especially France.

Charles de Gaulle (1890-1970, France) was a French general, resistant, writer and statesman. He was the leader of Free French Forces during the Second World War and the head of the Provisional Government of the French Republic from 1944 to 1946. After his retirement, De Gaulle wrote his *War Memoirs,* which quickly became a classic of modern French literature. In 1958, however, he returned to politics, founded the Fifth Republic and was elected as the 18th President of France, which he remained until his resignation in 1969. Under De Gaulle's reign, many of the French colonies, of which Algeria most notably, were granted independence. De Gaulle's memory remains influential in French politics today.

Milan Kundera (1929, Czechoslovakia) is Czech-born writer, playwright, essayist and poet. After the Soviet invasion in Czechoslovakia of 1968, Kundera's books were banned from libraries and he lost his teaching position at the Prague Academy of Music and Dramatic Arts, because he was a leading figure in the radical movement 'Prague Spring'. He emigrated to France in 1975, lost his Czech citizenship in 1977 and became a naturalised French citizen in 1981. Kundera's most famous work is *The Unbearable Lightness of Being* (1984), in which, like in the rest of his works, he combines erotic comedy with political criticism and philosophical speculation. Kundera is considered one of the greatest novelists of the 20th century and has won many literary awards.

Margaret Thatcher (1925-2013, United Kingdom) was a British stateswoman and politician who was Prime Minster of the United Kingdom from 1979 to 1990 and the leader of the Conservative Party from 1975 to 1990. She was the longest-serving British Prime Minister of the 20th century and is currently the only woman to have held office. Thatcher's nickname, the 'Iron Lady', refers to her uncompromising politics and leadership style. As Prime Minster, she implemented policies that have become known as Thatcherism. In 1995, Thatcher was appointed Lady Companion of the Order of the Garter, the highest order of chivalry in the United Kingdom.

Václav Havel (1936-2011, Czechoslovakia) was a Czech writer, philosopher, political dissident and statesman. He served as the last president of Czechoslovakia from 1989 to 1992 and became the first president of the "new" Czech Republic until 2003. Since his educational opportunities were limited by his bourgeois background, Havel first rose to prominence within the Prague theatre world as a playwright. Like Kundera, he participated in the Prague Spring, after which he became more politically active. Havel played a major role in the Velvet Revolution, which finally toppled communism in 1989. That same year he was elected president. Although his domestic policies were perceived controversial, he enjoyed great popularity abroad and is considered one of the most important intellectuals of the 20th century.

François Mitterrand (1916-1996, France) was a French statesman, who served as the President of France from 1981 to 1995, which makes him the longest-serving French president. Having started his political career on the Catholic nationalist right, Mitterrand moved to the left during the Fourth Republic, opposing de Gaulle's establishment of the Fifth Republic. He became secretary of the Socialist Party and attempted to unite the French Left. Mitterrand abandoned leftist economic policies early in his presidency and generally ruled as a pragmatic centrist. Together with German Chancellor Helmut Kohl, he forged the Treaty of Maastricht on European Union in 1991. He also appointed France's first female Prime Minister, Edith Cresson.

György Konrád (1933, Hungary) is a Hungarian novelist and essayist. He is author of famous novels such as *A Feast in the Garden* (1992) and *A Guest in My Own Country: A Hungarian Life* (2007) in which he describes his personal experiences during the Second World War and the Hungarian Revolution in 1956. Konrád is a famous advocate of individual freedom and has written numerous essays on Europe and European culture. He has received many prestigious prizes and awards, including the Herder Prize (1984), and the Goethe Medal (2000), and is former president of the literary PEN foundation.

Tommaso Padoa-Schioppa (1940-2010, Italy) was a well-known pro-European Italian banker and economist who was Italy's Minister of Economy and Finances from 2006 to 2008 and Chairman of the International Monetary and Financial Committee of IMF until 2008. He is considered the founding father of the European single currency and has received honorary degrees, such as the Order of Merit of the Italian Republic. Padoa-Schioppa has written over a hundred publications, many of them translated into English and French.

Edouard Balladur (1929, Turkey) is a French politician who served as Prime Minister of France under François Mitterrand from 1993 to 1995. Balladur started his political career in 1964 as an advisor to Prime Minister Georges Pompidou. From 1984 to 1988 he served as councillor of state, and was advisor to Jacques Chirac. Balladur later on joined Chirac's cabinet as Minister of Economy, Finance and Privatisation. He unsuccessfully ran for president in the 1995 French presidential election, opposing his former mentor Chirac, coming in third place. In 2009 Balladur presented his latest book, *A Union of the West*.

Barack Obama (1961, United States) is an American politician serving as the 44th President of the United States and the first African American to hold office. Before his presidency, Obama worked as a civil rights attorney and as a professor of constitutional law at the University of Chicago. Nine months after his inauguration, he was awarded the 2009 Nobel Peace Prize. A few of Obama's most notable accomplishments during his presidency are the Patient Protection and Affordable Care Act, also known as "Obamacare", the ending of the US military involvement in the Iraq War, the seizing of Osama Bin Laden and recently, the promotion of domestic policies on gun control and the normalising of US relations with Cuba.

Helmut Schmidt (1918-2015, Germany) was a German statesman and member of the Social Democratic Party of Germany (SPD), who served as the fifth Chancellor of West Germany, from 1974 to 1982. Before becoming Chancellor, Schmidt was Minister of Defence and Minister of Finance. As a Chancellor, he focused on international affairs, seeking political unification of Europe in partnership with the United States. Schmidt retired form Parliament in 1986, after which he became a leading figure in the creation of the European Monetary Union and the European Central Bank. He also was co-publisher, and director from 1985 to 1989, of *Die Zeit*, a nationwide German weekly newspaper.

This publication is an initiative of Forum on European Culture.

FORUM ON EUROPEAN CULTURE

The Forum of June 2016, titled Re:Creating Europe, is curated by Yoeri Albrecht (director De Balie) and Cees de Gaaff (director DutchCulture).
This publication was made possible through the generous support of:

Gieskes-Strijbis Fonds

GIESKES·STRIJBIS FONDS

European Cultural Foundation

EUROPEAN CULTURAL FOUNDATION

Editors:
Yoeri Albrecht
Mathieu Segers
For the Forum on European Culture:
Anne- Marijn Epker

Contributors:
Benno Barnard
Philipp Blom
Stella Ghervas
Tom Holland
Ivan Krastev
Kalypso Nicolaïdis
Larry Siedentop
Claudia Sternberg

Cover:
Van Lennep

With special thanks to the following persons/ organizations that granted permission to publish the historical texts in this book:
Curtis Brown Group Ltd
Editions Plon
The Federalist: a political review
Fondation Jean Monnet pour l'Europe
Friedrich Ebert Stiftung
Information office of the European
 Parliament in the Netherlands
The Isaiah Berlin Literary Trust
Konrad Adenauer Stiftung
Judit Lakner & György Konrád
Librairie Artheme Fayard
Margaret Thatcher Foundation
The Wylie Agency

For Product Safety Concerns and Information please contact our EU
representative GPSR@taylorandfrancis.com
Taylor & Francis Verlag GmbH, Kaufingerstraße 24, 80331 München, Germany

www.ingramcontent.com/pod-product-compliance
Lightning Source LLC
Chambersburg PA
CBHW070600270326
41926CB00013B/2373